D1774470

LITERATURE AND HISTORY
OF
AVIATION

LITERATURE AND HISTORY
OF
AVIATION

Advisory Editor: JAMES GILBERT

THE AMAZING MR. DOOLITTLE

A Biography of
Lieutenant General James H. Doolittle

BY
QUENTIN REYNOLDS

ARNO PRESS
A NEW YORK TIMES COMPANY

Reprint Edition 1972 by Arno Press Inc.

Copyright © 1953 by Quentin Reynolds
Reprinted by permission of Hawthorne Books, Inc.

Reprinted from a copy in The Newark Public Library

LC# 71-169434
ISBN 0-405-03778-3

Literature and History of Aviation
ISBN for complete set: 0-405-03789-9
See last pages of this volume for titles.

Manufactured in the United States of America

THE AMAZING
MR. DOOLITTLE

THE AMAZING MR. DOOLITTLE

A Biography of
Lieutenant General James H. Doolittle

BY
QUENTIN REYNOLDS

Appleton-Century-Crofts, Inc., New York

Copyright, 1953, by
QUENTIN REYNOLDS

All rights reserved. This book, or parts thereof, must not be reproduced in any form without permission of the publisher.

LIBRARY OF CONGRESS CARD NUMBER: 53-7155

The following quotations have been used with the kind permission of the publishers and copyright owners:

Excerpts from editorials in *The New York Times,* October, 1925, and April, 1944.

Ernie Pyle's column in the New York *World-Telegram,* June 6, 1944; reprinted in *Brave Men,* by Ernie Pyle: Copyright, 1944, by Henry Holt and Company. By permission of Scripps-Howard Newspapers and Henry Holt and Company.

Excerpt from "How to Make a Glider," by Carl Bates, in *Popular Mechanics,* Vol. 11, January-June, 1909, pages 386-388.

Excerpt from "The Flight From France to England," in *Popular Mechanics,* Vol. 12, July-December, 1909, pages 385 and 388.

Printed in the United States of America

Brigadier General Jack Allard
New Milford
Connecticut

Dear Jack:

This was your idea. Without your help it would have been impossible. Jimmy Doolittle was aghast when we told him we were working together on his story; Doolittle lives in the future, not in the past, and he wasn't the slightest bit interested in reliving his incredible life. But happily, at least two hundred of his friends (including you) were able to dig into the storehouse of their memories and emerge, each with his own picture of Doolittle. Generals and statesmen and pilots and industrialists and mechanics and professional boxers and scientists and great teachers and writers and miners were all happy to talk about Jimmy Doolittle and to tell how at one time or another he entered their lives. Everyone was anxious to talk about Doolittle—except Doolittle. He had neither the inclination nor the time. And so this book is based upon the memories of his friends.

You gave the full measure of your friendship to Jimmy back in 1918, when you and he and Brucie Johnson were kid fliers together. I'm grateful, Jack, that you had a little friendship left over to give to me, and grateful for the chance that brought us together a year ago when we decided that this story fairly yelled to be put into print. And so, Jack, I dedicate this book to you.

Sincerely,
Quentin Reynolds

1

One of the social highlights of Winston Churchill's visit to the United States in 1950 was a dinner tendered him by Henry Luce, publisher of *Life* magazine, at the Union League Club. Mr. Luce had invited one hundred of the most important men in America to attend the dinner. Governors, cabinet ministers, four-star generals, heads of industry and newspaper publishers were all there.

Among the guests was Lieutenant General James H. Doolittle. After Churchill had finished speaking Doolittle slipped unobtrusively out of the room; he was scheduled to catch a midnight plane to Los Angeles. Before leaving the club he phoned his wife to give her a report on the evening.

"I wish," Jo Doolittle said on the phone, "you'd asked Mr. Churchill for an autographed picture for my collection."

"I didn't get that close to him," Doolittle laughed. "After all, I only knew him on official business during the war. Why, he might not even have remembered me."

Doolittle hurried to the airport, chuckling at his wife's reference to her collection. By now she must have at least five hundred pictures and there were, he knew, 750 names embroidered on her tablecloth. It was in 1929 that she had started, that he remembered. It was during his experiments in blind flying at Mitchel Field that Jerry Land had signed his name boldly on Jo's white tablecloth and she had embroidered the signature in black silk thread. He was Captain Land then; now he was Vice Admiral Emory Jerome Land. That same night Elmer Sperry and Harry Guggenheim and Bill Brown, the scientist, and Ben Kelsey, the pilot, and Alex de Seversky had added their names, and all were embroidered neatly. Now, after more than twenty years, the tablecloth was crisscrossed with 750 names and Jo was very proud of it, because unlike most women who collect china or paintings or miniature silver Jo has always collected friends—and each of the 750 names represented a real friend. It is the only hobby she ever had, unless you could call cooking a hobby.

When Doolittle had told his wife that Churchill might not remember him he was quite wrong. As a matter of fact, a moment after Doolittle had left the dinner table Churchill showed that he most emphatically did remember Lieutenant General James H. Doolittle. Henry Luce had arisen and suggested that everyone adjourn to the lounge where old friends of the Prime Minister might renew their acquaintance on less formal terms than offered by the banquet table. While Luce was speaking Churchill was hurriedly scribbling something on a menu. He passed it to his host who looked at it, smiled, and then read aloud, "There are two men here whom I am very anxious to see [Churchill had written]. They are Bob Sherwood and Jimmy Doolittle."

Robert E. Sherwood looked startled but gratified. It was pleasant to be one of two men singled out by Churchill. He went into the lounge where Churchill waved him to a seat. Sherwood's book, *Roosevelt and Hopkins,* had just been published and Churchill wanted to debate one or two of Sherwood's conclusions. Finally Sherwood thought it time to yield his place to another guest. He arose and Churchill said, "Where's that Jimmy Doolittle? I want to discuss something with him."

But by now Doolittle was climbing into a westbound plane. What had Churchill wanted to discuss with Doolittle? It might have been something that had happened on the Tokyo raid which Doolittle had led. The doughty old warrior might have wished to refight some of the battles won by the Eighth Air Force when Doolittle had it. It was hardly likely but he might have wished to discuss the latest technological advances made in the petroleum industry—as vice-president of the Shell Oil Company, Doolittle knew as much about that subject as any man alive. He might have wished some technical advice about the new jet planes his country was building—Doolittle holds not only a master's but a doctor's degree in aeronautical engineering from M.I.T. He might have wished to ask Doolittle about speed flying—at one time or another Doolittle held virtually every racing title in the books. He might have asked him, though again it hardly seems likely, about boxing—Doolittle helped himself through school by fighting professionally under an assumed name. What did Churchill want to discuss with him?

It might have been almost anything, for Doolittle has had several careers. He can, with equal facility, demonstrate the fabled bobbing and weaving style of Jack Dempsey or discuss the Sulfuric Acid Alkylation Process which resulted in the production of octane improvement without hydrogenation. Boxer, stunt pilot, air force general, aeronautical engineer, scientist, gasoline salesman; he is a jack of all trades and a master of all trades. Doolittle? Experienced flying men say that Doolittle and Bernt Balchen are the two greatest pilots of the past thirty years. Doolittle laughs easily and his eyes are friendly but men who flew with him in combat say that he has ice water in his veins. Doolittle is generous, warmhearted, gregarious, but his best friend once said to him, "If you ever saw a tear you'd kick it in the face." That isn't quite true. He did cry—once. It's hardly likely however that Churchill would have wished to discuss that with him. Besides only one man was with Doolittle when he cried and now that man is dead. The incredible Mr. Doolittle is well worth knowing.

If there was one thing Tex Rickard hated, it was an amateur. Rickard himself was a professional gambler, which meant of course that he himself never took chances. Gambling followed inexorable mathematical laws, and although the few variables allowed the amateur to make an occasional killing, in the long run the percentage always won and the profits went to the house. Rickard saw to it that he was always on the side of the house. Men in Nome seemed to be too busy looking for gold to spend much time gambling, so Rickard, who could always cut his losses, concentrated upon running his saloon, a profitable venture, for men always had time to drink. The trouble with men who drank, however, was an unfortunate tendency to engage in physical combat, a form of violence Rickard took a very dim view of—there was no profit in the sight of two grown men belaboring each other with enthusiastic but unskilled fists. Rickard would shake his head sadly at such displays of unproductive and unprofitable energy. He noticed that next to fighting themselves, the male citizens of Nome best liked to watch others perform, and Rickard decided to take advantage of this strange human weakness. Tex began to stage boxing bouts as part of the vaudeville programs displayed by the local theaters. The vaudeville acts which reached Nome from the states were hardly the headline acts which featured the bill at New York's Palace, and the fights, if between crude, untutored sourdoughs, were at least vicious and not lacking in excitement. The youngsters of Nome looked forward with delight to the Saturday night imbroglios at the theater. They weren't a bit interested in the gold their fathers dreamed of; they didn't care about the profits you could make out of a bag of potatoes or a sack of flour; they didn't care about the dreary lessons they had to learn at school all week—they lived for the moment the bell rang and two husky young miners sprang at each other with mayhem in their hearts. They'd sit in the balcony of the theater, and their shrill cries would rise as one or the other of the gladiators would reel to the floor after a dose of brutal punishment, always alleviated by the $25 the genial Tex Rickard would pay each contestant for entertaining his patrons.

One of the youngsters who was always there when the bell rang was James Harold Doolittle. Doolittle was small for his age, but he could yell with the rest of them and he could thrill with the rest of them when some brawny-fisted fighter knocked an opponent out of the ring. When the show was over he'd run to the stage entrance to see what his heroes looked like up close. Sometimes a fancy boxer arrived in town, but the boys sneered at anyone so effete as to slip punches or to block roundhouse swings—defensive boxing was to them a running away, and they noticed that usually the hit-and-run fighters were eventually caught by the crude but persistently aggressive local maulers. Doolittle reserved most of his admiration for the fighters who kept boring in, ignoring punishment, to pound away at the mid-section. This to him was the epitome of fighting.

His father, Frank Doolittle, was a man with itchy feet and a restless heart. He had been born in Massachusetts and had followed the sun through sundry western communities to California. An itinerant carpenter, he finally settled in Alameda long enough to marry Rosa Shepherd and father a son he named James Harold. But his domestic status and his fatherhood were not proof against the itching feet, and when the magic word "gold" appeared in stories coming out of Alaska, he packed up his carpenter's tools, said good-by to his wife and infant son and chased the mirage of yellow riches, as so many thousands were doing just before the turn of the century. A carpenter could earn good money in Alaska then, and Doolittle senior would work in Dawson City or Nome until he had accumulated a stake—then he'd hie for the gold fields. He never did make the big strike, but he never did give up hope, and soon he sent for Rosa and his young son.

He had built a rough but serviceable-enough house on the outskirts of Nome, and it was here he installed his family. There was no running water in the house, no central heating, and young Doolittle was given the job of keeping the wood box filled and the water pails brimming. In the winter Jim with his mother would have to harness his father's dog sled and mush on to nearby Anvil Creek, where he'd fill the water buckets. Once, after a fairly long stretch of carpenter work, Doolittle senior decided to install running water in his home. This was fine until the first snow came, and then the water invariably froze in the pipes and the dogs had to be put into service.

Nome was a colorful city which had grown too fast for its own health. Almost overnight its population had increased from two thousand to ten times that. Nome was like a bag of flour tied too tightly in the middle; its people spilled over onto the beach on one side and into the rough tundra on the other. Eskimos, trappers, Indians, miners, gamblers, promoters, adventurers and their ladies filled the unpaved streets of the city. Nome was a lusty, bawdy, but tremendously vital community, and it was sheer paradise for a youngster who grew up in the midst of its noise and its smells and its tradition of settling all arguments with the bone-crunching blow of a fist.

Newcomers to Nome were called "Chee Chockers," an Eskimo word which might best perhaps be translated as "greenhorns." "Chee Chockers" were fair game to the long-established residents, some of whom had been around as long as five years. They could be swindled, cheated or beaten with impunity. Doolittle senior, of course, was regarded as a real native, but to the boys at school young Jimmy was nothing but a Chee Chocker. He was the smallest boy in the school, but this did not excuse him from having to conform to the tradition that you were a Chee Chocker until you were accepted by the rest of the school, and to be accepted you had to win your share of fights. There being no boys of his own size, Doolittle had to swing against the bigger targets of boys who outweighed him by twenty and thirty pounds. But nature had been kind to young Doolittle. As compensation for his small stature nature had given him a pair of hard hands and extraordinarily quick reflexes, and the ability to absorb a great deal of punishment. He fought the way his heroes at the theater fought—no fancy-dan stuff for him. Not for him the tantalizing tap of a left jab or the intricate but effective feint. Not for him the use of elbow to block blows or the deft footwork that enabled you to glide away from powerful punches. Doolittle, schooled in the Nome tradition, just lowered his head, started flailing his arms and kept on advancing. He seldom even felt the punches of his adversaries. And sooner or later his hard fists would find their mark and he'd be that much closer to losing the hated name of Chee Chocker. He found out that he could hurt anyone he could hit, a comforting thought in view of the fact that nature had shortchanged him on weight and reach. With this new discovery there came a great feeling of confidence, and now anyone, no matter what his size, who called Jimmy Doolittle a Chee Chocker would have to fight.

If you lived in Nome you did things for yourself. If your roof leaked or a window was smashed you did the fixing, and young Jim soon became proficient in the use of his father's tools. But he wasn't much good at tying knots. He even had trouble learning to tie the relatively simple bowline and after several failures his father shook his head sadly.

"Jim, my boy," he said, "I'm afraid you'll never set the world on fire."

Had the Doolittle family remained in Alaska it is quite possible that the only son might have wound up fighting for Tex Rickard's Saturday night shows; Jimmy didn't care much for school, he reserved his enthusiasm for fighting. But his mother had different ideas. To her son Nome was a delightful place, teeming with excitement; to her it was an evil jungle lying in wait to capture the unwary, and she resolved to take her boy back to California. Doolittle senior decided to remain behind to make just one more search for the big lode that was always right around the bend. Back in Los Angeles Jimmy finished grammar school and entered high school. He paid the same reluctant attention to studies as most American boys of his age; he certainly showed none of the intellectual brilliance which would one day gain the respect of the M.I.T. faculty and of the world of aeronautical engineering. Manual Arts High School did teach carpentry ("shop work" they called it), and there were machine shops and courses in the gasoline engine. Jimmy thoroughly enjoyed these—it gave you a chance to work with your hands, and he was discovering that the hands which could cause so much damage when clenched were also sensitive when working on precision problems set by a shop or engine instructor. He enjoyed using his hands, whether they were swinging punches or handling a lathe.

He also learned that you could fight without anger. There was an English teacher, Forest Bailey, who also acted as boxing instructor at Manual Arts, and he taught Jimmy the rudiments of boxing. He knew that the sturdy, short-armed little 105-pound firebrand would never become a good defensive boxer, but he did teach him to box and weave away from punches; he taught him to keep his right hand high when he went in to attack, and he taught him to hook instead of to swing.

"A straight line is the shortest distance between two points," he told Jimmy. "A straight punch doesn't have to travel as far as a roundhouse, and it has more force when it lands."

This made sense to Jimmy, and now when he boxed with gloves on (an effete custom that would have horrified schoolmates in Nome) he began to develop a certain skill in getting close to an opponent without stopping too many punches. Once he was in close he would tattoo his opponent's ribs with sharp left hooks, bring his guard down, and then throw that always-ready right hand. He had an additional incentive now to make a name for himself at boxing. His eye had been caught by a pretty schoolmate, Josephine Daniels. Jimmy was first attracted by her soft voice and intriguing accent. Her parents had recently moved from Louisiana to Los Angeles and Josephine spoke with the accent of the Bayou country. Jimmy was puzzled by her casual acceptance of his fistic triumphs in the gymnasium. They just didn't mean a thing to cool, detached Jo Daniels. Jimmy couldn't understand her indifference to what he considered so important. She was like his mother in this respect; she too displayed an irritating lack of pride when he came home bursting with the news that he'd just knocked out some 150-pounder. It began to be obvious that there were two worlds—a man's world and a woman's world. Jimmy shrugged his shoulders and immersed himself in the world in which he had been born.

He continued to fight, and soon he ran out of high school opponents. He entered the amateur tournaments and found the experienced amateurs easy. Forest Bailey thought he was ready for the big time. He entered his young protégé in the Pacific Coast amateur championships to be held at the Los Angeles Athletic Club, and Jimmy's fists cut a wide swathe through the state champions who had come to Los Angeles in search of the title. When it was all over Jimmy was the undisputed bantamweight champion of the Pacific Coast; they gave him a beautiful gold watch, and on the back of it was the engraved testimony acknowledging him as the champion. He showed the watch to Jo. She only asked, "Is it real gold?"

"Look," he said proudly. "Fourteen carat."

To a million boys of the early 1900's the man's world was best exemplified by the magazine *Popular Mechanics*. There wasn't much homework done by the youth of America on the day *Popular Mechanics* reached its young readers. By 1908 it had become an American institution. It told you how to make things; it told of the incredible one-man torpedo boat that went under the water; of the seven-masted schooner that had sailed into New York harbor; of the rival Polar claims of Peary and Cook; of Barney Oldfield, who had actually driven an automobile a mile a minute. Theodore Roosevelt was President of the United States, and pure food laws and federal meat-inspection acts were being passed in Washington. America was establishing herself as a world power. The Monroe Doctrine had been extended to Venezuela, and the country had acquired the Panama Canal Zone and was digging the biggest ditch ever dug. But who cared about these things? No one who read *Popular Mechanics. Popular Mechanics* gave a new hero to the boys of the nation.

He was Louis Blériot, the first man to fly across the English Channel. The newspapers, of course, had told of the phenomenal flight of Bleriot in his monoplane, but high school youngsters read only that part of the papers which contained the early comic strips featuring Happy Hooligan, Desperate Desmond and the Katzenjammer Kids. But when Blériot wrote his own story of the flight exclusively for *Popular Mechanics,* a good portion of America's youth read it—including the boys at Manual Arts High School. Doolittle thrilled as he read:

> At 4:35 in the morning the signal was given, and in an instant I am in the air, my engine making 1,200 revolutions, almost its highest speed, in order that I may get quickly over the telegraph wires along the edge of the cliff. As soon as I am over the cliff I reduce my speed. There now is no need to force my engine. I begin my flight, steady and sure, toward the coast of England. I have no apprehensions, no sensations.
>
> The French torpedo boat has seen me. She is drawing ahead at full speed. She makes perhaps 26 miles an hour. What matters? I am making at least 42½ miles. Rapidly I overtake her, traveling at the height of 250 ft.
>
> The moment is supreme, yet I surprise myself by feeling no exultation.
>
> Below me is the sea, its surface disturbed by wind, which now is freshening. The motion of the waves beneath me is not pleasant. I drive on.
>
> Ten minutes have gone. I have passed the destroyer and I turn my head to see whether I am proceeding in the right direction. I am amazed. There is nothing to be seen, neither destroyer, nor France, nor England. I am alone. I see nothing at all. For ten minutes I am lost. It

is a strange position, to be alone, unguided, without a compass, in the air over the middle of the channel.

I touch nothing. My hands and feet rest lightly on levers. I let the aeroplane take its own course. I care not whither it goes. For ten minutes I continue, neither rising nor falling nor turning, and then, twenty minutes after I have left the French coast, I see the green cliffs of Dover, the castle, and away to the west the spot where I intend to land. What can I do? It is evident that the wind has taken me out of my course. I press a lever with my foot and turn easily toward the west, reversing the direction in which I have been traveling.

Now, indeed, I am in difficulties, for the wind here by the cliffs is much stronger and my speed is reduced as I fight against it, yet my beautiful aeroplane responds.

Although I am confident that I can continue for an hour and a half, and that I might, indeed, return to Calais, I cannot resist the opportunity to make my landing upon this green spot. Once more I turn my aeroplane and, describing a half circle, I enter the opening and find myself again over dry land. Avoiding the red buildings on my right, I attempt a landing, but the wind catches me and whirls me around two or three times. At once I stop the motor. Instantly my machine falls, straight upon the land from a height of 65 ft., in two or three seconds, and my flight is safely done.

And then there was the great All American boy who for a brief time was the most glamorous figure in America. He was fourteen-year-old Cromwell Dixon. Almost every boy who made *Popular Mechanics* his bible dreamed of being another Dixon, just as his son of a later generation would dream of being another Lindbergh. Cromwell Dixon? Why, he was the world's youngest aeronaut—with the help of his mother (a seamstress) he had built a dirigible twenty-five feet long and ten feet wide. It was powered with his bicycle mechanism, and when he made his incredible eight-mile flight it was important news for the young readers of *Popular Mechanics*. Where had

Cromwell gotten his idea of a bicycle-powered dirigible? From *Popular Mechanics,* of course.

Doolittle devoured every issue of the magazine. "You can make it yourself" was the motto of the wonderful periodical, and its boast was an honest one; if you followed directions exactly you could make the household gadgets, the animal traps, the kites, the printing presses and the thousand and one exciting things displayed on its pages. And one issue carried an article by Carl Bates, "How to Make a Glider." Young Doolittle read the first paragraph of the article, and it was like discovering a new continent.

> A gliding machine is a motorless aeroplane, or flying-machine, propelled by gravity and designed to carry a passenger through the air from a high point to a lower point some distance away. Flying in a glider is simply coasting down hill on the air, and is the most interesting and exciting sport imaginable. The style of glider described in this article is known as the "two-surface" or "double-decked" aeroplane, and is composed of two arched cloth surfaces placed one above the other.
>
> In building a glider the wood material used should be straight-grained spruce, free from knots. First prepare from spruce planks the following strips of wood.

Jimmy read on, and for the first time heard the word "rudder" being applied to a winged contraption:

> The vertical rudder is to keep the machine headed into the wind and is not movable. This rudder is made of cloth stretched over a light wooden frame, which is nailed to the rudder sticks connecting to the main frame. The horizontal rudder is also made of cloth stretched over a light wooden frame, and is arranged to intersect the vertical rudder at its center. This rudder is held in position and strengthened by diagonal wires and guy wires. The horizontal rudder is also immovable, and its function is to prevent the machine from diving, and also to keep it steady in its flight. The rudders are fastened to the glider

by the two rudder sticks, and these sticks are held rigid by diagonal wires and also by guy wires leading to the sides of the main frames as shown in Fig. 1. The two arm sticks should be spaced about 13 in. apart and bolted to the long beams in the center of the opening in the lower plane where the operator is to take his position.

Jim decided to construct the glider. It seemed simple enough; he knew how to handle tools, and the spruce he needed didn't cost much. He labored long over the directions, and gradually his glider began to assume form. He wouldn't allow anyone to help him. A few blocks from his home a street had been cut through a hill. This he felt would make the perfect place from which to take off. He would run as fast as he could and leap from the top of the cut, and then glide gently to the street thirty feet below. He carried his glider to the spot early one morning. He took his place some forty feet from the edge of the cut, grasped the crossbar firmly and began to run. His small legs churned the turf, and then he leaped up. Theoretically the glider would now carry him into the air, and then it would settle gently to a landing. It did nothing of the sort. He leaped up and then came right down again. He tried it again and again. The glider refused to soar; it just fell limply to the ground.

Jimmy went back to the design to see where he had gone wrong, but he could find nothing the matter with his work. Once more he went back to the cut; once again he ran at full speed. He ran to the edge of the cut and then leaped. Doolittle and glider collapsed and began to slither down the side of the cut. When he picked himself up, the wreckage of the glider lay around him. One wing was completely smashed.

He brought the remains home and started to consider the various things that might have gone wrong.

It would be possible to rebuild the glider but a new issue of *Popular Mechanics* had arrived with plans for building the Demoiselle, a creation of the fabulous Alberto Santos-Dumont. Santos-Dumont was another real idol of the air age. He was so interested in popularizing flying that he refused to patent any of the planes he designed, built and flew. He gave the plans of his light 250-pound monoplane to *Popular Mechanics*. It was powered by a 30-horsepower engine. Doolittle decided to eliminate the smashed lower wing of his glider, repair the upper wing and install an old motorcycle engine.

Jimmy felt he knew why he had been so unsuccessful on his previous attempt. His small legs just couldn't generate enough speed to lift the glider. If you could go faster, the glider would take off without any trouble. The motorcycle engine would give you that speed. But even an old secondhand motorcycle engine cost money, and money was something that was seldom lying around the Doolittle household. When things were good up in Nome, his father would send a check. But Doolittle senior was a man who believed in everyone, and usually when he found himself ahead financially, someone would come along with a story that he knew where gold could be found— he only needed a stake. Again and again Doolittle provided the stake which gave him an interest in any gold that the prospector found. Some of the men he staked just disappeared; others came back discouraged.

If Jim were to buy a motorcycle engine he'd have to earn the money. He knew of only one way to do that—with his hard little fists. Once a week amateur bouts were held in downtown Los Angeles. The bouts were not exactly one hundred per cent simon pure. The boxers weren't paid, but were given watches which could then be sold back to the promoters for ten dollars each. Jim, under an assumed name, entered the amateur bouts and found that the competition wasn't too tough. He only weighed 105 pounds, but it was a chunky, compact 105 pounds. Most of his opponents were of the stringbean variety—made to order for his boring-in body-punching tactics. The crowd loved to see this little bit of perpetual motion in action—Jimmy never stopped punching. He took a lot of punches to the face, but though his opponents marked him up a bit they never hurt him. Three bouts, all of which he won, and he had enough money to buy his small engine.

He bought it, and now remodeled the glider as a single wing, or monoplane. The night before he was to give it its first trial, disaster struck. The glider was resting in the back yard when he went to bed. During the night a storm blew up. It caught the glider, and now it really did soar. It soared over the back yard fences and then, as a downdraft caught it, dove to the ground. In the morning there was nothing left but a smashed mess of wires and struts. It was probably the best thing that ever happened to Jimmy. He had not followed the *Popular Mechanics* design exactly; he had done a bit of improvising. The contraption he had created, although he didn't know it until years later, violated every single principle of aeronautical engineering. It might have actually taken Doolittle into the air, but it most certainly would have crashed immediately, with a good chance of killing its very amateur pilot.

Jimmy's mother was an understanding woman. He thought that his fighting had been carefully concealed, but when he came home with swollen lips and with bumps on his forehead, she knew exactly where they had come from. She knew that those years in Nome had left their mark on this restless, high-spirited son of hers. His desire to fight and to soar into the air on the wings of a glider were manifestations of his restlessness. She was wise enough to know that this intense energy couldn't be smothered; it had to find an outlet. If he kept on experimenting with homemade gliders he'd end by killing himself; if he kept on boxing he'd end up at best with a smashed, broken face. The wise mother provided an alternative to these two courses; she bought Jimmy a motorcycle on condition that he give up gliders and boxing.

The boy was overjoyed. His mother had been right. All of his spare time now was taken up tinkering with the engine, taking it apart, cleaning it, trying to coax more power out of it. When he wasn't busy with the engine he was practicing gymnastics with his two pals Bill and John Downs. He still boxed or wrestled at school with Lawrence Tibbett, the best singer at Manual Arts, and with Frank Capra, a dark, intense boy who acted in the school plays, and Bob Meusel, the star of the baseball team, but his real love was his motorcycle. He roared through the outskirts of sprawling Los Angeles with his cutout open and forgot all about flying.

At last he had something which did make Jo Daniels lose her indifferent air. Fighting and gliding seemed pretty silly to her, but no other boy ever screeched up to her house on a motorcycle. On Valentine's Day Jimmy bought his first present for a girl. He spent a dollar for a two-pound box of candy. Jo was really impressed by this gift, and by the tie he wore that day. Jimmy seldom wore a tie or for that matter a coat. Other boys occasionally gave her flowers, but she knew that the Japanese gardeners who grew the huge violet and carnation beds in the neighborhood sold their flowers very cheaply—you could get two bunches of violets for a nickel. And she knew this box of candy well; she knew it cost a dollar. For the first time she began to think seriously about Jimmy Doolittle.

Jimmy found that his motorcycle used plenty of gasoline, and gasoline cost money. Checks from Nome had been few and far between and he didn't feel that he could ask his mother to buy gasoline for him. Once again he had to resort to his fists. But he was through with the amateur ranks. He decided to fight as a professional under an assumed name. Every Saturday he'd hop aboard his motorcycle and disappear in a cloud of dust. He'd go to Long Beach or even to San Diego, or he'd go to the little towns in the valleys north of Los Angeles where fights were held every week. The promoters looked doubtful when he gave his age as eighteen, but they were always looking for new faces and they invariably signed him to a bout. His windmill style of fighting made a big hit with the boxing audiences, and now he could command up to $30 a fight. He didn't have too much trouble beating the spindly-shanked bantamweights in the small fight clubs, but one night he was put in the ring with an experienced old war horse who gave him his first real beating. He was Spider Kelly, and Kelly didn't fall apart under the fury of Jimmy's attack. Spider Kelly moved smoothly to his right and jabbed Jimmy silly; he stepped in and threw short jolts to Jimmy's ribs that had him gasping; he feinted Jimmy into leads and then countered with beautifully timed right hands that rocked Jimmy. Jimmy lasted, but the beating the ring-wise Kelly gave him made him forget boxing for the time being.

In his senior year at Manual Arts he asked Jo to marry him.

"Marry a fighter?" She looked her disgust. "You must think I'm crazy."

"As a matter of fact, I've given up fighting," he said. "This summer I'm going up to Alaska. I'll get a good job there, save my money and send for you."

"Jimmy, my mother would never let me go...."

"I'm going to marry you, not your mother," he said calmly.

"I think you're crazy," she said breathlessly.

When the school term ended Jimmy went off to Alaska. He could not have selected a more inopportune time. Alaska was in the throes of a real depression. The boom days had gone the way of all booms, gold had just about disappeared, and Alaska was the land of unemployed. He spent an unhappy, unproductive month and then took a job as a steward on a ship headed for Los Angeles. He had to face the scorn of Jo's mother, but that didn't bother him too much. He was cocky, completely uninhibited, and he had great confidence in his future.

"We'll just have to wait awhile, Jo," he said calmly.

"But, Jimmy," she said in exasperation, "I never told you I'd marry you . . . you take too much for granted. I really don't think I'll marry you."

"You talk just like your mother, Jo," he interrupted. "But you'll change."

That fall Jimmy entered Los Angeles Junior College. The courses he enjoyed most were those in mining engineering. He could never get interested in courses which were theoretical expositions of a subject; the engineering courses taught you something you could one day apply in a practical way. After two years at the junior college Jimmy matriculated to the University of California where he majored in mining engineering. He divided his time between the classroom and the gymnasium.

He discovered the parallel bars and the horizontal bar, and he became proficient on both. The knowledgeable gymnasium instructor told him, "You're lucky, Doolittle, you were born with a sense of balance." It was true enough that he was a natural athlete with extraordinarily quick reflexes. He was a watch-charm athlete, for even now at nineteen he weighed only 130 pounds. He had a catlike quickness, and he had learned the tricks of tumbling with ease. One day he was in the gymnasium going through his gymnastic routine when the gym began to fill up with students. One of his friends with whom he was practicing giant swings on the horizontal bar said that they were going to hold a series of elimination bouts to decide on the make-up of a team to box Stanford.

"Let's go over and watch them," Doolittle suggested.

Representatives in the lighter classes had all been selected. On this day they were looking for a middleweight to represent the university. Marcus Freed, the boxing instructor, had eliminated all but three of the 160-pounders. Two of them went into the ring, swung wildly and furiously at each other for two rounds, and then the instructor called a halt.

Two or three of Doolittle's classmates were in the crowd watching. They knew that Jimmy had done a lot of boxing, and one of them suggested he go and try his luck with one of the middleweights.

"I suppose you think he'll knock my brains out," Jimmy grinned.

"He probably will," one of the spectators said.

That was enough to prompt Doolittle to walk to the ringside and ask to try out for the team. The boxing instructor, who hadn't seen Doolittle in action, shook his head.

"These are middleweights, son," he said.

"I won't hurt them, coach," Doolittle grinned. "Let me have some gloves."

The coach shrugged his shoulders. The competition was open to everyone. Doolittle climbed into the ring and the coach motioned to one of the middleweights. He and Doolittle met in the center of the ring, touched gloves, and then the roof fell in on the middleweight. Doolittle had rushed him, had slipped under his long left hand, and had thrown a sharp left hook to his body that doubled him up. Then Doolittle threw his right accurately and with all of his power behind it. The middleweight was out for five minutes. A second middleweight was summoned. It took Doolittle the better part of a round to get through his guard and knock him out.

He was tired after that; the tumbling and gymnastic work he'd been doing developed muscles, but not the wind. The boxing coach called a halt and told this little buzz saw to show up tomorrow; there was one other man in the running.

The next afternoon the gymnasium was crowded. Practically all of his class turned up to watch the new sensation. The middleweight who provided the opposition today was a cut above the two who had preceded him. He had the good sense to keep Doolittle at long range with a left jab. When Doolittle did get in close, his bigger opponent managed to smother his desperate attempts to pump short punches into the body. Then he'd lean his weight on Doolittle. Jimmy was a tired young man at the end of the round. This was a good boxer he was up against. Well, he'd met good boxers before. He couldn't outmaneuver this fellow; he'd have to overpower him with the viciousness of his attack—and he'd have to do it fast. When the coach called them out for the second round Doolittle shot out of his corner with the momentum of a man catapulted from a cannon. He flailed away, throwing swift, hard body punches, and then as his opponent's head lowered, he smashed heavy uppercuts to the jaw. And in the midst of a furious exchange the middleweight sagged, stumbled and fell. It was all over and Jimmy Doolittle was middleweight champion of the University of California.

The meet with Stanford was the following week, and Jimmy put himself in the hands of the experienced boxing coach. Every morning he was out on the road; every afternoon he was punching the bag, trying to develop speed in punching. The coach noticed that Doolittle had that rare quality of exploding, or "snapping," a punch given to one out of a hundred fighters. Some of the biggest, most powerful men in the professional ranks were cream-puff punchers; they lacked this explosive ability. The classic example of the explosive puncher, the coach explained, was Bob Fitzsimmons, who at 165 had no trouble knocking out men who outweighed him fifty pounds. The boxing coach explained the art of punching to Doolittle. He had the knack of snapping a punch—you could never teach a man that, he told Jimmy—either you had it or you didn't.

"As long as you're strong," he said earnestly, "you can knock out anyone you can hit. But you've got short arms and not much of a defense. A clever boxer who can hit would weaken you in a couple of rounds and destroy your timing; take the sting out of your punch. You've got to get your man fast."

"I'll get him fast," Doolittle glowered. He was already feeling very unfriendly toward this unknown Stanford middleweight he was to box. Doolittle was not calm or detached—it would be many years before he would lose his sense of recklessness, his intensity.

The night of the fight arrived. Jimmy sat in his corner working himself into a rage. He looked across the ring at the smiling and rather surprised middleweight from Stanford. The Stanford man was wondering why they had put this midget in against him. He was a decent fellow, this middleweight, and he didn't want to hurt his pint-sized opponent. He'd just jab him a bit and take the decision. The bell rang and the Stanford man came out with his left hand high.

He smiled encouragement at Doolittle as though to say, "Come on, kid, don't be afraid, I won't hurt you." He glided nicely about the ring, jabbing easily. Doolittle started to come in, trying to get under the long left hand. He feinted a left to the stomach and the Stanford man dropped his right hand to catch the blow—and then Doolittle's own right whistled and landed exactly to the left of the chin where a nerve is located that sends messages to the brain. The Stanford man never heard the message but his brain did, and it stopped functioning for ten seconds. The referee counted him out while the California rooters screamed their tribute.

They helped the Stanford man to his corner. He shook the cobwebs out of his brain, grinned ruefully and hurried across the ring to shake Doolittle's hand. "My name is Pedley—Eric Pedley—nice work."

Jimmy, his rage gone now, shook hands and grinned. "I got in a lucky punch."

"Lucky my eye," Pedley laughed. "It was a beautiful feint, and I fell for it."

Doolittle looked closely at the smiling Pedley. He might have taught Pedley how to feint with a left hand, but Pedley was teaching him something about sportsmanship. Pedley actually meant what he said, and Doolittle felt just a bit ashamed of his rage of a few moments before. (A few years later, when Eric Pedley became a member of the International Polo Team, Doolittle was his biggest rooter.)

Engineering students were encouraged to work in the mines during the summer vacation, and after his junior year had finished Jimmy went to work in the Comstock mines at Virginia City, Nevada. It was hard work, but boxing and gym work had developed his muscles; he was small but sturdy and strong. Mines are either hot or cold; this was a hot mine. The temperature even far below the surface was high, and the water which seeped into the passages from hidden springs was boiling hot. July 4 was a holiday even in the Virginia City mines, but the seeping water took no holiday and Jimmy and an old-timer were given the unenviable job of caring for the pump during the twenty-four hours of the holiday. This was all right with young Doolittle—it meant overtime pay. The old-timer explained the operation of the pump to his young assistant. He told Jimmy that the pump had to be primed by hand to start it up. Once you poured some water into it and started it, she worked fine. But if you noticed that the water in the mine floor was almost all gone, then you reduced the power to keep the mine from going entirely dry—if it went dry the pump would stop automatically, and then you'd have to prime it again. He then fell asleep. The pump chugged along nicely and Jim didn't think watching it would make it work any more efficiently, so he too fell asleep. He awoke an hour later with wet feet. When he saw what had happened he yelled to his experienced mate to wake up. The old-timer rubbed the sleep out of his eyes and looked at Jim with disgust.

"I warned you to watch the pump," he said sadly, "but you didn't. And it kept on and drained every bit of water out of the mine. With no water coming into it the pump stopped by itself. Then the water started seeping into the mine again, and now it's covered the pump."

"What'll we do?" Jim asked.

"What'll we do? Nothing. It's you who'll do it," the old man growled. "You've got to take this hand lever, get down there and prime the big pump. Then it'll start up again."

"But that water is almost boiling," Jim protested.

"That's right. And it's getting higher every minute."

Jim took the hand lever, and then dropped into the three feet of hot water. He had to bend to fix the hand lever in place, and the hot water burned through his clothes. It was sheer agony, but he attached the hand lever hurriedly, primed the main pump and then, when it started to chug, he climbed out. He took his heavy shoes and socks off; his feet were lobster red.

"Okay?" he asked the old miner.

"Okay," the miner said, and then he added, "You're okay too, son. Took a lot of nerve . . . that did."

The regular miners didn't have much respect for the college kids who worked with them each summer. As a rule the youngsters couldn't take the hard work, the cramped spaces and the bad air. Many of them quit after a week or two. To the miners Jim Doolittle was just another college kid—a little fresher than most, but no more useful. It was seldom that they accepted any of the part-time workers as one of themselves, but Doolittle finally made it. One day Jim was working with a group of men reopening some drifts at the 2,700-foot level. The Comstock mine had the conventional shafts leading from the surface to the various levels. Drifts were the passages leading from the shafts to the ore deposits. A mine foreman and one of the men stepped into the cage at the 2,500-foot level, intending to be lowered another two hundred feet to investigate conditions at the 2,700-foot level. The cage began to descend when the cable snapped, plunging the cage and the two miners to the abandoned 2,900-foot level. Jim and the others who were working in the drift leading from the 2,700-foot level ran to the shaft. There was silence below.

"We've got to lower someone fast to see if those men are alive," the drift foreman said. "Who'll it be?"

"I'm lightest," Jimmy said. "Give me that rope."

The foreman tied the rope around Jimmy's waist. Four strong men started playing out the rope, and Jimmy began to drop into the black, yawning chasm. The only light was that which came from the carbide lamp he wore on his cap. His light began to flicker. There wasn't enough oxygen at this depth to keep the lamp burning.

"Light's going," Jim yelled up to the foreman.

"We'll get some oxygen down to you," he heard the foreman cry. They had no oxygen containers at that level, and there wasn't time to send to the surface for any. The experienced foreman grabbed a hose and started to pour a stream of water down the shaft. There is always a certain amount of oxygen in water, and, in addition, the stream of water started the air circulating and brought a downdraft which contained at least some of the precious oxygen. The water was a mixed blessing; it gave him purer air, but it also doused his carbide lamp. He finally reached the cage. It had landed hard and it was nothing but a twisted mess of cable and wreckage. Soaking wet, gasping for breath, he reached the two men. He felt for their pulses; both were dead. He gave the signal and was hoisted up. He reported what he had found, and suggested that another man be sent down with him. Together he thought they could attach a cable to what was left of the cage and raise it with the two bodies. Once more he was lowered the two hundred feet into the dark shaft. Another man followed him down. The heat was intense, and the metal of the cage almost unbearably hot to the touch, but they attached a cable. Both men were hauled up and then the cage, with its tragic burden, was raised to the 2,700-foot level. After that Doolittle was accepted as one of them.

2

Young Doolittle discovered in September, 1917, that there was a real war going on in Europe and that America had committed herself in a big way. The war fever had caught up with San Francisco, and Doolittle found that many of his classmates at the University of California had joined up. It was quite a shock to walk into the almost hysterical atmosphere of San Francisco after the isolation of the little mining town. The newspaper in Virginia City hadn't paid much attention to a war going on five thousand miles away. It was different in San Francisco, where every victory or defeat of the Allies was headlined in the newspapers.

Doolittle decided to get into this show—it seemed to be the thing to do. The mundane routine of the Infantry didn't appeal much to Doolittle. The Navy apparently wasn't taking a very active part in the war. There remained aviation. That, Doolittle thought, might be fun.

Doolittle had no special enthusiasm for flying. He was seriously interested in only two things—mining engineering and Jo Daniels. But there was something glamorous about flying, and Doolittle thought he might even make a hit with Jo's mother if he appeared at the Daniels' home in uniform.

Actually, in 1917 there was no such thing as an Air Corps or Air Force. The pitifully weak Air Service was merely an unimportant branch of the Signal Corps. Doolittle enlisted as a flying cadet in what was known as the Signal Reserve Corps, Aviation Section. He was told that they would notify him when they needed him. It seemed rather purposeless to register for his senior year at the University of California when he might be called up in a few weeks. So he decided to get a job.

The only kind of job that had any attraction for him was a mining job, and he heard that they needed men at the January Jones Quicksilver Mine in Napa County, California. The mine superintendent looked thoughtfully at this 133-pound youngster and asked, "Are you a miner?"

"Damn right I'm a miner," Doolittle said emphatically.

"Okay," the shorthanded superintendent said with considerable misgiving. "Go over there and join those drillers."

To make his initial job more difficult, he was assigned to drilling holes in the back or ceiling of the drift, a tiring job to any but the most experienced driller. He struggled for an hour or so, and then the superintendent took a look at what he had accomplished.

"You're no miner," he said in disgust. "Go over there and start mucking."

A mucker was the most unskilled of unskilled labor. After the holes were drilled, filled with dynamite and rock-blasted, the muckers loaded the crushed rock into the cars, which then went to the smelters where the ore was extracted. The indignity of being demoted from a driller to a mucker was embarrassing, but after a couple of weeks of it Doolittle was ordered to report to the Aviation Ground School at the University of California. Here he was given basic military training, lectures on military science, and went through the routine of what is now known as preflight training.

At Christmas the cadets were given a vacation, and Doolittle hurried down to Los Angeles. The uniform, to Jimmy's delight, had the anticipated result—at least with Jo.

Her mother still thought that her auburn-haired daughter could do a lot better than marry an irresponsible flying cadet. Without benefit of parental blessing Jimmy and Jo went to the Los Angeles City Hall on Christmas Eve to be married. Jo had a five dollar bill her mother had given her for Christmas and she paid for the license. They emerged from City Hall a little dazed by the wonder of it all. The only one to greet them was a frowzy woman who begged for a dime. The radiant Jo gave her a fifty-cent piece.

"You crazy?" Jim yelled. "We haven't got twenty dollars between us and here you are throwing money away to a ginned-up tramp."

"It'll bring us luck," Jo said, and then she turned to her brand-new husband. "We've been married three minutes and you're fighting already. I'm not sure . . ."

"Listen," he said. "Remember I'm taking the same chance that you are."

They spent their honeymoon in nearby San Diego. San Diego's chief advantage lay in the fact that there were a dozen cafeterias which gave food away to service men and their girls.

A few weeks later Jimmy was ordered to Rockwell Field, San Diego, for his flight training. He was assigned to the tender mercies of a civilian flight instructor named Charles Todd. His first instruction was to be in the dual control Curtiss JN-4 trainer which was never called anything but a Jenny. Doolittle climbed into the front cockpit, and under Todd's watchful eye buckled the safety belt. It was the first time that he had ever been in an airplane. He looked at the instrument board, which seemed fairly familiar after his preflight training. One thing bothered him a little. He was so short he could just see over the side of the cockpit.

Todd began to warm up the motor. Training planes were taking off and landing in a steady stream. Todd was about to taxi down the runway when there was a tremendous crash almost overhead. A plane taking off had collided with one coming in. Todd and Doolittle scrambled out of their plane and ran into the wreckage of the two planes. One pilot was dead, and another pilot and student horribly injured. The fire truck and an ambulance roared up. After the injured men had been removed Todd and Doolittle walked back to the Jenny.

"You all right?" Todd asked his pupil.

"Of course," Doolittle said, a little puzzled.

Todd looked at him curiously. The youngster seemed to have no nerves. He might just possibly be that one out of a hundred who could be made into a good pilot.

"Okay, let's go," Todd said.

The plane lumbered down the runway and then was airborne. Doolittle sat back in his pilot's seat completely relaxed. As Todd gained altitude, a feeling of exhilaration gripped his young student. During those brief moments Doolittle had fallen in love with flying. In those few moments his whole future was charted.

Todd began to give him instructions. Doolittle's hands moved almost instinctively over the controls, and his feet pressed just as instinctively on the rudder bar. Six hours of instruction and the cadet soloed.

Doolittle was commissioned a second lieutenant in the Aviation Section, Signal Reserve Corps, on March 11, 1918. His instructors were more than satisfied with the progress made by the fledgling pilot.

"The kid really has the feel of an airplane," they said—which was the ultimate in praise from the harassed instructors accustomed to handling ham-handed youngsters who were completely out of their element once they left the ground.

With the rest of his graduating class Doolittle waited impatiently for the orders that would send him overseas. The orders finally came, and the class left for France, but without Second Lieutenant James Doolittle. Doolittle was ordered to Camp Dick, Texas, to await orders. Dick was called a concentration camp long before that term was given the sinister significance it earned later. Pilots were stationed here, and from here assigned to either overseas duty, instructing, or advanced flying. The day he arrived, Second Lieutenant John

Allard, who had been trained at Ellington Field in Houston, Texas, also landed at Camp Dick.

Allard was a tall, handsome lad who had been working in a Boston bond house for a couple of years. He and Doolittle were first brought together by the fierce resentment each had toward the fate which had dropped them at this spot in Texas, when their hearts were set on being in France.

"I don't know what you're going to do tonight, Doolittle," Allard said, "but I'm gonna get out of this hellhole and have a few drinks."

"That suits me," Doolittle said.

The six-foot-two Allard and the five-foot-five Doolittle strode grimly to nearby Dallas. Allard, a free-wheeling spender, wangled a hotel room, sent out for a bottle of Scotch, and in the process of consuming it a lasting friendship was forged between the two completely dissimilar pilots. Their backgrounds were entirely different; Doolittle talked in the crisp tones of the Westerner, Allard with the broad A and soft accent of the Bostonian, but they found they had many things in common, not the least of which was the knack of being able to handle Scotch whiskey without any trouble at all.

A few days later the newly commissioned officers were assigned to various camp duties. There were no planes to fly at Dick, no instruction to take, but the commanding officer knew that he had to keep these exuberant young officers busy or they'd find ways of raising hell; they were given the job of painting barracks.

One of the pilots, looking for a way out of any of these onerous duties, sold himself to the C.O. as a boxing instructor. His name was Bruce Johnson, and he came from upper New York State. Each Saturday night Johnson would spar with some of his prize pupils. Bruce Johnson (who occasionally stuttered) had joined the Air Service direct from Cornell University, where he had been the college boxing champion. One night he ran out of sparring partners, and Doolittle, who had been watching, volunteered.

"Okay, take off your shirt," Johnson said cheerfully.

"What for?" Doolittle shrugged his shoulders.

"Take off your shirt and get into a pair of gym shoes," the instructor stuttered.

"I don't need gym shoes," Doolittle said disdainfully, "but if it'll make you any happier I'll take off my shirt."

The two men faced each other, Johnson smiling easily—Doolittle grim, a little contemptuous. Johnson threw a tentative left jab and then another. He was a good boxer. He kept his right hand high, his right elbow in close to his body, and he kept peppering his sparring partner with long but easy jabs. Doolittle ignored them. He kept shuffling in, and when he got in close he threw short hooks to Johnson's body that hurt. Johnson stopped smiling. This man could fight, and Johnson sighed happily. He wouldn't have to pull his punches against this opponent. He found it easy to jab Doolittle, and he found it easy to evade most of Doolittle's hard hooks. But when Doolittle did land a punch it hurt.

They boxed three rounds, and for more than thirty years they've been arguing as to which had the better of it. Doolittle's face was marked by the long jabs and occasional right hands that had reached it; Johnson's ribs felt as though they'd been tattooed by a well-shod horse.

"You're an easy guy to hit," Johnson laughed, shaking hands, "but a terrible guy to miss." Like Pedley, Johnson could fight without anger.

"Let's go out and get a drink somewhere," Doolittle grinned.

Johnson, Allard and Doolittle left the camp. They talked for hours of their delight in flying, of their dislike for all commanding officers, of their common affinity for whiskey. They talked about airplanes and about boxing, and discussed ways and means of getting to France. They were the same age—twenty-one.

Doolittle and Johnson were sent to Wright Field for courses in the maintenance and repair of engines. They were sent to Camp Dix, N. J., headed they thought for overseas, but instead they were shipped to Gertsner Field at Lake Charles, Louisiana, for advanced flying instruction. To their delight they found Jack Allard waiting for them.

"What's it like here?" Doolittle asked.

"Another hellhole," Allard said cheerfully. "I tell you, Jim, the mosquitoes here are big enough to saddle and ride. But at least they got airplanes."

"Jennies?" Johnson asked.

Allard shook his head. "Fast pursuit ships."

The Thomas Morse single-engined biplane was about the hottest thing in the local skies in 1918. Its Le Rhone or Gnome rotary engine which was lubricated with castor oil was capable of about 100 horsepower. It was not an easy plane to fly. It seemed to have only two speeds—off and wide open. The Gnome engine had no throttle—it was controlled only by the ignition switch. When you wanted to land you shut off the engine and glided in. It had no "brakes," and casualties were high among instructors and students. But Doolittle, Allard and Johnson felt the same excitement when given a Thomas Morse that a young pilot of today feels when given his first jet plane.

The week they finished their advanced training at Gertsner, disaster struck the airfield. A severe hurricane hit Louisiana, and Gertsner was almost literally blown off the map. The three hundred flyable airplanes were all demolished. The hangars, the barracks and the administration buildings were all smashed beyond repair. Gertsner Field as an air base ceased to exist, and the three young pilots were transferred to Rockwell Field, San Diego, to act as instructors.

At Rockwell they began what was then probably the most dangerous job in any service—the advanced instruction of youngsters many of whom nature had never intended to be flyers. The casualty among instructors teaching combat flying and aerial gunnery was high. In those days, any young man who was physically fit and was able to pass ground school examinations was taken into the Air Service. There were no such things as aptitude tests. Fundamental weaknesses which completely disqualified a man for flying could not be ascertained until you got him in the air and turned the controls over to him. Then he was very apt to go into a mental tailspin, freeze to the controls and destroy himself, his instructor and the airplane.

It wasn't long before Doolittle was recognized by his fellow instructors as being exceptional. He was patient with his students and, unlike many of the instructors, was conscious of their limitations. When he went to the C.O. to "wash out" some of his students, his decisions were received without question.

"I could teach these fellows to fly airplanes," he'd say, "but I can't teach them to be hot pilots. Unless we get rid of them, they'll destroy some good airplanes."

When he said "good airplanes," he was giving the crude, clumsy Jennies and Thomas Morses all the best of it. They weren't good airplanes, but they were the best ones available.

At periodic intervals Doolittle, Allard and Johnson would make fervent pleas for assignment to combat duty abroad, but the C.O. shelved all such requests. (It would be twenty-four years before Doolittle would ever fire a shot at or drop a bomb on an enemy.)

They were assigned to Ream Field, one of Rockwell's auxiliary training spots. Ream Field was an advanced gunnery and pursuit flying school. The instruction duties were not particularly difficult here, because only the very best of the students were selected to fly the expensive and scarce new fighter planes. For the first time Doolittle was able to do a little experimenting in the air. Reports had come back from France of the maneuvers perfected by Richthofen, by the Canadian Billy Bishop, by the American Eddie Rickenbacker, and Doolittle familiarized himself with the loops, barrel rolls and tight turns used in combat. As his knowledge of what a plane could do increased, so did his inventiveness. How much strain could you put on an airplane before it became uncontrollable?

This is what the instructors discussed, sitting around their tents after the day's work was done (there were no barracks at the field).

Meanwhile Jo was working for a shipyard in Los Angeles. Back at Manual Arts her favorite member of the faculty had been the librarian and her ambition had been to emulate friendly smiling Mabel Dunne. She had studied the intricate business of cataloguing and cross-indexing and now in the offices of the shipyard she made her training pay off. She kept the records and made more money in a month than did her husband. She visited San Diego week ends, staying at the Coronado Beach Hotel. She realized now that she would always have to share Jimmy with his other love, flying, and she accepted it without question. She accepted Allard and Johnson in the same spirit, knowing that their friendship meant a great deal to her husband. It wasn't long before their friendship meant just as much to her.

One morning Jimmy told her that he was going to take her for her first flight. It would have to be done without his commanding officer's knowledge for there was a rule forbidding pilots to fly civilians. He would pick her up about three miles from the hotel. She was waiting when he landed his Jenny. He motioned her to climb into the front cockpit. Jo looked up in dismay. She was wearing a tight hobble skirt and the wing seemed very high.

"How can I get up there?" she yelled trying to be heard above the roar of the engine.

"Climb up," Jimmy yelled back impatiently.

There was only one thing to do. She raised her skirts above her knees and scrambled up to the wing. Then feeling thoroughly ashamed of herself and hoping that no one was within seeing distance, she climbed over the side of the fuselage into the cockpit. A pair of goggles lay on the seat; she adjusted them and then was conscious of a faint sick feeling.

"What's that horrible smell?" she cried to Jim but busy with his controls he merely nodded his head encouragingly. The

Jenny took off, lurched sickeningly and then began to climb. The horrible smell was the castor oil which lubricated the engine. Jimmy wanted to show off to his bride. He put the Jenny through every maneuver he had learned, never realizing that his bride was being thoroughly sick in the front seat. He thought he was giving Jo a rare treat but the combination of rough air and castor oil fumes was too much for her. When he finally landed the Jenny she could barely climb over the side.

"That smell," she gasped and was promptly sick all over again.

"I got to get back," he yelled. He waved a careless hand and sent the Jenny roaring down the field. Jo stood for a few moments trying to regain her strength and her composure. The smell of the castor oil had gone with the Jenny but now she was conscious of another and equally nauseating odor. She looked about her and saw a factory in the next field—a potash factory whose chimney was spewing forth the fumes of potash. She hurried away as fast as her legs would carry her. She reached the hotel and staggered into the lobby. The long corridor to the elevators was known as Peacock Alley. Here the elite of San Diego gathered each afternoon to sip tea. Jo was puzzled by the attention she received as she strode toward the elevators. Every man and woman seemed to be staring at her intently. When she reached her room she realized why her appearance had startled the lobby-sitters. Except for small areas around her eyes which had been protected by the goggles her face was coal black. Her lovely dress was splattered with oil and stained by the castor oil fumes. Jo threw herself on the bed and sobbed. She resolved never to fly again. She kept her resolve, too, for nearly a month.

Jimmy had been lucky in having as his C.O. at Ream a fellow Californian who was a Stanford alumnus. Lieutenant Robert Worthington was in charge of Ream, although Colonel Harvey Burwell was the commanding officer of Rockwell and its auxiliary fields.

"I saw you knock out Eric Pedley," Worthington grinned

when he first saw Doolittle at Ream. Worthington, twelve years older than Doolittle, did his best to tame the exuberant young pilot, but when he found that to be impossible he just tried to keep Doolittle out of official trouble.

When Doolittle wasn't flying he was tinkering with engines. He always had a screwdriver or a pair of pliers or a spare spark plug in his pocket, and his uniforms were invariably stained with grease spots. Colonel Burwell took a dim view of this. Worthington felt that Doolittle had within him a great potential talent not only for flying but understanding airplanes. He wanted Jimmy to stay in the Army, but he felt that as soon as demobilization began Doolittle would be one of the first to be let out; commanding officers had no liking for irresponsible fliers who dressed like grease monkeys. Smart Bob Worthington had met Jo; now he pleaded with her to come and join Jimmy at Rockwell. She could keep him in line—could keep his uniforms clean. So Jo quit her job and joined Jimmy at Rockwell. He was overjoyed.

Worthington even found and rented a home for them not far from the field. It was a charming house with a two-car garage, with three bedrooms and a sun porch. Jo was entranced with it until she learned the rent. It was $55 a month, which put quite a bite into her husband's $147-a-month pay check. The first thing she did was to rent the garage and take in a boarder, Lieutenant Fonda Johnson. Then she decided she would learn to cook. Jo's mother had never allowed her daughter to enter her kitchen. She had never even boiled an egg or made a pot of coffee. She confided her problem to Louise Worthington. The wife of the Ream Field C.O. was a trained cook and she took Jo in hand.

"You may as well start from the beginning, Jo," she said earnestly. "Think of cooking as an art, not as a chore. When you are cooking you are creating something."

Under the guiding hand of Louise Worthington she learned quickly. As often as not Allard and Johnson would come home with Jimmy for dinner. Jo made the Fanny Farmer Cookbook her bible and gradually she began to have the same enthusiasm for cooking her friend Louise had. Jo was falling into the pattern of the army wife.

Meanwhile Jimmy was learning a great deal about flying an airplane. He tried dozens of experiments in the air. He was gradually learning a little about the science of aeronautics, but he knew that he didn't have the technical engineering training to properly evaluate or use this knowledge. Meanwhile, his daring experimental flying had earned him the reputation as a daredevil stunt flier, a reputation which displeased Colonel Harvey B. S. Burwell no end.

Doolittle was constantly in hot water with Burwell. Cecil B. de Mille, who was making an aviation picture, obtained permission to set his cameras up at Ream Field to get a few shots of military aircraft. Doolittle and Lieutenant John McCulloch had been having a little quiet fun engaging in some strictly nonmilitary aerial maneuvers. Doolittle had read of some barnstorming pilots who had entertained crowds with wing-walking. This presented a challenge to a youngster whose delicate sense of balance and timing had been developed on the parallel bars, the rings, the horizontal bar and the tumbling mat at the University of California. With McCulloch acting as pilot, Doolittle found wing-walking was absurdly simple. Within a few days Doolittle found that he could go through a dozen gymnastic gyrations on the wing of the plane. It wasn't long before he became just as much at home climbing along the wings, riding piggyback on the tail, or dangling from the landing gear, as he was in the cockpit.

One afternoon de Mille, peering through his camera, saw a rather strange sight. An airplane was approaching for a landing with someone sitting, quite at ease, below the fuselage on the axle connecting the two landing wheels. Automatically he began to turn the handle of his camera. McCulloch landed the plane skillfully, and Doolittle, quite unconscious of the fact that his stunt had been recorded for posterity, got up from his precarious seat and walked off the field with McCulloch. That night the eminent director showed Burwell the shots he had taken. They sat in a darkened room watching the routine flights, and Burwell was well pleased.

"There's a shot coming up that's a little bit out of the ordinary, Colonel," de Mille said mildly. "I suppose it's part of your training program."

Just then the plane with Doolittle sitting so nonchalantly on the landing gear appeared on the screen. Burwell exploded and turned to his aide.

"Tell Doolittle he's grounded for a month," he cried angrily to his aide.

"Are you sure that's Doolittle, sir?" the aide said, peering toward the screen. It was impossible to see the face of the man on the landing gear.

"He's the only one here who's damn fool enough to try anything like that," Burwell said. "Confine him to the post for a month and ground him."

Doolittle was made permanent Officer of the Day, with a term of thirty days. It was a dreary, tiresome assignment, relieved only by the fact that the Officer of the Day was given a motorcycle with sidecar to facilitate the routine checks he had to make all around the field. Doolittle relieved the monotony of the thirty days by putting the motorcycle through a lot of fancy maneuvering. He took out his frustration on the hapless motorcycle, and finding that with a little tinkering he could soup up its tiny engine, he used the broad expanse of Ream Field for experiment.

One day he was putting the motorcycle through its paces on the landing field when a Thomas Morse pursuit plane came in for a landing. Just as it was about to touch ground, the motorcycle circled in front of it and the pilot pulled it up sharply. Twice more the fast plane tried to land, and each time the motorcycle crossed its path. Finally the Thomas Morse landed at the far end of the field and an angry, sputtering pilot stepped out demanding to know what maniac was out there on that motorcycle. The understandably irate pilot was Colonel Harvey Burwell.

"Who is on that motorcycle?" he demanded of the senior officer present.

"It's Lieutenant Doolittle, sir."

"Confine him to the post," Burwell yelled.

"He is confined to the post, sir."

"Well, ground him," Burwell roared.

"He is grounded, sir."

"Well, damn it, do something with him," the frustrated Burwell said.

Doolittle was given an additional two weeks on the ground. He chafed under the restraint and began to build up an entirely unwarranted resentment against Burwell. Army discipline at that time meant very little to the twenty-one-year-old second lieutenant. He had much more respect for the primitive but effective way differences among men had been settled in Alaska or in Virginia City. But he realized that he would be grounded permanently if he followed his natural inclination to walk up and take a punch at his commanding officer. This sort of thing just wasn't done in the United States Army, where all officers were presumed to be gentlemen.

There was a physical director at Rockwell Field named Charles "Doc" Barrett whose job was to keep men and officers fit. Doc Barrett was a civilian who had been training football players at Williams College. Doolittle and he were good friends. Doolittle found out that Colonel Burwell liked to box. Burwell was an enthusiastic and fairly experienced boxer, and Doolittle conceived a truly Machiavellian scheme. He suggested to Doc Barrett that a special bout be added to the usual Saturday-night boxing program. The men, he suggested, would get a great kick out of seeing their commanding officer box. Doolittle said that he would be very happy to act as Colonel Burwell's sparring partner.

"The Colonel is a pretty good boxer," the physical director

said. "But, Jimmy, you're practically a professional. It wouldn't be fair. You'd knock his brains out."

"That's just what I want to do," Doolittle said grimly.

The physical director agreed to approach Burwell. The commanding officer listened to his proposal. Both Doolittle and Barrett had underestimated Burwell's intelligence. Burwell's initials, "B.S.," had made him rather vulnerable to the inevitable derisive nickname pinned on him by Doolittle, Allard, and the other pilots who sweated under his discipline. But Burwell was actually a capable if untactful commanding officer who thought that part of his duty was to keep the pilots in his command alive. Few of the breaches of discipline committed by Doolittle ever found their way on any official report made out by Burwell. He knew that Doolittle had within him the germ of flying greatness, but he also knew that left alone, Doolittle might easily kill himself.

He knew Doolittle's background thoroughly, and when Doc Barrett so blandly suggested that he and his problem boy put on a boxing exhibition, he knew just what Doolittle had in mind. Burwell knew that Doolittle kept himself in perfect physical shape, that he had been an amateur champion of note, and that he could easily have become an outstanding, perhaps champion, professional.

"Not a bad idea," he said to the trainer casually. "I'll tell you what we'll do. I'll box three rounds with Lieutenant Doolittle, and after that I'll box three with you."

The physical director knew a great deal about conditioning men, but he had been a football player who knew the rudiments of boxing but nothing more. He looked at the Colonel, saw the twinkle in his eye, and realized that Doolittle needed a few more years of experience before he could fool an experienced old regular Army man like the commanding officer. He knew that while Doolittle might do some damage to Burwell, when it was over Burwell would certainly dole out plenty of punishment to him.

"I guess it wasn't such a good idea after all," he said casually.

"Doolittle might hurt his hands and you would be losing one of your best pilots."

"Okay, Doc," Burwell said pleasantly, and Barrett had to report to Doolittle that their scheme had misfired. (Doc Barrett afterwards became the football trainer at Columbia University, and generations of Columbia athletes learned to love the genial Irishman.)

His period of chastisement over, Doolittle went back to flying. Some really outstanding pilots were being developed at Rockwell. In addition to Worthington, Doolittle, McCulloch, Allard and Bruce Johnson, D. W. Watkins, H. H. Bass, W. S. Smith, Albert D. Smith, "Red" Mosier, Lewis Dayton and H. L. Williams were all capable of the most advanced acrobatic flying. A group of Rockwell Field pilots under the leadership of Major Albert D. Smith had made a cross-country flight from San Diego to New York. The flight received considerable publicity. Bruce Johnson was one of the pilots, and when he returned he couldn't resist gloating over his ground-based pal Doolittle. The flight had taken place while Doolittle was Officer of the Day. Now that he was free to fly, he thought of something that would not only be interesting but that would reflect credit on the field. He took his idea to Colonel Burwell.

"A flight from San Diego to New York doesn't mean anything, Colonel," he said earnestly. "It's just a stunt. But a flight from Rockwell Field to Washington would mean something."

"What would it mean, Doolittle?" Burwell asked mildly.

"Well, Colonel, it would not only demonstrate how well we've learned navigation here, but if you could give us a message to deliver to the Army brass in Washington, it would demonstrate the value of an airplane to deliver confidential messages."

Doolittle was a persuasive salesman. Burwell listened as he pointed out on a map the various spots where the planes could be refueled. It was obvious that Doolittle had planned the flight thoroughly. Burwell was quite pleased. Young Doolittle was beginning to realize his undoubted potentialities. He was beginning to realize that there was more to flying than madcap stunting.

To Jimmy's amazement, Burwell said, "Go ahead with your plans. I'll let you pick out two other pilots."

Doolittle selected Walt ("Sump") Smith and Charlie Haynes. Four days later the three pilots took off from Rockwell Field for distant Washington, D.C.

The first leg of the trip was without incident. They made Indio, and the next morning set out for Needles. They reached Needles all right, but found there was no airfield there suitable for landing the Curtiss planes. But they had carried gasoline enough only to take them to Needles. Now they *had* to land. Doolittle spotted a concrete highway just outside the city. He landed without mishap, as did Smith, but Haynes in the third plane ran out of gasoline just short of Needles and cracked up in the midst of a pile of rocks. Doolittle phoned Colonel Burwell and said that everything was fine. The trip was going according to schedule.

"Just one slight mishap, Colonel," he said casually. "We lost one airplane and now there are only two of us left."

The next morning the two remaining planes took off from the highway, which was flanked by telegraph poles. Doolittle got off all right, but Smith hooked one of the telegraph poles with his right wing, spun around and cracked up the plane beyond repair. Doolittle saw the accident from the air. He came down to see if Smith was all right. Then he went to the telephone to tell Burwell the bad news.

"You'd better return to Rockwell Field," Burwell said icily, "before you get hurt."

3

Doolittle took off and headed for Rockwell Field. While flying over the mountains in the Imperial Valley section of California, he ran into heavy weather. He found it impossible to get above the overcast so he had to go below it. One part of this valley section looked like another and Doolittle had no idea where he was. He flew on, hoping that the overcast would lift, but the weather kept getting worse. He spotted a field below him that looked smooth enough and he landed. Unfortunately, it was a freshly plowed field and his wheels tangled in the furrows and then tripped the plane so that it nosed over to land on its back. Neither the aircraft nor Doolittle was hurt much. However, when the ship turned over, oil from the engine had showered on Doolittle, covering his face and his uniform. As he extricated himself from his awkward position under the plane, he caught his trousers on some obstruction and completely ripped out the seat. Two inquisitive farmers came up to see what strange monster had landed in their potato field. With their help, he turned the plane over. They pulled the plane to an adjoining field which was not yet plowed. The unpredictable California sun now burned the overcast away. Doolittle found out from the farmers just where he was, made the minor repairs necessary, and took off for Rockwell Field.

He immediately walked into Colonel Burwell's office. Burwell took one look at his oil-covered face, his filthy uniform, took a deep breath, and calling upon his long army experience launched into a tirade. He talked for ten minutes, and even the unhappy Doolittle had to admire the effective use his commanding officer made of profanity. Burwell never repeated himself. Doolittle realized that the tough miners he had known at Virginia City were amateurs in their use of invective. But finally even Burwell ran out of breath.

"Will that be all, sir?" Doolittle asked respectfully.

"That is all—for now," Burwell snapped.

Doolittle saluted and turned around to leave the office, completely forgetting that he had lost the seat of his trousers.

Burwell took one look at the pink expanse which confronted him. He could only put one interpretation upon Doolittle's lack of a trouser seat. Doolittle was extending to him the time-honored but usually unspoken invitation proffered by most junior officers toward their C.O.'s.

"You damned Chinese Ace!" he bellowed. "Get out of here."

Honestly bewildered for a moment, Doolittle was startled by the almost hysterical anger in his C.O.'s voice, and then he realized what Burwell was thinking. Doolittle, a devout disciple of the broad, rowdy humor much a part of the young Air Service, could only grin with delight.

"I'm sorry, sir," he said. "My trousers were ripped when I was getting out of the plane."

"Doolittle," the irate C.O. cried, "you can't even keep your ass in your pants."

Beyond the verbal castigation, Doolittle received no further disciplinary action. But for a long while he was the Chinese Ace to his fellow pilots. The expression had arisen out of the then-prevalent belief that Chinese army pilots destroyed virtually all of their own planes by clumsy flying tactics. It was true that by now Doolittle had cracked up some seven or eight planes, at a cost to the taxpayers of some $80,000. But pilots who didn't have frequent crack-ups were rare.

An influenza epidemic hit the West Coast, and Ream Field was put under strict quarantine. No visitors were allowed to enter the base, and none of the pilots allowed to leave the field. Two weeks of this and everyone at Ream was jumpy, uneasy and bored. Lieutenant Robert Worthington sold Colonel Burwell on the idea of letting a few of the boys take a Sunday morning flight to a lovely valley about a hundred miles away.

"There's a fine place to land there," he said earnestly. "There's a lake. We can all have a swim and be back before sundown. Nobody up there at all," he added casually, "just a nice-looking natural valley."

Burwell thought it a good idea. He knew that his pilots were restless. He didn't know that Worthington had landed in this "uninhabited" valley before and had found the hospitality of the natives quite overwhelming. It was a warm Sunday morning when four of the planes took off for the valley. Doolittle and Johnson formed the crew of one Curtiss. It was a beautiful day for flying, and as was their custom, they took turns flying the airplane. The Curtiss, designed for instruction, had dual controls. Johnson was in the front cockpit. Doolittle shouted something to him which he thought was a suggestion that he abandon the controls and let Jim take over. Johnson relinquished the stick, leaned back, and relaxed. For some unaccountable reason the plane didn't seem to be handling well. It took a few sudden lurches, but Johnson put this down to the turbulence one often found flying over the hills and valleys of southern California. It banked very sharply to the left, then slowly righted itself. Wondering what in hell Doolittle was trying to do, he turned his head and was horrified to see the rear cockpit empty. Doolittle had disappeared. Then he heard a shout from the left. Doolittle was sitting nonchalantly on the lower wing of the plane, his legs wrapped around the strut that connected the two wings.

"I thought you were flying this plane," Johnson yelled.

"I told you to keep it, I was going for a walk," Doolittle

shouted back. By now the plane was heading directly for an unfriendly looking mountain. Johnson grabbed the stick, pulled it back sharply and got it under control.

Doolittle finally tired of enjoying the crisp California air out on his precarious perch. He climbed back into his rear cockpit, and a few moments later Worthington, who was leading the flight, banked into a valley and started down for a landing. The rest of the flight followed. Worthington knew this place well. It was a rich farming section peopled by well-to-do families who lived so far from the large cities that they had to find their own amusement. The visit of an airplane was enough to startle and delight them all; the visit of four planes was the biggest thing that had ever happened to the community. The propellers of the planes had hardly stopped whirling when the crowd came running. People looked at the young pilots as though they were Olympian gods who had condescendingly come to brighten life for the poor earthbound mortals. The pilots were quite happy to be received in this fashion. They'd had two weeks of quarantine; they were all young and they were definitely ready for whatever hospitality the local citizens were prepared to mete out. Worthington had timed the arrival of the planes well. He knew that the local custom was to have a big Sunday dinner at noon, and it only lacked a few minutes of that hour now. The pilots only had to stand around looking godlike and nature took its inevitable course. A comely widow of about forty approached Doolittle and Johnson and asked if they would come to her home for dinner. They would; they did.

The comely widow not only served them a wonderful dinner but the meal was enhanced by the server—her young and attractive niece. Doolittle and Johnson played the part of modest Olympian gods and allowed the admiration and worship of the widow and the niece to flow over their hypocritical heads. The roast chicken, the masses of snow-white potatoes swimming in butter, the homemade wine, the apple pie and the after-dinner drink of brandy made the two young pilots forget all about the two dreary weeks of quarantine they had endured. Life was good—but it was three o'clock now, and take-off had been scheduled for three thirty. With intense reluctance Doolittle and Johnson, with promises to be back, left for the field. Their colleagues, all equally well fed and some with memories of hospitality that transcended the conventional, were waiting for them.

It was Doolittle's turn to fly. He took off and headed for the end of the valley. He had reached five hundred feet when a huge gray goose appeared just ahead of the plane. "Let's get that goose," he yelled, and Johnson nodded. The goose, a fast-flying bird, knew this valley better than Doolittle did. It flew straight ahead and then whirled to the right. Doolittle banked right after it. Now the plane was closing in. Johnson raised his eyes and his bones turned to butter. The goose had led the plane into a cul-de-sac.

"Get her up, Jim," Johnson roared, and then and only then did Doolittle take his eyes away from the goose. He saw cliffs on either side of him and the high expanse of a steep hill straight ahead. His wings were almost touching the cliffs on either side. He couldn't turn and yet couldn't clear the hill that seemed to be approaching at diabolical speed. He could only pull back the stick and hope for the best. The nose of the plane raised slowly, but it did raise. The plane skirted the slope of the hill, it clipped the branches from a hundred trees and then slipped rather gently into the shrubbery of the hillside. By some miracle (and some inspired piloting) the plane managed to avoid the tree stumps that dotted the hill. It collapsed fairly easily, its undercarriage smashed, its prop broken, but its two crew members unaccountably alive. Doolittle and Johnson climbed out of their plane, which now leaned dispiritedly against a huge boulder. They shook themselves, they felt for broken bones, and then they looked at each other.

"You damned Chinese Ace!" Johnson yelled.

Doolittle pointed above. A large bird was circling overhead.

It came lower, and then after a few raucous cries of triumph flew back to its valley. The goose had won a notable victory over the Air Service.

"Let's sit down and take it easy," Doolittle said calmly. "They'll come looking for us."

They did. Their late hostesses had seen the accident. So had half the inhabitants of the valley, and they all trouped up the hill to view the remains. They were amazed to find the two pilots sitting calmly beside the wrecked plane. Burwell had instilled the Air Service rules and traditions into his pilots. If you cracked up a plane but were not injured yourself, your first thought must be the safety of that airplane. Either you or a crew member must remain with it until your base was notified and assistance sent.

"You wrecked it, Jim," Johnson said. "I'll go back with these kind folks and phone headquarters."

Doolittle winced, but he knew the rules too. "Tell them to hurry," he urged.

Johnson said, "You know how the Old Man is. He'll only be concerned about the airplane."

"Okay, I'll stay here until he sends someone. But I don't want to spend the night here."

"It'll be dark in half an hour," Johnson reminded him. "We don't have anyone who could find this valley in the dark. Just make yourself comfortable, Jim. With any luck the Old Man will have someone here by morning."

Johnson went back with the kindly widow and her lovely niece. He phoned Rockwell, got Colonel Burwell and reported the accident. Burwell promised to send a wrecking crew to salvage what was left of the plane, but it couldn't arrive until morning.

"There's no hurry, Colonel," Johnson said smoothly. "Doolittle insisted upon staying with the plane. It's a warm night and he'll be comfortable enough."

"How about you, Johnson?" the irate C.O. said.

"Me? Oh, don't worry about me, Colonel, I'll be all right."

He hung up the phone and turned to the rapt faces of his hostess and her niece.

"Is there a hotel in the valley where I can get some sleep? I didn't realize it, but I'm afraid that crack-up hurt me more than I realized. . . . In fact," he said weakly, "I feel a little faint."

"Don't you worry about a thing," the widow said happily. "There is no hotel in the valley, and we'll be glad to take care of you."

They took very good care of him. Doolittle spent the night on the side of the hill swearing at all geese in general, but with special attention to the goose that had led him to this uncomfortable spot. That afternoon a stiff, sneezing Doolittle and a smug, contented Johnson flew back to Rockwell, where Doolittle again had to face the wrath of his C.O.

Doolittle took his instructing duties with deadly seriousness. It was just about the first time in his life he had been really serious about anything—except Jo. More than once he saw cadets who had been hurried along too fast by careless instructors, come to grief. This he resolved would be one sin he'd never commit. Each instructor was given four men to train. It was up to the instructor to decide when his students were ready for acrobatics. Doolittle had one batch of four rather exceptional students. They were bright, relaxed, air-minded, and all eager to attempt the advanced tests. One day he felt that they were all ready. He gave them their final instructions and then helped the first student into the cockpit of a Tommy Morse. The plane took off nicely, banked sharply and then for no apparent reason plunged to the ground. It burst into flames, and the student died in this burning pyre. The other three students stood frozen with horror. Doolittle called out crisply, "Who's next?" The three men looked at him, their faces white, but one of them nodded. Doolittle walked to another plane with him, in cold steady tones gave him his final instructions and then stepped away from the plane. He performed his rolls and stunts creditably. So did the remaining two students.

"What in hell have you got in your veins—ice water?" a fellow instructor barked at Doolittle. "Doesn't that kid's death mean a thing to you?"

"I'll think of that kid tonight," Doolittle said, tight-lipped. "Meanwhile my job is to make flyers out of these men. So is yours."

He did make flyers out of many of them, and by sifting out some who could never make the grade he probably saved more than one life. Doolittle didn't like instructing, but as long as they'd handed him the job he felt he had to do it well. He was beginning to have a pride in this Air Service to which he belonged. The war itself was very remote, but the Air Service was not. He went back to practicing his loops, his spins, and his Immelmann turns. Allard, Bruce Johnson, Clem McMullen, L. S. Andrews, John McCulloch and Steve Cavanaugh were all doing the same thing. And then Doolittle suggested that they try these stunts in formation. With a little practice, they found that formation stunt flying was not the suicide maneuver it had always been considered. It took a steady hand on the stick to keep your wings from brushing those of the planes on either side of you, but these pilots were all born with steady hands.

A visiting British Air Mission came to Rockwell Field and Burwell told his pilots to put the pursuit ships through their paces. This was just what Doolittle had been waiting for. Burwell and the British brass watched in amazement as Doolittle and his fellow pilots went through all of their tricks. It was the first time on record that pilots had ever stunted in formation.

"Never saw anything like it," the British general said to Burwell.

"Neither did I," the perspiring Burwell answered.

"You've certainly trained these pilots well, Colonel."

"I do the best I can," Burwell said weakly.

After that Burwell declared a truce in his war against Doolittle. Burwell was smart enough to know that he had an exceptional group of pilots here, spark-plugged by Doolittle. Life was more pleasant for Doolittle after that.

Bruce Johnson and Jack Allard lived at the Coronado Beach Hotel, in its biggest and most expensive suite. Bruce Johnson, although a second lieutenant, had the taste of a general, and like Allard he didn't have to live entirely on his Army pay. They both loved flying, and when they weren't flying they liked to talk about flying. With Doolittle they would stay up until the dawn arguing amiably about ways of getting more speed or maneuverability out of the planes they flew during the daytime. When Johnson bought a broken-down yellow Dusenberg racer for ninety dollars and had the Ream Field mechanics soup it up, the three young pilots were completely happy.

Los Angeles planned a monster air show, and Colonel Burwell was asked by the Army to provide some of the entertainment. He still had no love for Doolittle, but he had never forgotten the look of amazement on the British general's face as he watched Doolittle and his friends go through the stunt formations. He assigned Doolittle, Bruce Johnson, and Lieutenants H. E. Sturken, Lewis Dayton and F. B. Johnson to represent Rockwell Field. They practiced eight hours a day for a month and they were ready. More than two hundred airplanes performed in the greatest air show ever presented up to that time. Aces, back from France, went through combat maneuvers, and pilots, later to become famous (Major Carl Spaatz was one of them), gave spectacular exhibits of their flying skill. But the real thrill was furnished by the aerial acrobatic team. They dove, looped, spun, in perfect unison, acting, the *Los Angeles Times* said the next day, as though they were operated by a single hand. Colonel Burwell was well satisfied with the work of Doolittle and his colleagues. He was showered with congratulations which he accepted modestly. Shortly afterwards he was transferred and a new Commanding Officer arrived at Rockwell Field. His name was H. H. Arnold, but he was better known as "Hap." Before Arnold had the opportunity of impressing the force of his personality upon Doolittle, the war came to an end.

Now what? Allard was anxious to get back to civilian life. He tried to persuade Doolittle to do the same. He couldn't see any future in Army life or, for that matter, in aviation itself. They'd all had a lot of fun flying, but now the war was over.

"I'm going to stay in," Doolittle told them one night.

"I think I will too," Bruce Johnson agreed.

"What future is there in being a pilot?" Allard asked.

"Someday aviation is going to be real big business, I think," Doolittle said. "I'm going to stay in the Army and let the government teach me everything there is to be learned about airplanes. The hell with being a mining engineer. I'm going to be an aeronautical engineer. Then when I've learned everything the Army can teach me, I'll be ready to take a good job in the aviation industry."

"What in hell good are airplanes," Allard growled, "except in war?" (Later on Allard would make his living in the airplane business, but that was in the dim future.)

"Transportation, Jack," Doolittle said. "As soon as they make airplanes safer, they'll make them bigger. Why, in twenty years the train will become obsolete."

"All right, try it for a couple of years, you two suckers," Allard said. "Then come up to Boston and I'll get you both decent jobs."

Doolittle settled down to learn the business of being a soldier. Now that he had made up his mind that his future lay in aviation, he became more amenable to discipline. When he was appointed Executive Assistant to the Commanding Officer of Rockwell, his first impulse was to rebel. But then he realized that there was more to aviation than mere flying, and that sooner or later he would have to learn the administrative side of the game. This new post cut down his flying, but added immeasurably to his knowledge of the ground work done by the mechanics and maintenance men at the field.

Many of the World War flyers had organized barnstorming groups, and more than once Doolittle was sorely tempted to join them. It was a hazardous way of earning a living, and the mortality was high among the flyers, who were trying to cash in quickly on their World War I fame. Their limited resources prevented them from buying good planes, and the ramshackle craft they used often came apart in mid-air. It wasn't the personal danger that kept Doolittle from joining their ranks; it was the financial insecurity. As long as he remained in the Army, he and Jo were at least certain of a roof over their heads and three meals a day.

After a few months he was transferred to the Mexican border, where he flew with the Border Patrol. The Border Patrol was supposed to stop smuggling, but as all of the smuggling was done at night and Army planes at that time were hardly useful at night, the Border Patrol could not be said to be very effective. But there were a few thoughtful, far-seeing officers now, men like Billy Mitchell and Hap Arnold, who realized the potential strength that airplanes might one day supply; and they were doing everything they could to keep the tiny Air Service alive. The Border Patrol was merely an excuse for developing young pilots like Doolittle and keeping them enthusiastic.

The progressive men in the Air Force had another weapon —not a very good weapon, but they'd use any means to keep appropriations earmarked for the purchase of airplanes. A great many newspapers started a "Look Out for Mexico" campaign. They actually began to arouse the public about the possibility that Mexico might declare war on the United States. This completely absurd fear played beautifully into the hands of the Air Service. It gave the little Border Patrol some excuse for existence, and the Army brass, which for the most part still considered airplanes to be expensive toys, was forced to spend some of its appropriation to keep the Air Service alive.

One Border Patrol station was located at Eagle Pass, a sleepy Army outpost which offered little in the way of either excitement or comfort. Bruce Johnson went along with Doolittle, and both were disgusted at the austerity of Eagle Pass life. To begin with, they lived in pup tents. Living in any kind of a tent was bad enough, but pup tents had no flooring, no warmth, no protection against the occasional rains or the more usual blistering sun. But they had a fine C.O., First Lieutenant H. D. McLean, who had known Doolittle and Johnson at Rockwell.

The flying duties were not too onerous. The Border Patrol flew DH-4's. Bruce Johnson was sent to San Antonio to secure some much-needed supplies. Lieutenant McLean told him what was needed and then added casually that if he saw anything else at San Antonio which might come in handy, to get it. Johnson saw plenty of things at San Antonio he thought might come in handy. To begin with, there were rifles and shotguns—not for any anticipated combat with Mexican smugglers but for himself and Doolittle to use on the deer, the duck, doves, quail which abounded in the region the Border Patrol policed. While he was about it he managed to requisition a piano. The piano was put in a tent on its arrival, and the guns and ammunition divided among the pilots.

Now life became a bit more bearable at Eagle Pass. Until the arrival of the hunting guns, Doolittle's chief diversion had been the "buzzing" of deer as he flew over them. Now he and Johnson made many "forced" landings, climbed out of their planes, and a few hours later arrived at the base with cockpits filled with birds and game.

Doolittle spent five months there and then sent for Jo. Lieutenant McLean wangled a house of sorts from the post commander but there wasn't a stick of furniture to be had. There were plenty of crates and plenty of lumber around and with the help of a few other amateur carpenters Jimmy made a couple of tables and five or six chairs. He decided to give Jo a shock. He grew a beard. When she stepped from the train there was her husband with a full reddish chin-growth. He waited expectantly for the anticipated explosion but Jo said nothing. She chatted about her trip and about friends who had sent messages and the more she chatted the more silent the frustrated Jimmy became. They reached the post, went into their new home, and finally Jimmy couldn't control himself any longer.

"Can't you even see I've grown a beard?" he stormed.

She peered at him closely. "You know, Doolittle," she said slowly, "I did feel that you looked a little bit different. I guess it is the beard."

Life at Eagle Pass was primitive and complicated by the fact that the regular Army men at the post looked upon the pilots with something less than enthusiasm. The pilots earned extra pay for flying and this caused considerable jealousy. There was virtually no fraternizing between flying men and the regular officers attached to the post. Jo was an accomplished cook by now and her beaverboard house was usually filled with pilots munching on the cookies she made so expertly. She took a few lessons in pastry-making from the Chinese cook stationed at the post and she learned how to make the Mexican dishes so popular in border posts. From Eagle Pass the Doolittle family was sent to the border cavalry post of Del Rio. The cavalry too looked with scorn upon the flying men. By now Jo had become resigned to the fact that she would forever be an Army wife. She would never have a permanent home, never be allowed to grow any real roots. But life with Jimmy was an exciting adventure. Like her husband she made friends easily and her home, no matter where it was, immediately became a clubhouse for Jimmy's fellow pilots. Jack Allard was back in New England working for the Gillette Safety Razor Company. Bruce Johnson had left the Army to handle his father's farming properties in upper New York State. But these two men now seemed part of the Doolittle family and they kept in constant touch with them.

In 1920 Doolittle was commissioned a first lieutenant in the regular Army and assigned to the Air Service Mechanics School at Kelly Field, San Antonio. Here he had a chance to experiment with a dozen different types of aircraft. He began to realize that these World War I planes were on the whole clumsy, primitive aircraft that were too slow and too temperamental. He learned how to soup up engines, and he began to study ways of reducing wind resistance. He developed theories of what later would be known as streamlining.

In 1921 he was sent to Langley Field in Virginia, to take part in some interesting experiments to be conducted by General William Mitchell. Mitchell at that time was the most controversial figure in the Army. As early as 1919 he had prophesied in the magazine *Air Service* that in another few years commercial air passengers would be as familiar a sight as train passengers; that distances between the West Coast and East Coast would be figured in terms not of miles but of hours.

Mitchell never stopped preaching of the possibilities of air power. He cried out that "the entrenched admirals in Washington are too stupid to face the fact that sea power is done for." The one thing, above all, Billy Mitchell hated was the battleship. He said that the battleship was an absurd anachronism that could be sunk easily enough from below by a submarine or from above by an airplane. The old-line admirals and generals disliked General Mitchell intensely.

Right after the war the United States Navy had in its possession several former German warships, including the big battlewagon *Ostfriesland*. Mitchell pleaded for a chance to demonstrate his theories on these German warships, but the Navy was obdurate. When Mitchell told a Congressional committee that it was his belief that a fleet that had twenty airplane carriers could always annihilate a fleet of twenty ordinary battleships, a storm broke about his head. Oddly enough, some high-ranking officers and an obscure Assistant Secretary of the Navy named Franklin D. Roosevelt agreed with him.

Mitchell, in his fight to make the country air-minded, did not hesitate to use every weapon which he could get his hands on. He even violated all service traditions by enlisting the aid of the press. Former Secretary of the Navy Daniels, whose influence at that time was considerable, declared contemptuously that he would stand bareheaded on the bridge of any battleship during any bombardment by any airplane "and by God, expect to remain safe."

The controversy as to whether or not Mitchell should be allowed to use the obsolete German ships as targets even reached the White House, and strong pressure was brought to bear on President Harding to prevent the experiment from taking place.

Meanwhile, Mitchell had gathered a group of pilots at Langley Field for training in bombing. They flew twin-engined Martin Bombers and DH-4's. Doolittle was made engineer officer and a flight leader in a DH Squadron. The DH-4 was a two-place biplane powered by a Liberty 400-HP engine. It wasn't much of a plane, but it was capable of carrying bombs. While Mitchell fought his fight in Washington, Doolittle and the rest of the group went through intensive test flights, many of which were held at night.

Doolittle and his crew were told to try some night bombing. A sergeant in charge of a detail was sent to an island off the coast of Virginia and ordered to build a huge fire just before night fell. This fire would be the target for the bombs. Doolittle and his crew took off with four one-hundred-pound bombs suspended beneath each of the lower wings of the plane. They proceeded on course, and soon saw a fire burning brightly. Doolittle made his bomb run, signaled to his crew, and the eight bombs flew through the night. All of them landed on or very close to the fire. They returned to Langley Field, well satisfied that they had done a good job. The next morning Doolittle called in the sergeant who had been sent to light the fire, to check up on the accuracy of the bombing.

"How many of our bombs landed within fifty feet of the fire?" he asked the sergeant.

"What fire, Lieutenant?" the sergeant said, puzzled. "Didn't they tell you? The boat that was going to take us out to that island had something wrong with its engine, so we never did get there and we never did light a fire."

Doolittle swallowed hard and waited for the complaints that would come in from angry campers. He couldn't think of anyone else who would have a fire roaring at night on an uninhabited island off the coast. But no reports were made, and Doolittle never learned whose fire it was he had bombed nor did he ever get a report on how accurate the bombing had been.

Mitchell finally won, and the historic experiment was conducted by the Langley Field bombers. The *Frankfurt* was hit and sunk in eleven minutes, and the unsinkable *Ostfriesland,* which had withstood the heaviest Naval gunfire in the Battle of Jutland and which had made port after a mine had exploded directly under her, followed. The next day Billy Mitchell was a national hero. The Army and Navy brass took a dim view of this unorthodox air general, and the Joint Army and Navy Board, after investigating the bombing tests, issued an incredible report which stated that nothing conclusive with regard to air power had been proven. The report added that planes were a valuable auxiliary, but could not be depended upon by themselves. The battleship was "still the backbone of the fleet and the bulwark of the nation's sea defense." The report was signed by General Pershing.

Mitchell answered the report in what was intended to be a confidential memo to Major General C. T. Menoher, his chief. Somehow Mitchell's vitriolic answer, which spared neither the admirals, the generals nor Pershing himself, became public. Not long after that Billy Mitchell was assigned to Fort Sam Houston, Texas, where he reverted to his permanent rank of colonel and was made Air Officer of the post.

By now Doolittle had become a devout disciple of Billy Mitchell. He too believed that neither armies nor navies could exist in warfare unless the air above them was controlled. Hap Arnold, Tooey Spaatz, and a dozen other progressive young officers were doing their best to persuade the Army that Mitchell was right and that Secretary of the Navy Wilbur was living in a dream world when he said, "The Atlantic and Pacific are still our best defense." Air power was on its way, but it would be years before it would be accepted.

Doolittle felt now that he would like to tackle a cross-country flight. Bad luck had attended most previous attempts by Army pilots to span the continent, and only a few months before, Lieutenant W. D. Coney, taking off from Pablo Beach, Florida, in what was intended to be a one-stop flight to San Diego, met his death. Lieutenant Alex Pearson, trying to span the continent, had been forced down in Mexico by engine failure.

Doolittle had studied the various attempts and he thought he knew the answers to some of the problems which had defeated most of the pilots. He asked for and obtained permission to tackle the cross-country flight.

He took one of the DH-4 biplanes to the San Antonio Air Depot where it was stripped of every excess part. Once he had lightened it and eliminated the second seat he was able to fit it with extra gas tanks. But before taking off from Pablo Beach he wanted to fly to McCook Field near Dayton, Ohio, to see if they had anything new in the way of navigation instruments. He wired Washington for permission to fly there first. There was no answer so he decided not to wait. He took one of the conventional two-place DH-4's and carried Lieutenant L. S. Andrews, who had just married Jo's sister, as a passenger. Andrews wanted to visit his folks at Napoleon, Michigan, not too far from Dayton. They arrived in Washington and Doolittle, according to the tradition of the service, checked in with General Mason M. Patrick, Chief of the Air Force. Patrick, a grave, correct officer, asked Doolittle if he had obtained official permission to make the flight to Washington.

"Well, sir, I did apply for permission," Doolittle said seriously, "but it didn't arrive and I . . . well, I assumed it was all right, so I just took off."

"Suppose, Doolittle," the General said in his most official tones, "that when you landed here you had discovered that permission for the flight had been refused. What would you have done?"

"Sir," Doolittle said gravely, "I would have hopped into my plane and immediately returned to San Antonio."

"Quite right," the General said, completely mollified.

"Now I would like permission to go to McCook Field to pick up any new instruments they might have."

"That is granted." General Patrick nodded his dismissal.

"One thing more, General," Doolittle asked. "I have my brother-in-law, Lieutenant Andrews, with me. He has leave to visit his parents who live near McCook. May I drop him off there?"

"Yes, yes, go on," Patrick said, and Doolittle, with Andrews in the rear cockpit, headed for Napoleon, Michigan.

"Go to Jackson and then I'll steer you, Jimmy," Andrews said. "We've got a field back of the farm—plenty of room to land."

They found Jackson, and then Andrews guided him to Napoleon. From the air all the farmhouses looked pretty much alike, but finally Andrews spotted his parents' homestead. Doolittle circled the white farmhouse.

"Andy," he yelled, "you said there was a big field where we could land. Where is it?"

"It seemed awfully big when I was a kid and had to plow it," Andrews said sadly. "But I guess it shrunk a bit."

Doolittle headed back for Jackson where there was a field of sorts, and they hired a car to take them to Napoleon. From there they went to McCook and Doolittle picked up a crude bank and turn indicator; it wasn't all that he wanted but it was the best instrument of its time. And then they headed back to San Antonio.

The flight had attracted some attention from the press, and when Doolittle went to Pablo Beach near Jacksonville, Florida, he found that for the first time in his life he was something of a celebrity. Pablo Beach was perfect for a take-off. At low tide the sand made a hard-packed runway, completely unobstructed. Doolittle had complete confidence that he would be able to lift the heavily overloaded plane from the beach without any trouble at all.

On the morning of August 6, 1922, more than a thousand Floridians turned out to watch Jimmy's take-off. He warmed up the engine and grinned cheerfully at the crowd. Then he sent the biplane roaring down the beach. He gave the engine full throttle, but then allowed the plane to veer too close to the water. The left wheel hit a soft, wet spot in the sand and the plane slowed abruptly, veered toward the ocean, buried its nose in the sand and turned gently over.

Doolittle was tossed clear of the plane. He landed in the water, his helmet down over his eyes; his goggles over his nose. Dazed by the shock of landing, his vision cut off by the helmet, he began threshing his arms wildly to get out of the watery depths into which he had fallen. He felt the fuselage of the plane and pulled himself up—when he pushed his helmet away from his eyes he found, to his embarrassment, that he had landed in water only two feet deep. The cheers of the crowd had changed to laughter, and young Doolittle wished fervently that the earth would open and swallow him.

The plane had sustained only superficial damage. Four weeks later, after it had been repaired, he tried again, this time without benefit of crowd. The heavy DH-4 took off without any difficulty, and Doolittle headed for Kelly Field, Texas. He flew at an altitude of 3,500 feet and at a speed of 105 miles an hour. Two hours after his take-off he flew right into a severe thunder and lightning storm. He tried to pick out familiar landmarks every time the lightning flashed. He flew out of the thunder and lightning and into a heavy rainstorm which stayed with him until he reached New Orleans. Then the weather cleared and he made Kelly Field without any trouble. His time was ten hours and five minutes.

He stayed at Kelly only long enough to refuel, and then

aimed for San Diego. A few days before he had left Pablo Beach he had written to his old friend Lieutenant John McCulloch, who was now Adjutant of Rockwell Field. In discussing the flight with McCulloch he said the only thing that worried him was the fact that he might fall asleep during the last two hours of the flight. He asked McCulloch to send a couple of boys out to meet him, to keep him company on the last lap. When Doolittle reached Yuma, two planes were circling, waiting for him. They were flown by Captain William Randolph and Lieutenant C. L. Webber. Doolittle had been sleepy, but the sight of the two planes acted as a cold shower. He touched down at San Diego eleven hours and fourteen minutes after he had left Kelly Field. He had crossed the continent in twenty-one hours and nineteen minutes, and his average speed was a hundred and one miles an hour.

This flight put Doolittle's name on the front page of every newspaper in the country. It was an affirmation of some of Mitchell's popular theories. Doolittle was hailed as the greatest pilot in the service. Never again would he be able to live in anonymity—henceforth in the service he would be regarded as a man "to watch." Civilians would regard him as a harebrained, death-defying pilot. Doolittle enjoyed both reactions. He had developed an intense love for the Air Service and for the men who were trying to develop it. As for public acclaim —he didn't mind it a bit. This was something he could take in his stride.

"Looks like I'm married to a hero," Jo said to him one day.

"Maybe, Doolittle," he said complacently. "But hell, I haven't started yet."

4

The Florida-to-California flight was merely one of many pioneering flights by Army pilots that year. A month after Doolittle's flight, two other Army pilots, Lieutenant Oakley J. Kelly and Lieutenant John A. Macready, attempted a nonstop flight across the continent. The flight failed. So did a second attempt. Then Kelly and Macready made a new world's endurance record for sustained flight by remaining in the air for thirty-six hours. They then successfully made the first nonstop transcontinental flight. The Army knew that there were a great many unknown factors which had to be thoroughly explored before further progress could be made in flying and they encouraged their pilots to venture into the realm of the unknown.

The Air Corps Engineering School had been established at McCook Field to study these problems. Doolittle was sent there to study all of the problems connected with flying, and to do research. Airplanes frequently came apart in the air for no apparent reason; pilots themselves cracked up under the strains and tensions of fast flying. The Army wanted to know why. It wanted to know the answers to dozens of flying problems, and the pilots doing research at McCook Field were the guinea pigs selected for experimentation.

For the first time Doolittle now had the opportunity of really studying an airplane from the tip of its nose to its rudder. He had always realized that flying was more than a matter of giving the engine full throttle and sitting on it until you reached your destination. But he had never realized that there were so many questions which aeronautical engineering still couldn't answer. He knew that he couldn't attempt to find the answers until he was thoroughly familiar with the fundamentals of the science. For the first time in his life he embraced classroom studying with enthusiasm. He found that his immense practical knowledge of flying was of great help to him in learning something about the theory of plane construction, of stress and strain under various flying conditions.

He had been at McCook Field a year when the University of California, in recognition of his Florida-to-California flight and of his study at the Air Corps Engineering School, had conferred the Bachelor of Arts degree upon him, the degree he had missed by passing up his senior year at the University. In July, 1923, he had completed virtually all of the prescribed courses. There was a report that the Army was going to sponsor an around-the-world flight, and Doolittle was desperately anxious to be one of the pilots picked. Captain Ed Aldrin, who was in charge of the Engineering School at McCook Field, and Lieutenant Sam Mills, his assistant, tried to discourage Doolittle, but Doolittle's imagination was captured by the thought of being among the first to circle the globe by air. Mills then presented his case to Jo Doolittle.

"Jimmy has shown a great aptitude," he told Jo, "for engineering research. The Army is inaugurating a new project. We are sending six students to the Massachusetts Institute of Technology for advanced work in aeronautical engineering. I'd like to see your husband spend two, maybe three years at M.I.T."

"But where do I come in?" Jo asked, puzzled.

"You might be able to persuade him to enter M.I.T.," he said. "Jimmy has a fine scientific mind. At M.I.T. they will teach him everything that is known about aeronautical engineering and subjects allied to it. We have plenty of pilots in the Air Force capable of handling long flights, but we don't have many engineering brains like Jimmy's."

"I'd like to help you," Jo said helplessly, "but I will tell you how our family operates. I take care of the children and the cooking. Jimmy never interferes with me. I'd never think of interfering with him when it comes to flying or his career. He has to decide these things for himself."

"All right, Jo," Mills said, discouraged. "I only hope he doesn't spoil what can be a brilliant career just for the sake of a spectacular flight."

Mills recommended that Doolittle be one of those selected for the special postgraduate engineering courses at M.I.T. When time came to enroll in the fall, the Army turned down Doolittle's plea to participate in the round-the-world flight. He was sent to M.I.T., and so once again Jo packed up, and headed for Boston.

By now Johnny had come along to join young Jimmy. Jo had become accustomed to packing up the family and moving; it was part of the job of being an Army wife. She found a floor in a three-family house in Dorchester, not far from Cambridge. The $65-a-month rent she had to pay put a big dent in her husband's $160-a-month pay check.

M.I.T., then as now, was one of the most exacting of all scientific institutions. It had attracted perhaps the most brilliant group of engineering instructors ever to assemble at any college. Men like Woods and Bailey, and the nearly blind mathematician, C. M. E. Moore, and the aeronautical engineering genius Edward Warner, were exacting taskmasters. During the first year Doolittle was often discouraged, often felt out of his depth, but he stuck doggedly at it. He knew you could never find the answers that the whole aviation world was looking for until you had thoroughly mastered all of the theoretical knowledge available. Once you had this knowledge you could use it as a springboard, and from it leap into the unexplored regions and perhaps eventually return with some of the right answers.

He would return home every night to Dorchester mentally exhausted, always with pages of scribbled notes taken down during the day's lectures. Jo saw an opportunity to be of help to him. Back in her Manual Arts days when her only ambition had been to be a librarian, she had studied typing. Now if she could only type out Jimmy's daily lecture notes and file them, they would always be available for quick reference. But, unfortunately, the ordinary typewriter did not have the mysterious mathematical signs upon its keyboard. A typewriter did not speak the language of trigonometry or of integral calculus. Jimmy, however, found that one company made a mathematical typewriter with five shifts (including one for Greek). He bought one and now each night when he came home and while the lectures were fresh in his mind, he dictated to Jo, and that night she would type his notes up neatly. Every morning over his hurried breakfast he would read them over.

He was blessed, he discovered, with a remarkable memory —an essential requisite if one were to get through the highly concentrated mass of knowledge hurled at the M.I.T. students by their professors.

It was inevitable of course that the Doolittle home would be, as usual, a gathering place for the friends whom both Jimmy and Jo always attracted. Ted Lonnquest, Red Townsend, George Chapline, Clarence Lober, Ed Sorenson, instructors like Bill Brown and professors like Ed Warner were frequently in and out of the small Doolittle apartment. Somehow out of her limited budget Jo always managed to have beer in the icebox and cheese and crackers in the pantry. They would sit far into the night discussing some of their more esoteric problems. Jo would sit quietly as they talked what to her was a foreign language. But she was always busy. The day just wasn't long enough to do all the things that she wanted to do. There was the matter of china, for instance. Her budget would only allow her to buy plain, undecorated china. But Jo had a talent for painting flowers, and she learned how to paint the plain china. While her husband and his classmates were argumentatively exploring the higher echelons of mathematics, she would sit in the corner contentedly painting her dishes, her cups and her saucers.

Jo also found that the university sold student tickets for the Boston Symphony. Betty Brown was secretary to Professor Warner. Once a week Jo would deposit three-year-old Jimmy and one-year-old Johnny in Professor Warner's office, and Betty would take care of them while Jo hurried off to Symphony Hall.

At the end of the college term Doolittle was sent back to McCook Field for a temporary assignment. The Army was planning an expansion program for the Air Corps and was considering the purchase of a great many new pursuit planes (it would be another twenty years before they would be referred to as fighter planes). Before specifications for the new planes were decided upon, there were a few things the Army wanted to know about the flying characteristics of the planes it was tentatively considering. The top brass wanted to know, for instance, if the formulae then in use to calculate design strength were valid. How much strain could the wings of an airplane stand before they disintegrated? Were the present safety factors correct? It was the kind of a job which Doolittle delighted to undertake.

The government-sponsored National Advisory Committee for Aeronautics had been given the job of doing research for both Army and Navy planes. Information about acceleration in flight was sadly lacking and both military and commercial planes were being plagued by too many unexplained crashes. The aviation world wanted to know not only how much strain a plane could stand—but how much strain the human body could stand before it collapsed. It was really a matter of investigating and charting the effect gravity had on plane and human under varying flight conditions. A man standing on the ground has a normal pull of gravity, which science arbitrarily defined as one G. But suppose you are at 5,000 feet and you are streaking along at 250 miles an hour and you decide to make a sharp turn? A little thing called centrifugal force enters the picture then. If you turn sharply to the right, natural forces tend to hurl your body to the left. Suppose you threw your plane into a steep drive? Gravity doesn't bother you until you try to pull out of the dive. Pull out sharply and you are fighting gravity and gravity can be a remorseless foe, quite capable of collapsing either aircraft or human frames. These all came under the heading of the subject Doolittle was assigned to study.

Brilliant Ed Warner, perhaps the best-known man in his field, had taught Doolittle a great deal about how much stress wings would take. Only a pilot with scientific knowledge and with rare flying ability could test these planes with a reasonable chance of staying alive and of bringing back information of value to the engineers. For two months Doolittle put all of the new planes through every possible maneuver. He would climb to 18,000 feet, and then nose over and with full throttle plunge the plane toward the ground. When he thought the wings were just about ready to sheer off the plane, he would pull it up out of the dive. Recording devices which were attached to the planes brought back the story of the speed reached at the zenith of the dive. He did loops at every possible air speed; he performed single and multiple barrel rolls; power spirals; tailspins; half loops and half rolls; Immelmann turns. He put every plane he flew through the most extreme maneuvers possible. Several times he came close to disaster, but he was always impatient at fellow pilots who urged him to be more cautious.

"I calculate every risk I take," he would say curtly.

Invariably after putting a plane through the most difficult stunts, he would examine it thoroughly. A recording accelerometer and various other instruments which were always mounted on the plane were immediately grabbed by the test supervisors; but Doolittle always wanted to inspect the plane itself. Once after he had dived a pursuit plane and had pulled it out at the height of its dive, he landed to find that both wings had already begun to crack. He found that the paint had literally peeled in strips away from the wings. He knew that had he attempted one more dive the wings would have flown away and he would have had no time at all to bail out. Instead of frightening him, the discovery of the cracked wing-ribs delighted him. Now he knew exactly what the breaking point was in this particular airplane. The wing had failed when the acceleration had reached 7.8 G's. The design strength was 8.

The N.A.C.A. immediately rushed Doolittle's report into print and gave it the prosaic title, "Report No. 203—Accelerations in Flight." It created a considerable stir in engineering and aviation circles, for it was the first authentic information on the subject to emerge, not from the drawing board or mathematical formulae, but from the experience of a test pilot who was not talking theory but was giving data gathered from actual experimentation. Doolittle presented tables and charts which showed the effect of acceleration upon the plane while it was going through single and multiple barrel rolls, as well as during the various loops he sent the Fokker PW-7 with its Curtiss D-12 engine through. Of vital interest to pilots was his report on the effect severe accelerations had upon the human body. Doolittle wrote:

> From the results of these tests it is apparent that serious physical disorders do not result from extremely high accelerations of very short duration, but that accelerations of the order of 4.5 g., continued for any length of time, result in a complete loss of faculties. This loss of faculties is due to the fact that the blood is driven from the head, thus depriving the brain tissues of the necessary oxygen. To the pilot it seemed that sight was the only faculty that was lost. The flight surgeons at McCook Field are of the opinion that sight is the last faculty to be lost under these conditions, even though the pilot may be under the impression that he retains all the others.

This opinion is based on the observation of men undergoing rebreather test. The acceleration which an individual can withstand for any length of time depends upon his blood pressure, the person with the higher blood pressure being able to withstand the higher acceleration. Upon the condition of the heart depends the ability of the individual to recover quickly from the effect of prolonged acceleration. If the heart is in good condition, there is no danger in undergoing such a strain unless the acceleration is continued for a period in excess of 10 or 12 minutes, after which death will result. The same is true of the rebreather test; unconsciousness will result from the deprivation of oxygen and death will result if this is continued for the same length of time.

This was the kind of information which would explain some of the recent crashes and which would point out the road to safer flying. So important was the report that it was translated into half a dozen languages and within weeks had become as well known in Warsaw as it was in Washington. Back at M.I.T. Jimmy plunged into the difficult curriculum. There was one course he didn't bother much about—the course Acceleration in Flight given by his friend Bill Brown. He knew more about this subject than any pilot alive. When time came for the final examination Brown pulled a fast one on him. He asked a lot of questions more theoretical than practical and Doolittle just didn't know the answers.

"I can't flunk you, Jimmy," the irate Bill Brown said. "After all you've written the book on flight acceleration. But damn it all, I just want you to know that you're the worst student I ever had."

"And you're the worst teacher I ever had," Doolittle grinned.

"Okay," Brown sighed. "Now let's take a few days off and go deer hunting. There's a man up in Maine . . ."

The results of the tests he made at McCook during those two months were invaluable. When the Army engineers forwarded their specifications to the aircraft companies and asked for bids on pursuit planes, some of the findings he emerged with immediately became part of aeronautical engineering law.

Merely as an economical necessity he had to put in several hours a week flying time. This was the only way he could retain proficiency and qualify for his flying pay. The C.O. at the Boston Airport was Captain Robert Brown, an old friend, and Doolittle usually spent week ends flying whatever type of aircraft Brown happened to have around his airfield. Jack Allard was living in nearby Melrose manufacturing and selling shoes, but he had retained his reserve officer status, and he usually went along with Doolittle on his week-end flying excursions. There wasn't much excitement in flying the standard JN-4's and DH's which were based at Boston Airport, so Allard and Doolittle inaugurated a game of follow-the-leader. They would take turns in leading. If Doolittle flew the lead plane and he decided to fly under a bridge, Allard had to follow. If Allard dove an old Jenny and didn't pull out until he had only three hundred feet left, Doolittle would have to emulate him. It was a wonderful, crazy game, and it gave Doolittle just the kind of mental relaxation he needed after five days and nights of intensive study.

The Boston Airport was situated on reclaimed land that jutted out into Boston Harbor. When you landed on it you approached over the water. The surface of the field itself was about three feet above the water. One day when Allard was leading the game, he decided to see if he could touch down at the very end of the field. He skimmed the water. Doolittle's plane was right behind him, his wheels just a foot or so above the placid surface of Boston Bay. Just before Allard reached the edge of the field he pulled the stick back gently, but the ancient Jenny was slow in responding, and instead of clearing the lip his wheels hit the edge of the runway, his undercarriage sheered off with a frightening scream, and the Jenny promptly rose on her nose. Doolittle veered sharply to his right to escape hitting Allard's plane. He made exactly the same kind of landing that Allard had made. His undercarriage too was washed out, and his old Jenny rose sharply on its nose.

Allard climbed shakily out of the wreckage of the Jenny and walked over to Doolittle's washed-out plane. Doolittle emerged unhurt. "Wise guy," he said to Allard. "I suppose you thought I wouldn't follow you."

"You don't think I meant it that way, do you, Jimmy?" Allard said in horror. "I just miscalculated and hit the lip of the field."

"I thought you'd made up a stunt you thought I wouldn't duplicate," Jimmy said. "Now what in hell are we going to tell Bob Brown? We've washed out two of his planes."

Just then a car roared up and stopped with a screech. Captain Robert Brown leaped out.

"Are you two all right?" he cried anxiously.

They assured him that they were. Brown looked at the two planes which were smashed beyond all repair. Then, instead of turning the anticipated wrath upon Doolittle and Allard, his face broke into smiles.

"You've done me a great favor, you two," he said. "I've been trying to get rid of this junk for a long while. Rube Fleet is making some good airplanes up in Buffalo. I've been after Washington to let me have a couple of them. They said I could have some as soon as any of my Jennies became unflyable. And you must admit," he added, grinning, "these two crates you've wrecked are most certainly unflyable."

With his master's degree in his pocket, Doolittle now went after the big one—the doctor's degree in aeronautical engineering. For his subject he picked wind velocity gradient and its effect on flying characteristics. He wrote to some twenty of the country's leading pilots asking them if they could be sure of the wind direction when they were aloft and too high to see an airfield stocking or a flag on a pole. They were unanimous in saying confidently that they could tell the direction of the wind at all times. Why they could "feel" it, some boasted. Suppose, Jimmy asked them, that the weather was too bad to allow them to see the horizon—could they still be sure of the attitude of the plane? Again the barnstormers and stunt men and Army pilots answered in the affirmative. Of course they knew whether the plane was flying level no matter what the weather.

Then Doolittle proved them to be one hundred per cent wrong. He made flights in the worst possible weather and discovered that there was no accurate way for a pilot to know how the wind was blowing or how level his plane was, unless he had visual aid. Once he had tested and verified his observations and had proven them he lost interest in his paper. He knew the information was valuable and he knocked off his thesis quickly. To his disgust it was turned down by the faculty board which considered theses for doctorates. His friends on the board told him it wasn't profound enough.

"You've obviously written this for other pilots, Jim," Professor Warner said. "It's simple down-to-earth language that they'll understand. But, Jimmy, you're being considered for a doctor's degree. You must use the esoteric language of the scientist. Rewrite the thesis in those terms," Warner chuckled.

He did. He wrote a rather abstract mathematical treatise and the board solemnly praised it and without hesitation gave him the coveted degree of Doctor of Science in Aeronautical Engineering.

"That first paper might have done some good," he grumbled to Warner. "Pilots would read it and learn something. But this thesis will be locked away and never be read by anyone."

"You're absolutely right, Jimmy," Warner said sadly. "But that is the fate of most theses."

When Doolittle left Boston and M.I.T. in June, 1925, he was twenty-eight years old. He was recognized in the Army as one of the finest pursuit and acrobatic pilots in the service, if not in the world, and he was recognized by the aviation industry as an aeronautical engineer who was not only brilliant but sound. At that time there were not a hundred men in the world who held a doctor's degree in aeronautical science. Doolittle still retained the exuberance, the gaiety and the passion for practical jokes that had characterized him seven years before when he had been the despair of Colonel Harvey Burwell at Rockwell Field. The master's degree and the doctor's degree had in no way tamed his irrepressible spirits. He still laughed at life, but he no longer laughed at the business of flying an airplane. Flying would never again be a happy-go-lucky adventure to him. Flying was a serious business. His three years at M.I.T. had given him a vast respect for the drawing board and the mathematical table. He would take risks—hundreds of them—but they would always be carefully calculated risks. He would never stunt merely for the fun of it, or try to make an airplane perform maneuvers which it had not been designed to perform.

He felt now that the time had come to leave the laboratory, which was what he considered M.I.T., and do more speed flying. He did not look upon this type of flying as a mere stunt. Aviation could only progress if there was a satisfactory marriage between the laboratory and practical demonstration. Speed tests and air shows were necessary to center the attention of the public on the fact that the Air Corps was an important element in the national defense.

Like most Air Corps pilots, Doolittle believed fervently in Billy Mitchell's theory of a separate air force which would not be a mere stepchild of the Army. It was common gossip that the Army old guard was readying a court-martial for brilliant Billy Mitchell, but virtually all of the Air Corps was behind the courageous, blunt-spoken Brigadier General.

The Air Corps, desperately trying to gain the favor of the public, planned a gigantic air show to be held at Mitchel Field, the nearest military airport to New York City. Doolittle, after leaving M.I.T., had been sent on a temporary assignment to the Naval Air Station at Anacosta, near Washington. The Army had lent Doolittle to the Navy in order that they might teach him how to fly a seaplane properly in the

Schneider Cup Races which were to be held in Baltimore, October, 1925. Italy and England would be represented in the international event. Doolittle had flown every type of land plane, but he had never handled a really fast seaplane. He spent a month learning the tricks of flying a speedy plane equipped with pontoons instead of landing wheels. He flew all of the Navy's fastest pontoon-equipped aircraft. Then he was sent to Mitchel Field to be assigned to the Joint Army-Naval Test Board. He continued to experiment with the heavy-footed Navy planes, utilizing all of his scientific knowledge in an effort to coax more speed out of them.

He took time off to join several of his former flying mates from McCook Field who were to demonstrate what Army planes could do in the Mitchel Air Show. Doolittle and Lieutenant Cyrus Bettis decided that the best way to attract New Yorkers to the Mitchel Field show was to do a little advance advertising. On Tuesday, October 6, as the Manhattan offices were beginning to empty at lunchtime, Doolittle and Bettis roared over the city, and the papers estimated the next day that three million necks craned and three million pairs of eyes gazed skyward. Doolittle and Bettis went through all of the spectacular loops and rolls which were routine maneuvers to them but which seemed to be death-defying gyrations to the gaping citizens of New York. They played tag with the skyscrapers, flying below the surface of the Woolworth Building, skimming almost at treetop level over Central Park, and then zooming to dizzy heights only to dive down on the massed crowds gathered at the Battery in lower New York.

New Yorkers had never seen anything like this. That night Doolittle and a group of Army pilots put on a night show for New York. They flew over the city in V-formation. Different planes were equipped with different-colored lights, and from the ground the whole formation looked like a crystal Christmas tree sparkling with red, green and white lights. The planes climbed to 8,000 feet and then released fireworks which exploded and filled the night with great hanging clusters of fantastically colored patterns. It made New York conscious of the fact that the Air Corps was going to display its talents in New York's own back yard two days later.

The show was under the direction of General J. E. Fechet. His Chief of Staff was Major Carl Spaatz, famous even then because he had brought down five German planes in World War I. The rest of Fechet's staff was made up of Captain Ira C. Eaker, Major H. H. (Hap) Arnold, Major J. S. Jouett and Captain Ralph Wooten.

The first day of the show was taken up with races and stunts by civilian pilots, and was marred by tragedy. Clarence Chamberlin had entered his old monoplane built in 1918 in one of the races. In tests before the race Chamberlin had found that his plane was wing-heavy on the right side. The right wing had an annoying tendency to pull down. But he had added 15 HP to his motor, and Chamberlin, rightly enough, had enough confidence in his flying ability to think he could correct the wing-heaviness. As he taxied down the runway to take off, a man streaked across the field, leaped on the wing of Chamberlin's plane and then edged his way into the empty rear cockpit. Chamberlin couldn't stop. He took off with his unwelcome passenger. The passenger was Lawrence Burnelli, brother of Vincent Burnelli, a well-known airplane designer. Chamberlin had added ballast to his plane to counteract the wing defect. The extra weight added by his hitchhiker caused the plane to handle badly. He was only able to gain three hundred feet altitude when his craft began to wobble. Then it nosed down, and not even Chamberlin's great skill and deft handling could bring the nose up. He tried desperately to gain altitude, but the plane dropped. A wing caught a telegraph wire and it crashed. Burnelli was thrown sixty feet away and killed instantly. Chamberlin was pulled from the wreck with a broken ankle and a badly injured back. That incident resulted in government regulations which put all air shows under the supervision of inspectors.

During the day the Air Inquiry Board, composed of Senator

Randolph Perkins, Senator Hiram Bingham of Connecticut, Senator Dwight Morrow of New Jersey, Congressman James S. Parker of New York, Judge A. C. Denison of Michigan and General J. G. Harbord, flew from Washington to Mitchel Field in two hours and ten minutes. This routine flight caused almost as much excitement as did the more thrilling exploits of the Army pilots. The trip, happily, was without incident, and all of the distinguished members of the Board (only Senator Bingham of Connecticut had ever been in a plane before) professed themselves to be delighted with air travel.

The air show delighted the public but the hard-bitten opponents of spending money on an air force didn't see it. In Washington the skids were being carefully greased for Billy Mitchell who had dared to advocate a separate air force. The Mitchel Field air show dramatized how pitifully inadequate America's air power was. Three groups of fifteen airplanes each put on the show. These forty-five airplanes were actually the nucleus of America's air power; they were the only really up-to-date aircraft the little air force owned.

The N.A.C.A., however, had been given half a million dollars with which to pursue experimentation, and this board on a joint Army-Navy contract had purchased four Curtiss racing ships. Three were to be used for speed tests while the fourth was a guinea pig used to test wing loads and stress.

The Pulitzer race was to be one of the features of the air show. Lieutenant Alford Williams, one of the Navy's finest speed and acrobatic fliers, was to pilot one of the Curtiss racers while Cy Bettis would pilot another—with Doolittle acting as his alternate. Bettis' little plane, over which he and Doolittle had worked long hours in an attempt to coax every bit of extra speed out of it, was black with gold wings; Al Williams' ship was wearing the Navy colors—dark blue and gold. The Navy was confident that brilliant Al Williams would cop this event.

The race was to feature the day's program but the officials thought they'd give the crowd a preliminary treat. They asked

Doolittle to take a Curtiss pursuit plane up and do his stuff. He did. He took the little plane up to 10,000 feet and dove at the field; he came out of it at 500 feet and then went through every loop and stunt he could think of. He gave the spectators their biggest thrill by flying upside down, a maneuver not quite as difficult as it looked but one which at that time hadn't been performed very often. He finished off his display of aerial pyrotechnics by chasing a mass of balloons which officials had released and pricking them with his wings and propeller. Doolittle and his fellow army pilots knew that these stunts didn't mean a thing—but they were out to catch the eye of the public, and if the public wanted stunts they'd oblige. If the public really became air-minded perhaps some pressure might be exerted on Congress; perhaps Billy Mitchell could be saved.

Then came the Pulitzer race between Williams and Bettis. The race was around a closed course of four laps. Bettis and Doolittle had been practicing tight turns around pylons, while Williams used the conventional wide sweep. It was this margin which gave Cy Bettis and the Army the victory. Bettis shot his Curtiss racer around the course at an average speed of 248.99 miles per hour, a world's record for this type of course. The plane had hardly landed before Bettis and Doolittle were at work on it preparing it for the Schneider Cup race only a few days off.

Doolittle would be the pilot and Bettis the alternate for this event. They removed the landing gear of the little plane and replaced it with pontoons. Doolittle had studied Bettis' approach to the pylons carefully. He had admired the iron nerve and skillful hand of his friend Cy who had almost brushed the pylons.

"I've thought of something, Cy," he said. "We've been approaching the pylons rather low. We bank sharply and then of course lose quite a bit of speed as we turn. Suppose I get a bit more altitude and then instead of approaching the pylon on a level fly downhill toward it. That'll give me some added speed. It'll compensate for the speed we lose in banking."

"Sounds good, Jim," Bettis nodded.

As soon as the pontoons were attached, Doolittle tried out his new theory. It seemed to work pretty well. He had only two days of practice and then the plane was shipped to Chesapeake Bay where the race would be held.

The Schneider Cup Race was the World Series of seaplane racing. Enormous prestige went to the winning pilot, to the designer, to the engine manufacturer, and to the company which made the plane. England had won the race twice, Italy had won it twice, and the United States had scored only one victory two years previously. England was the favorite this time. Captain Hubert Broad, Bert Hinkler and Captain Henry Biard had brought three Gloster-Napier racers with them. The three British pilots were quietly confident that there was nothing which could match the speedy Gloster-Napier. They refused to tell newspapermen who were covering the preliminary trials just how fast their planes could travel, and the newspapers promptly dubbed the British seaplane "the mystery plane." The newspapers said that the British machines had done well over two hundred miles an hour in practice runs.

Two days before the race Captain Biard wrecked one of the British planes in a test flight. The next morning Bert Hinkler took his plane out on the waters of Chesapeake Bay, where the race was to be held. The water was rough and the waves smashed one of his rear struts. The remaining strut broke under the strain, and before Hinkler could cut his engine his whirling propeller had cut deeply into both of his pontoons. With two planes out of the race, the British hopes rested upon Captain Hubert Broad.

Italy had sent her two greatest speed pilots, H. Ricardo Morselli and Giovanni de Briganti. Between them these brilliant pilots held a dozen European speed records. They had brought over two Macchi-Curtiss flying boats, odd-looking, with the motor mounted on struts above the pilot's cockpit.

On the morning of the race, Morselli's plane developed engine trouble and he had to withdraw.

There were three American planes entering in the event. Lieutenant George Cuddihy, Lieutenant Ralph Ofstie of the Navy, and Doolittle were the pilots of the three Curtiss racers. Major General Mason M. Patrick, Chief of the Army Air Service, and Admiral W. A. Moffett were on hand hoping that their pilots would make a respectable showing. Glenn L. Martin, Grover Leoning, C. M. Keys, president of the Curtiss company, and a host of the world's greatest aircraft designers and manufacturers were present. Weather conditions were ideal for record breaking. There was a gentle wind, and the bay, which had been so fractious the day before, was now quiescent.

The pilots were to take off at five-minute intervals and fly the 350-kilometer course seven times. Doolittle was the first to take off. As he gave his engine full throttle the spray cascading high above the plane almost buried his little black-and-gold racer. And then he was air-borne and heading for the first pylon.

Captain Broad then sped his sleek white Gloster-Napier into the air, followed by Cuddihy, Ofstie, and finally Briganti, who had won the event in 1921.

Instead of making the customary wide turns around the pylon Doolittle approached it from above diving toward it and whirling his little Curtiss around the pylon in a vertical bank. He had discovered that when he used too much aileron in turning, it caused a wind drag and cut miles off his flying speed.

The record for the Schneider Cup Race had been established by Lieutenant David Rittenhouse, U. S. Navy, when he had won the 1923 event at Cowes, England. His average then had been 177 miles per hour. After three laps it was obvious that Doolittle was in the process of completely mutilating that record.

Both Cuddihy and Ofstie developed engine trouble and had

to drop out. But Captain Broad and Briganti kept doggedly after Doolittle. When, after the fourth lap, Doolittle's average time was announced as better than 230 miles an hour while Broad and Briganti were both ambling along averaging less than 200 miles per hour, it was no longer a race but merely a brilliant exhibition. When Doolittle finished the seventh lap, landed and taxied up to the judges' stand, the knowledgeable spectators gave him a roaring ovation. His average speed of 232.57 miles per hour was the fastest a seaplane had ever flown. It was only sixteen miles an hour slower than Bettis' time in the Pulitzer event, and Bettis, of course, had carried merely a light landing gear instead of the heavy pontoons. Doolittle had broken every seaplane record from three to 350 kilometers. He had flown the race fifty-six miles faster than it had ever been done before. Captain Broad's time was 199.16 miles an hour, while the Italian Macchi-Curtiss monoplane had averaged only 168.44 miles an hour for the seven laps.

Dwight F. Davis, then Secretary of War, wired Doolittle that afternoon:

> Your splendid accomplishment in winning the Jacques Schneider Cup once more proves America's position among the nations of the world. The victory was won through your superior knowledge of aeronautics. It is especially pleasing because of the worth of your competitors. The War Department is proud of you. I am certain the entire personnel of the American Army desires to add its congratulations.

In a long editorial the following day the *New York Times* heaped lavish praise on Doolittle and some fun-poking ridicule at our Navy flyers. Said the first paragraph of the *Times'* editorial dig at the Navy:

> The insatiate United States Army won the race for the world's premier seaplane trophy, the Schneider Maritime Cup, on Chesapeake Bay Monday, in spite of rooting by Father Neptune for the naval entries. As the Army holds

nearly all the world records for flying in the Aircraft Year Book, it must have been a grievous sight to sailors when Lieutenant James H. Doolittle, U.S.A., putting pontoons on his landplane, romped away with the cup which Lieutenant David Rittenhouse of the Navy brought over from England two years ago. But that was not the worst of it. The naval lieutenants Cuddihy and Ofstie had engine trouble, dropped out of the race and were "towed to safety." The Army men never seem to take tows in Neptune's realm.

Everyone but Doolittle was satisfied with his record-breaking performance. He felt that he could stay even closer to the pylons and knock a few additional seconds off the record. That night he asked the race officials if he could make an official attempt to set a record on a straightaway course. Representatives of both the National Aeronautical Association and of the Fédération Aéronautique Internationale had supervised the Schneider Cup event, and they granted the permission. They would pick the timer, and if Doolittle did break a record it would have official sanction.

He simply screamed through the three-kilometer course three times, and when he sat the little Curtiss down they told him that his average speed had been 247.17 miles per hour, a new world's record for seaplanes. Then he and Jo returned to Dayton, Ohio. If Jo could call any place home, it was McCook Field at Dayton. Their friends in Dayton had a surprise waiting for them. They were given a civic reception and driven through the city—not in the conventional automobile, but in a boat rigged to an automobile undercarriage, and across the boat in gay colors was the inscription, "Admiral James H. Doolittle." It was the first time that a first lieutenant in the Army had been given the honorary rank of admiral.

His success in record breaking brought him a new and, to him, highly desirable assignment. He was made Chief of the Flight Section at Wright Field—the top job. His task was to supervise and take part in test flights which would demonstrate whether or not experimental developments were sound. As often as not these developments which looked like fine improvements on a drawing board showed inexplicable bugs when tried out in the air. For a year he worked alternately between drawing board and cockpit. He was almost too busy to do more than grin his thanks when he was presented with the coveted Mackay Trophy, awarded annually to the outstanding flier in the country. He was more interested in investigating the possibility of an experimental tab control. Billy Mitchell had seen this control on a plane in Europe and had suggested that its possibilities be probed. The gadget consisted of a small section in the trailing edge of the control surfaces which was operated from the cockpit of the plane by a stick about the size of a lead pencil. Its purpose was to give greater stability in the controls and to enable the pilot to operate them with less effort. The tab was built at Wright Field, and Doolittle, with a fellow pilot, Lieutenant James E. Hutchison, decided to try it out. With Hutchison as a passenger Doolittle took the plane up to 5,000 feet. New developments could only be okayed if they had been subjected to maximum strain. In one of the tests of the tab control a terrific vibration was set up in the rudder, and before Doolittle could neutralize the controls the rudder control snapped off. Now Doolittle found himself in much the position of an automobile driver who at full speed suddenly loses his steering wheel.

"Want to jump?" he shouted to Hutchison in the rear cockpit.

"What about you, Jim?" Hutchison shouted back.

"I think I may be able to bring it down," Doolittle yelled.

"That's good enough for me. I'll stay with you."

Doolittle had often wondered whether it was theoretically possible to keep a rudderless plane under control enough to land it. He had an idea that might conceivably work; now was an opportunity to try it out. He cut the power gradually and then pulled the ship up into a stall. At stalling speed the plane was directionally controllable; at higher speeds it was not. He virtually "stalled" the plane down, and then as it was about to pancake on the field he gave it the gun, straightened it out, and made a gentle landing. It was an amazing exhibition of piloting skill, and some of the junior pilots who had watched it shook their heads and said, "Doolittle is the luckiest pilot in the world." Actually, no luck at all had attended this feat—long ago he had envisioned the possibility of losing a rudder and had worked out what he thought to be a feasible plan of landing the plane safely.

A few years before, when he was cracking up ship after ship at Rockwell Field, he had no sense at all of the value of a plane. Now a plane to him was a precious commodity that could be ditched only as a very last resort. By demonstrating that a rudderless plane could be landed he not only saved the plane he was flying—he had taught other pilots that losing a rudder did not mean that you automatically bailed out and let your plane crash.

In a desire to expand the foreign market Clarence Webster, president of Curtiss Export, and C. M. Keyes, president of Curtiss Wright, went to Army authorities and asked if they'd allow Doolittle to have a leave of absence to demonstrate the new Curtiss fighter in South America. In 1925 the civilian test pilot with a knowledge of military planes was almost unknown. The Army, grateful to Curtiss (and other companies) because the research and development of military planes was too expensive for it to handle and the job was in the main being done by private industry, lent Doolittle to Curtiss.

Doolittle and the plane, a P-1 fighter with a Curtiss D-12 engine, were shipped to Santiago, Chile. Boyd Sherman, a Curtiss technician, supervised the assembly of the plane at El Bosque, the military airport. Doolittle discovered that he wasn't the only salesman wooing the Chilean government; there were German, Italian and English pilots on the spot hoping to prove their planes better than the Curtiss. The night before the planes were to be demonstrated, a group of Chilean army pilots entertained Doolittle at the Officers Club. It was a convivial party and the talk turned to the reigning film favorite, Douglas Fairbanks. The Chileans loved his acrobatic antics, and they asked Jimmy if Fairbanks was exceptional or were all Americans such incredible athletes.

"This Fairbanks leaps from a balcony in a theater to the stage," an officer recalled ecstatically. "He swings on ropes; he does handstands—sometimes on a window sill."

"That's nothing," Doolittle said with innocent eyes. "All American kids are trained to do those stunts. Watch."

He touched his hands to the floor, threw his body back and up and began to walk around the room on his hands—one of the most elementary of the gymnastic stunts he'd learned as a youngster at college.

"But Fairbanks stands on his hands on window ledges," an officer objected.

"We can all do that," Doolittle said calmly. He had to sell these men airplanes, and to do that he'd do much more than stand on his head. He walked to the window and noticed that there was a two-foot ledge outside. He hopped over the sill and went into his handstand routine. The officers were now really impressed. Their applause stimulated Jimmy to further efforts. He lowered himself close to the ledge and then extended his legs out into space and parallel to the ground. "Bravo," the officers cried, and then to Jimmy's horror the soft stone of the ledge began to crumble. Ledge and Doolittle dropped twenty feet to the ground. Doolittle lay there for a moment dazed, and then he felt sharp pains in both ankles.

At the hospital they said both ankles were broken. They encased his legs in heavy casts. He'd be all right, the doctor said—he just needed a couple of weeks uninterrupted rest. Doolittle winced. He was not only throwing the Curtiss people down, the Army itself would take a very dim view of a pilot who had broken his legs as the result of a hilarious party at an officers' club. He called for Boyd Sherman.

The President of Chile and all of his high-ranking military

officials were at the field to watch the tests. They had sent expressions of sympathy and regret to Doolittle, and were a bit surprised to see a mechanic warming up the American airplane. The other planes had been demonstrated when an ambulance rolled up to discharge a Doolittle on crutches. Sherman slipped two heavy flying boots over the encased legs. He boosted Jimmy to the cockpit of the little racer and then slipped his feet through two clips which he had attached to the rudder bars. Now Doolittle would be able to control the plane—to some extent. His feet were almost riveted to the controls.

He took off, and the beautiful little P-1 didn't let him down. He was in agony every time he had to put pressure on the controls, but the little plane rolled and dove and banked and then flew upside down.

When he landed the crowd broke into wild applause. Then Ernst von Schonabeck, a war ace who had fought with the famed Richthofen Squadron, took up his Dornier, powered with a 260-HP B.M.W. engine, to show off its wares. Doolittle had nothing but respect for the man who had been a combat pilot during a war which he had been forced to sit out, but the Dornier company had sent a salesman along with von Schonabeck and Doolittle remembered that this salesman had done a lot of arrogant boasting at the ill-fated party at the Officers Club a few days before. He sat in his plane watching the Dornier go through its paces, and knew he had a better airplane under him than the one in the air.

"I'm going up," he said to Boyd Sherman, "and show that plane up for what it is."

Sherman nodded with delight, gave the prop a few spins, the engine caught, and Doolittle streaked down the runway and into the air. He joined von Schonabeck at five thousand feet and the German waved a friendly greeting. Doolittle made a pass at the Dornier and von Schonabeck caught the idea. They would hold a mock fight up here in the thin clear air. He nodded agreement, grinned, and then banked to dive at the Curtiss.

The little Curtiss plane would obey Doolittle's whisper; it climbed easily, turned, and now Jimmy dove at the German. He came so close that the spectators watching the show were positive that he had raked the wing of the Dornier with his wheels. Actually the German plane was cumbersome compared to the Curtiss product, and Doolittle literally flew circles around it. He dove under it, zoomed above it, and showed von Schonabeck how the Immelmann roll should really be executed. Finally the German had had enough. He glided to the ground. So did Doolittle, but just before he touched his wheel he shot up, rolled the plane on its back and buzzed the field upside down.

When he landed the spectators yelled with sheer Latin abandon. Doolittle didn't care about what emotions he had aroused in the breasts of the spectators. They weren't buying airplanes; they were here just for a free show. But he saw Webster's beaming face, and the left eye of the Curtiss official dropped in a wink. Doolittle knew that he had sold the airplane to Chile.

He noticed that a crowd of Chilean air officers were gathered around the German plane. They hurried over to join him.

"You brushed across his wing with your wheels," one of them gasped. "Just look."

Doolittle looked. Sure enough, a large piece of canvas had been ripped from the wing.

"That's the greatest exhibition of flying I've ever seen," the head of the Chilean air force said to Doolittle. "You actually played tag with the Dornier and yet touched it so gently that the pilot never knew you had done it. But we here on the ground could see you make contact with the wing."

Doolittle smiled modestly and looked at the grinning Webster. There was no use telling the Chileans that he'd do a lot of things in an airplane, but he'd never risk another man's life, and such a stunt would almost certainly have caused the

Dornier to get out of control. There was no use telling the happy Chileans that the canvas had ripped from the wing because of the wind friction created by the dives von Schonabeck had been performing. Webster brought back a nice order from Chile.

The schedule drawn up weeks before couldn't be altered now, and Doolittle had to fly the Curtiss to La Paz to show it off to the Bolivians. Both casts had cracked and broken under the strain. The doctor who had set the ankles refused to have anything more to do with this obstreperous patient, so Boyd Sherman found an artificial limb maker. He made two strong casts, using old-fashioned corset stays as reinforcements. Doolittle was helped into the plane by Sherman, again had his feet clipped to the controls, and then headed for Bolivia. His reception was less than cordial. Bewildered at first by the open hostility, he learned that Bolivia and Chile were on very bad terms, and that anyone arriving from Chile was immediately suspect. Doolittle was taken to the Strangers Club. Shortly thereafter an angry crowd had gathered outside to shout imprecations at the suspected Chilean spy. The army had to be called out to disperse the crowds. Doolittle exhibited the plane the next day, but the Bolivian officials, crushed by the pressure of public opinion, refused to buy. They were apologetic but firm; they liked the plane better than anything they had seen, but after all—they shrugged eloquent Latin shoulders.

Doolittle was happy to streak back to friendly Santiago.

Then he headed for Buenos Aires, a rather hazardous flight under any conditions. It was the first time an American pilot had flown across the Andes, and Doolittle had done it without wearing a parachute. A 'chute would have been completely useless had trouble developed. He couldn't have jumped with two broken legs. But he made it; he put on his show; the Argentinians bought the plane and Doolittle headed for home, to face an unmerciful kidding from his family and his flying mates.

He was immediately hustled to the Walter Reed Hospital. The doctors winced when they saw the horribly swollen ankles —muscles, tendons, and tissues were a hopeless mess. It would take a year, they said, to repair the damage done to the two ankles. They removed the limb maker's cast, and after studying X-rays once more put the legs in plaster casts. Jo, who by now was beginning to take such incidents in her stride, moved Jimmy, Jr. (age six) and John (age four) to an apartment near the hospital.

For six months Doolittle lay in bed. It was a frustrating period for the flyer. Aviation was suddenly throwing off its swaddling clothes. The commercial airlines were booming. Civilian pilots were making all kinds of record flights. The oil companies were doing research in fuel, trying to produce something more powerful than the standard octane. Engine manufacturers were constantly experimenting with newer, lighter motors. A young airmail pilot named Lindbergh was planning a solo flight to Paris. Richard Byrd had announced that he would try a nonstop trip to Paris. Doolittle lay in bed fuming. When they let him sit up he immediately called for a drawing board and pencil. If he couldn't fly, he could at least fool around with designs and with paper stunts. And out of this came an idea that was to eventually land him in the headlines again and to contribute a great deal to the science of aeronautics.

Lying in bed propped up against the pillows, he considered the possibility of doing the impossible—flying an outside loop. No man had ever performed this gravity-defying maneuver. Many had tried and many had died. For years pilots had been "looping the loop," a relatively simple maneuver to an experienced pilot with a pair of sturdy wings on his aircraft. The inside loop wasn't difficult because as he "loops" the pilot is forced tightly into his seat by centrifugal force. In an outside loop the pilot would be literally flying the outer course, and centrifugal force would be straining him out of his seat. Few pilots thought that the human body could stand the strain of an outside loop. You might find straps strong enough to keep you from flying out of your cockpit, but what about the soft vital organs on which the same tremendous pull would be exerted? Wouldn't they be pulled horribly out of place? Most pilots felt that the blood vessels would burst, and doctors were inclined to agree with them. Even if by some miracle the human frame did withstand the pressure, there seemed little chance that an airplane could stand it.

This latter problem was an engineering one on which the drawing board might shed some light. The stress and strain on wings and fuselage was something that could be worked out with a fair degree of accuracy. By the time he left the hospital after six and a half weary months, Doolittle had made up his mind that the airplane could survive the strain of an outside loop. He had no idea whether or not the pilot could withstand it.

Once again Jo packed the family belongings and headed for McCook Field. He found that the enforced rest had not impaired his flying ability at all. The ankles had healed perfectly, and the rudder bars still acted sensitively to the touch of his feet. He began kicking a Curtiss pursuit ship with a 450-horsepower engine all over the sky above the Ohio plains. He'd reach 15,000 feet, safe from prying eyes, and begin his dives. He flew upside down, constantly bringing the plane up to a partial loop, and then he'd land to see what his own physical reactions had been and to see how the wings and struts had reacted. He found that although there was considerable personal discomfort when he attempted the partial outside loop, there was no bursting of blood vessels, apparently no tearing away of vital organs, and no black-out. And the sturdy Curtiss fighter showed no signs of disintegration at all.

Each night Doolittle recorded his observations. He knew that the centrifugal force encountered in doing the outside loop was three times the normal weight; he weighed 150 pounds now, and flying the outside of the loop a force of 450 pounds would be straining against him, and he'd need a safety belt strong enough to contain a force of 450 pounds. On May 25, 1927, he decided to try it. Only a few fellow officers knew what he was going to attempt when he took off that morning in the Curtiss.

He pushed the plane up to 10,000 feet and then dove it straight at the ground. With the throttle wide open he roared earthward at 350 miles an hour—maximum speed for this airplane. Then instead of pulling the stick back as one would in the conventional loop, he pushed it forward. The plane responded, and now at the bottom of the loop he was flying upside down with his head dangling toward the earth. He felt the blood rush to his head, and now he was in the real danger zone. Would he black out? Would the wings stand the horrible strain? Then the plane began to climb up and up to reach his approximate starting point. He had done it; had flown on the outside of a huge aerial circle.

His fellow officers mobbed him affectionately when he landed. That night the newspapers carried page-one stories of the incredible outside loop. One reporter asked Jimmy what made him try it.

"Just on the spur of the moment," he said in a dead-pan voice. Only the officers at Wright Field knew that he had been working out the details of this loop for many weeks and had approached the problem with the detachment of the scientist. He hadn't attempted it until his tests, his human reactions had convinced him that its success was a mathematical certainty. If there was a risk (and there was, of course), it was a "calculated risk."

Once again Curtiss asked the Army to lend Doolittle for a South American tour. Again the Army was glad to oblige Clarence Webster. William H. McMullen, one of the few civilian pilots capable of demonstrating pursuit planes, went along as did two good mechanics, Van Wagner and Todhunter. Doolittle and Bill McMullen were to demonstrate the P-1 and the O-1, an observation plane Curtiss had developed.

"Take care of yourself, Doolittle," Jo said when she said good-by.

"I always take care of myself in airplanes," Jimmy said, a bit startled at what he felt was Jo's lack of confidence in him.

"Oh I know that, dear," Jo said sweetly. "I never worry about you when you're flying. I mean take care of yourself in those officers' clubs."

Their first demonstrations were at Peru and then the Curtiss troupe headed for Bolivia. The political atmosphere was much clearer now than it had been a year and a half ago, and even the crowds which had thought Doolittle to be a Chilean spy now cheered him. Both little planes were equipped with pontoons as well as conventional landing gear. In an effort to convince Bolivia that it should have a naval air force (despite the fact that the country had no seacoast), Doolittle decided to demonstrate the P-1 on the water of Lake Titicaca. This is the highest large body of water in the world, but he was confident that given a break in the weather he could take off even in this rarefied air. The weather break he needed was a stiff breeze and a few white-tipped waves. But on the day set for his flight the water was like glass. There wasn't a breath of wind. He tried everything but his P-1 refused to leave the placid surface of the lake. In desperation he tried a rather dangerous tactic. He gunned the engine and then when the plane had achieved full speed he tried rocking it alternately to the right and the left—dipping the wings dangerously low and then raising them, but even this maneuver failed to work and the Bolivians still have no naval air force.

He did, however, quite unwittingly start a commercial airline in the country. He met Charles Wallen, the manager of a large gold mine located just over the Andes at Tipuani. The manager had just returned from his mine and he was a tired man—the trip had taken him nine days.

"Had to make it though," he said wearily. "I need some medical supplies badly. Some of my men were hurt, and unless

I get back pretty quick I'll have a lot of dead Indians on my hands."

"How were they hurt?" Doolittle asked.

"Playing a little game called *Probando la suerto,*" Wallen said dryly.

"Testing your luck?" Doolittle translated freely but correctly.

Wallen nodded. "My Indians are all from the headwaters of the Amazon," he said, "and for a hundred years or so they have been called simply the Bad Indians. They have a strong aversion to paying taxes, and for many many years the Bolivian government has been sending one tax collector after another to Tipuani to collect taxes from them. The mortality among tax collectors," he shook his head sadly, "has been very high.

"Well, my boys—and I might add that I get along fine with them because I pay them well and do not collect taxes—like to play rather rough. They play *Probando la suerto* whenever things get dull. Things have been dull since they stopped sending tax collectors to Tipuani, so they had a little session of their favorite game just nine days ago. They play it this way. Some forty men stand in a circle just close enough so their outstretched arms will touch. Then they take a quarter stick of dynamite, attach a long fuse to it, light the fuse, and start passing it from hand to hand. They pass it quickly and expertly, but always there is that last man who has it when the dynamite explodes. He is considered unlucky. And that," Wallen ended gloomily, "is why I am here to get some badly needed medical supplies. I've got a doctor there trying to keep a dozen of them alive with whiskey and quinine."

"How far is your mine?" Doolittle laughed.

"Nine days by burro," he said. "We have to climb up the Andes, come down the other side and then go by jungle trails to Tipuani. In a straight line I suppose it's less than a hundred miles."

"Get your medicine and meet me at the airport," Doolittle said. "I'll have you there in no time."

"But my mine is in the midst of a jungle," Wallen protested. "You could never land there."

Doolittle shrugged his shoulders. "We'll drop the medicine to your Bad Indians."

They located the mine without any trouble, and as the O-1 swooped low, hundreds of Indians looked up in awe. Wallen pointed out a small clearing and Doolittle dropped the packaged medicine. An hour later they were back in La Paz enjoying a drink.

"I've got a thousand Indians working for me," Wallen said thoughtfully. "It would take them about a week to clear the ground for an airfield. A plane would come in mighty handy for taking the gold out."

"It's a nice little airplane," Doolittle said, "easy to fly; it allows you to make an occasional mistake. Great little engine."

"I'd better look up your Mr. Webster," Wallen grinned. Webster had gone along for Curtiss this trip also, and the next morning Wallen bought a plane from him. A year later he bought a fleet of planes and started Bolivia's first commercial airline.

In Chile Doolittle was received with enthusiasm, but this time he stayed away from the Officers Club. Some visiting British naval air force officers were in Santiago and they were very much interested in the O-1 equipped with pontoons. One of them, Commander Bruce Jones, asked Doolittle if he could try out the plane.

"You've flown this type before?" Doolittle asked.

"Of course, about a thousand hours," the British pilot said confidently.

"I'll go along as ballast," Doolittle grinned. "Take it over."

Jones climbed into the front cockpit while Doolittle sat in the observer's seat in the rear cockpit. The British officer revved the engine and started down the bay. Then Doolittle was struck with the horrible thought that the man had no idea of what to do next. The plane, now roaring at full speed, began to careen madly, it swayed from side to side, its wings getting closer and closer to the water. And then the inevitable happened. One of the wing pontoons hooked a wave, the plane cartwheeled over and the pilot, who had forgotten to fasten his safety belt, was thrown fifty yards away. As the plane began to sink, Doolittle unfastened his belt and swam clear. The shock of the impact had knocked the British officer out and Doolittle got to him just as he was about to go down. The pontoon had been knocked clear of the wreckage of the plane and Jimmy grabbed it with one hand while hanging on to his pilot with the other. Crash boats had seen the accident and they were hurrying. The cracked pontoon was gradually filling with water. So were Doolittle's heavy flying boots. Jones became heavier and heavier each moment. It was a question whether or not the speeding rescue launch would reach the two waterlogged pilots and the equally waterlogged pontoon in time to save any of them. The launch arrived just as the pontoon gave up. But the sturdy O-1 plane went to a watery grave, which annoyed Doolittle and McMullen considerably. Now they only had the pursuit plane left.

Doolittle and McMullen had kept their engines hot during the first months of the tour. Wherever they had gone, government officials and military men had wanted to be "taken for a ride." The two young pilots had fallen completely in love with their Curtiss planes, and to sell them they would have flown them without wings had they been requested. Sometimes Doolittle had made as many as nineteen flights in one day carrying government representatives. But now the O-1 was gone; it was too late to have another one shipped to South America, and he was forced to concentrate on the single-seater. He decided that the best way to dramatize its exceptional qualities (and for its time it was an exceptional plane) was to establish a few new records. This presented no particular problem, for no plane superior to the P-1 had ever been flown in South America.

Jimmy flew from Santiago to Buenos Aires in five hours and forty-five minutes to clip nearly half an hour from the previous record. After his exhibition in the Argentine capital, the Minister of War gave a dinner in his honor. To the delight of his audience he returned the flowery compliments of his host in Spanish. It was pretty good Spanish, too, for Spain, and he was puzzled by the chuckles and then guffaws which greeted his sentiment of how he enjoyed coming down from the mountains to fly over the lush flatlands of the plains. His Spanish was correct enough—the word "chata" he used meant "flatlands"—but unhappily in the Argentine the word "chata" was used exclusively to mean "bedpan," and the audience was understandably amused to hear their guest say how much he enjoyed looking down upon the bedpans of the country.

After exhibiting the P-1 in Asuncion, Paraguay, he flew across the Matte Grosse—the great jungle of Brazil—to Rio de Janeiro. This flight, never before attempted, was complicated by the fact that the jungle was virtually uncharted. It was a long flight for the little fighter plane, but he installed extra gas tanks which he figured would give him nearly seven hours' flying time. For the last hour over the jungle he flew in dense fog, and when he came out of it he had no idea of his exact location. To his surprise, he saw railroad tracks beneath him, but his map didn't indicate that there should be a railroad here. He came down, followed the tracks to a station and then circled to catch the name of the place. He caught the name MICTORIO on the little wooden shack which served as a station, but there was no Mictorio on his map. Thoroughly bewildered, he followed the tracks another fifteen miles to another station. Again he tried to pick up its name, but this too was called MICTORIO. He shot away to find a third railroad station—this was labeled MICTORIO.

Giving up any thought of visual help, he headed in the right general direction and did manage to hit Rio right on the nose. The bottoms of his gas tanks were wet when he landed, but that was all; his time had been seven hours and ten minutes.

"I would have made it sooner except for a place called Mictorio," he growled when he landed. "That place has three railroad stations."

"That name is on every railroad station in our country," the air force captain who met him said solemnly. "It means 'Men's Room.' And now, Lieutenant Doolittle, we have your favorite drink waiting for you."

He led Doolittle to a shaded terrace and introduced him to the government and air officials present. Then he pointed to an empty seat. In front of it on the table stood a quart pitcher of chilled orange juice.

"We have read that orange juice is your favorite drink," the officer said, "and we managed to get some for you."

"Captain, you read wrong," Doolittle said solemnly. "That story has chased me all over South America. I told a reporter in Santiago that I never took a drink before flying—except perhaps some orange juice. He misunderstood my Spanish. He wrote that I never drank anything but orange juice."

"Then you will have something else," the delighted captain said.

"Captain," Doolittle said, "I think after flying over your Matte Grosse a man deserves something stronger than orange juice."

"You are a real Latin," the officer beamed. "Would you like a drink of Scotch?"

"I know of no finer Latin drink than Scotch," Doolittle said gravely.

In all, he spent six months in South America, and State Department officials in Washington kept getting delighted messages from their ambassadors. Doolittle was invoking the Good Neighbor policy long before the term had become part of the language. He was not only demonstrating and selling planes; he was making friends wherever he went. The public and the newspapers called him "Geemee." It had been a tremendously successful and pleasant trip, but now it was time for "Geemee" to get to work.

5

In the 1920's many veteran pilots had nothing but contempt for the instruments which were on their planes. They gloried in the fact that they flew by instinct, or "by the seat of their pants," and thought pilots who depended upon instruments did not have the romance of flying in their veins. These pilots, great natural fliers that they were, didn't even know the rudiments of physics—how angular turning acceleration affected the little liquid level in their inner ear, the vestibular labyrinth, causing them to think they were flying straight and level when they were in an ever-tightening circle. In fine weather these veterans found it easy enough to ignore their instruments. In bad weather they just didn't fly, or, if they did, they hedgehopped under the ceiling and when caught blind, many spiraled and crashed to their deaths. Younger pilots, coming along, who manned the new and struggling air mail lines, felt differently, and eagerly learned how to fly blind by the gyroscopic turn and bank indicator which had been available since early in 1918.

Trains traveled on schedule; air travel was still haphazard and schedules were a big "if." Airline operators and pilots knew that until their planes could keep reasonably close to announced schedules they would never rival the railroads as common carriers. But trains worried very little about the weather; only a blizzard stopped a train. Heavy rain, snow, fog, winds of gale proportions—these all threw airline schedules off kilter, and the air routes were dotted with the remains of aircraft and pilots who had tried to fight the weather with stubborn recklessness.

Doolittle now felt that aeronautical science had given pilots reasonably safe airplanes to fly. They were at least structurally sound. At M.I.T. he had earned a doctor's degree on the subject, which was a major contribution to the art. You seldom heard of wings falling off. The undercarriages had been developed to a point where they would easily absorb clumsy landings, and engines were more powerful and ran a longer time between overhauls. But science had not licked the weather. Fog was the factor now responsible for the many crashes and deaths each year. If a pilot ran into a thick fog he could fly blind by instruments—if he knew how—and could be helped by radio, but if he didn't come out of it and find a place to land before his gas gave out, he would come a cropper every time. Doolittle was an expert instrument-flier and had no patience with any pilot who claimed he could do it without these mechanical aids. He knew the problem and already had a solution—yet to be worked out in detail.

In 1926 Harry Guggenheim, president of the Guggenheim Fund for the Promotion of Aeronautics, with Captain Emory "Jerry" Land, vice-president, formed a world-wide group for the study of the various problems connected with flying in fog. A great many experiments were financed and much valuable information accumulated. In 1928, they decided to establish the Full Flight Laboratory to make planes available for testing out devices and schemes which might help in this problem. Doolittle was naturally the best qualified to head this work. He had the nerve and the knowledge. Guggenheim persuaded General Fechet, Air Corps leader, to give Doolittle a leave of absence and things began to happen. Once again Jo had to move her family—this time to Mitchel Field,

Long Island. Young Jim was now eight and John six, and the base was taking on more than they realized!

It didn't take Doolittle long to get started. Guggenheim and Land backed him completely. He selected a Consolidated N.Y. 2 for the testing of special instruments and a Corsair O-2 U-1 higher speed ship for cross-country flights to get what was needed in a hurry. He had these two planes rebuilt by their manufacturers to his own specifications and arranged for Jack Dalton, his old chief mechanic, to take care of them in a hangar assigned to them at Mitchel Field. Since he needed a good instrument and radio man he persuaded his professor at M.I.T., Bill Brown, and Lieutenant Ben Kelsey to join him and they soon had the Bell Telephone Laboratories and the Radio Frequency Laboratory at Boonton, New Jersey, working on special radio equipment for the planes.

Blind flying and blind landings to Doolittle were primarily a matter of getting the proper equipment. The first essential was the radio beams to guide them to the airport. They planned to fix up and use the aural beacon already located at Mitchel Field for the long-range approach beam, and in addition Bill Brown laid out a low-powered landing beacon system installed in a small house on the field itself. This beacon was patterned after the one being developed at College Park, Maryland, by Diamond and Dunmore of the Bureau of Standards and the Department of Commerce. A vertical marker beam was to flash a signal in the cockpit marking the edge of the airport.

Second, a reliable altimeter that would at all times tell you how far above sea level you were was essential. When you landed "blind," you had to have precision instruments—not instruments which would merely approximate your position. They investigated the possibility of turning the runway localizer beam at 90 degrees to provide a radio path to glide down to the field. Doctor Kolster, Diamond and Dunmore were making experiments on this. But the high frequency used here ran into ground reflections which delayed the immediate use of it. It was perfected later on and is in use today.

In 1928 there was no such thing as a true altimeter. At best, pilots could get only an approximation of their height above sea level. Doolittle decided to try the principle of the Fathometer developed by Doctor Fessenden of Boston. This instrument utilized the sonic principle to give the depth of the sea. Sound waves were sent from a ship to the sea bottom. They hit bottom and bounced back. The Fathometer, a knowledgeable instrument which knew that sound traveled 4,000 feet per second in water, measured the length of the round trip, divided by two, and the skipper of a ship could tell instantly how much water he had under him. If you had a similar gadget in your airplane, Doolittle reasoned, you might conceivably be able to get a pretty good idea of how high above the ground you were. He fixed a horn to the under-fuselage of the plane, installed a microphone and tried it out. Over this distance the noise of the airplane drowned out the echo from the ground. It was not good enough.

Word of the experiments being made at Mitchel Field spread rapidly. Everyone in the country who had any idea at all of how to fight fog weighed in with his idea. One proposed by Harry Raeder of Cleveland seemed interesting enough to warrant investigation. Raeder wrote that he had been able to dissipate the heaviest fog by using gigantic blowtorches. He said that he had noticed that when men were breaking rock in quarries near Lake Erie they used blowtorches to expand the rock, which then broke off from the still cool, unexpanded portion. When this quarrying was done in fog, Raeder had noticed that the flames from the blowtorches had made huge gaps in the fog. Why, he asked, couldn't this be done on a large scale—large enough to clear an airport of ground fog? Harry Guggenheim opened his checkbook and sent for Mr. Raeder. Raeder set up his enormous blowtorches and waited for fog. It was nearly two months before Long Island obliged, and then a real pea souper drifted in over Mitchel Field. The confident Raeder lit his blowtorches and blue flame shot into the fog. He was right; it did clear the space affected; it cleared it for a moment or two, and then as more fog rolled in, the clear space immediately filled with its fleecy thickness. Mr. Raeder's experiment would be successful only when there was fog but absolutely no wind. Mr. Raeder was thanked, given a check and sent back to Cleveland. At a later date the idea was picked up and became a success when installed first at Arcadia and then at Los Angeles airport.

Doolittle discarded this idea just as he discarded dozens of others. Inventors from all over the country were sending gadgets to Captain Land, and those he thought worthy of investigation he turned over to Doolittle. At this time Doctor Brombacher, of the Bureau of Standards, reported that a young man named Paul Kollsman had submitted a barometric altimeter to him for tests which was way ahead of anything that he had ever seen before, and he thought it might be of use to Jimmy. Doolittle got Kollsman's address from Brombacher and immediately got in touch with him. Paul Kollsman was a mild-mannered genius who had worked for Pioneer Instrument Company, but when he voiced disapproval of Pioneer's altimeter he was fired. To prove his point he decided to make a better altimeter himself, and had built this instrument in his garage back of his house on Junius Street in Greenpoint, Brooklyn. A graduate of one of Germany's leading scientific schools, Kollsman was a perfectionist. He not only had great vision, but he was meticulous in his design. When he started to make his altimeter he went to some Swiss watchmakers he knew in New York.

"I want you to cut me a better gear for this altimeter than you ever cut for a watch," he said. "It must be more precise, more accurate than the best watch ever made. We will first rebuild your gear-cutting machines."

They thought he was crazy, but these Swiss soon realized that Kollsman knew what he was talking about. When he replaced the crude chain that wrapped around the shaft that turned the pointer by these accurate gears, he was enabled to put another speeded-up pointer on his instrument that indicated altitude in feet. He also developed a much-improved diaphragm for his altimeter which had no hysteresus, or lag, in its spring. Thus the reading was accurate and the same at all times. When Doolittle arrived, Kollsman was putting a barometric pressure adjustment on his altimeter to make it read accurately in feet above sea level irrespective of changes in atmospheric pressure. Doolittle told him what he was doing and asked him if he could try out the altimeter. Kollsman was delighted, and they made many test flights together. The altimeter was so sensitive that it was found necessary to seal the case of the instrument and connect it by a tube to the static line of the air speed indicator, to eliminate pressure changes in the cockpit. Soon Doolittle had in his possession the finest and most accurate altimeter ever constructed, which would tell him within a few feet just where the ground was. Bill Brown could radio the barometric pressure so Jimmy could set it in the altimeter just before using it for a landing. Doolittle now knew he could be at the proper altitude when he passed over the radio signal which marked the edge of the field, as he was coming in on the radio beacon. Also, as he let down, the altimeter would tell him when his wheels were about to touch the ground.

Finally, an instrument was needed that would give the exact direction of flight. The only instrument which pilots had available was the magnetic compass, satisfactory enough in smooth air but virtually useless under turbulent conditions. The magnetic compass, for instance, had a tendency to swing past the course being flown, and it required considerable time to settle and indicate a true course. When a plane was flying north and the pilot started a turn to the right, the magnetic compass, due to the dip of the earth's magnetic field, would indicate that the plane was turning to the left. This phenomenon is known as the "northerly turning error."

As to the second basic problem (an instrument giving true direction of flight), Doolittle felt that the ultimate solution lay in a light, compact gyroscopic compass. But he was looking for an immediate solution for flying accurately in "blind" weather, and he decided it would be better to build a small gyro on which was mounted a compass card and which could be set on "north" at will, by checking with the conventional magnetic compass. This he felt was a rather cumbersome arrangement, difficult for the pilot to execute, but for the moment it would have to suffice.

He went to see Dr. Elmer Ambrose Sperry, a famous pioneer in the electrical industry—perhaps the one man in the country who could help Doolittle. The Sperry gyroscope was known wherever man flew or navigated ships. Actually it was Leon Foucault of France who in 1852 created the word "gyroscope" for an apparatus designed to demonstrate the rotation of the earth. He took the term from two Greek words: *gyros,* meaning "rotation," and *skopien,* meaning "to view." Foucault suspended a weight from the dome of the Pantheon in Paris with a wire two hundred and twenty feet long. There was nothing new about the pendulum, but Foucault's observation of this swinging pendulum was new. He for the first time appreciated the fact that the swinging pendulum would maintain the plane of its motion and so would establish a plane of reference in "inertial space." From this it was a logical step to his analysis that the axis of an idealized spinning rotor must have a similar property. Foucault well understood the mechanics of the ideal spinning body, but a useful gyroscope could not immediately spring from his experiments. It had to wait for the development of some means of sustaining the rotation. In the first part of the twentieth century Doctor Sperry invented a successful gyrocompass, using electric power. In 1913, Sperry applied the gyroscope to the stabilizing of airplanes. One of the most spectacular events of early aviation history occurred when Doctor Sperry's son Lawrence, flying a Curtiss flying boat, won a prize of fifty thousand francs in a contest for stabilized planes held in France in 1914. Sperry had the only gyroscope entry.

Doctor Sperry was now nearing seventy, and his reputation

was world wide. Doolittle approached him with diffidence. He found the elder statesman of science affable and kindly.

"I need two of your gyroscopes, one for indicating the horizontal position of my plane and the other for direction," said Doolittle.

"I don't quite understand," Sperry said cautiously

"Here's what I want—" And Doolittle explained what he was doing. He made some sketches of the approach and landing radio beams and how he proposed to make his blind landing at Mitchel Field.

"Why don't you use a Gyro Stabilizer? You know, my son Lawrence flew blind with one in 1915," Sperry asked.

"Fine. Have you got one?" replied Doolittle.

"No, but we have the original model in the stock room. You know the bottom fell out of aviation and there has been no demand for anything of this kind. Why don't you use our Turn and Bank Indicator that goes on the panel board? Lawrence made the first accurate turns, totally blind, with this instrument in late 1917. These are being made in very small quantities and are available at the Pioneer Instrument Company, our licensee."

"I've tried it," said Doolittle. "I can maintain a course in the approach beam far away from the field, but even then with difficulty. And as I get close in and the beam gets narrower, I've got to have instruments which give me positive readings and not rate of turn. I've got to fly into the runway localizer beam, say at right angles to it, and then snap right around, ninety degrees precisely, and bring my wing down absolutely level and at the same time so that I won't go through the beam and have to come back to it again."

"Yes, indeed." The eminent Doctor Sperry was excited now. "We can take the gyros out of the stabilizer and put them on the instrument panel. My son Elmer will fix them up for you. With the horizon gyro and directional gyro you can make precise angular turns, find the radio beam and go right down it to the landing field, by Jove!"

A man of strong religious principles, Doctor Sperry never allowed himself the luxury of using any expletive stronger than "by Jove." The men who worked for him knew that when he used the expression he was mighty, mighty interested. He guided Doolittle to his son's office and told Elmer to work closely with the experimenter. Elmer and Doolittle found they spoke the same language. Elmer Sperry was an affable young man only three years older than Doolittle, and Doolittle's enthusiasm immediately infected him. He gave up all his other activities to work with Doolittle. Within a week he had become a virtual member of the family, and now at Mitchel Field Jo automatically set an extra place each night for Elmer Sperry. His father had once said of Elmer, "What I especially like about my son is the fact that he never slams a door when he leaves the room." Equable, placid and painstaking, Elmer Sperry fitted in beautifully with Doolittle and Bill Brown.

Elmer did not take the gyros out of the stabilizer, as his father had suggested. He took two others which were more suitable and rigged them up for Doolittle's instrument panel. Doolittle made a series of test flights to check these instruments under the worst possible flying conditions. Elmer received many unscheduled thrills as a passenger-observer on some of these flights. Doolittle would set the directional gyro on zero while flying a straight course just over a stretch of track on the Long Island Railroad, so low that his wheels were practically on the track. When road crossings or approaching trains got in the way, he would zoom over these—clearing them by what seemed to Elmer only inches. After flying around for a while he would come back to the same track again to see how much the D. G. had drifted off. Bearings were changed, friction reduced and balance perfected until the gyro would maintain its direction consistently. The D. G. had a compass cylindrical dial on it. But the horizon gyro had no indicator as yet. Doolittle just looked through the window at the gyro itself. It was quite a problem to figure out how to put some kind of an indicating pointer on it, but Doolittle solved the problem in his characteristic way.

"Since we call it an artificial horizon, why not put a pointer on it that behaves just like the real horizon? It will be like looking at the real horizon through a porthole," Doolittle said.

Elmer then worked out a mechanism to operate the pointer that would allow the airplane to bank ninety degrees and climb and dive eighty degrees without knocking the gyro off its horizontal position. He also put a setting knob on the directional gyro. These two instruments are still used today as standard equipment on all commercial and military aircraft. The equipment was now about complete.

Visiting scientists who dropped in at Mitchel Field were often amazed that the apparently carefree practical joker they found in Doolittle was the man who had written the two erudite and scientifically sound theses at M.I.T. As often as not they found him on his knees boxing furiously with his nine-year-old son, or they would walk into his quarters to find him singing Russian songs lustily with Sachinka Toochkoff and Alex de Seversky. These two Russian pilots, both making names for themselves in American aviation circles, had represented the old Moscow regime and were in America when the Revolution had engulfed their country. They decided it would be nicer to be live American citizens than dead Russian Czarists. So they remained in the United States. Seversky, an internationally known speed pilot, was working on a new bombsight which utilized the Sperry gyroscope, and he wanted to keep in touch with Doolittle's experiments with the gyro. Toochkoff had been chief of naval aviation in Russia.

Visitors usually found the Doolittle menage something of a madhouse. Jo was an ingenious provider of food and drink. She had discovered that the secret of making good beer lay in the quality of the hops, and she had friends in California who were growing the best hops produced in the country. All Army pilots had been alerted by Jo to pick up hops for her any time they left California. When a plane from the West Coast touched its wheels to the runways at Mitchel Field, there was usually a bag of hops somewhere in the aircraft. A visiting scientist might arrive in time to hear the exuberant Toochkoff sing the praises of Jo's beer.

"Beer have I had in Moscow," he would cry, seizing Jo's hand and kissing it. "Beer have I had in Leningrad and in Copenhagen and in Vienna and in Munich, and in every damn place. But, Jo, there is no beer like your beer."

Jo had moved her family into a long-vacant, temporary officers' quarters built in a hurry for World War I personnel at Mitchel Field. They had three and a half units, so there were plenty of rooms in the ancient beaverboard shack, but the beams had long since been taken over by termites. Doolittle, working at his drawing board in a small office with Kollsman, Sperry, Brown, Land, Morgan, Basset and a host of others connected with the work, didn't worry about the termites or the condition of the house.

The Doolittles had a Negro maid who did the laundry, washed the dishes and made beds—the kitchen itself was Jo's domain. When dinner was ready—and there might be anywhere from five to fifty waiting for it—Jo would always produce a masterpiece. Through the years she arranged a very complete file of the favorite dishes of her various friends. Among her specialties were meat balls, chili con carne, chow mein, and broccoli with Jo's own lemon mayonnaise sauce. At large parties Jo would serve dozens of wonderful little cakes, made and iced by herself. After dinner there would be dancing on the wavy, rickety floor. One time the victrola fell through it. Jo would always caution that people danced at their own risk. She had once gone through the floor herself.

Jo took some flying lessons and was surprised to find how easy it was. But she soon gave it up—her husband's oft-repeated, "Come on to dinner with us" chained her to her beloved kitchen. She did, however, fly with her husband on many of his test flights. She especially liked to fly over New York at night, and when they'd land and Jimmy would go into a huddle with Bill Brown, she found them unresponsive to her descriptions of the lighted fairyland which was New York from the air.

Doolittle made many blind landings at night and even in fog before he felt that he was absolutely ready for the official test. It actually occurred on September 24, 1929. That morning he awoke, looked out of the window and yelled to Jo, "Perfect weather, just what we've been waiting for!" Jo hurried to the window and winced—a mass of real thick fog had rolled in from Long Island Sound. Doolittle called his gang and then went out to the hangar to wait for the group who were to witness the official test. Harry Guggenheim and Jerry Land and Lieutenant Ben Kelsey had arrived with the other official observers.

"Just one suggestion, Jimmy," Guggenheim said. "I want Ben to be in that second cockpit—just in case."

"In case of what?" Doolittle was actually startled.

"In case anything goes wrong," Guggenheim said. "If it does, Ben may get enough visual aids to land the plane."

"But nothing can go wrong, Harry," Doolittle said. "We've got this thing all taped. It's a simple matter of trusting our instruments."

"I'll feel better, Jim, if Ben is along—just for insurance. Why, you might meet another plane in the air and not see it."

During the months of the research and experimentation, Guggenheim had become very fond of Jimmy Doolittle and of his wife Jo. He knew Doolittle's insistence that he never took an uncalculated risk, but Guggenheim knew, too, intangible elements of risk were always entering into any pioneering operation. There wasn't one chance in fifty thousand that there was another plane in the sky, but Guggenheim didn't even want to take that risk.

Ben Kelsey climbed into the front cockpit and Doolittle, with a cheery wave of his hand to Jo, slipped into the rear one. To him this flight called for the display of no more courage than that presented by any scientific problem. He had, he felt, already solved this problem on paper and proven these theories twenty times in flight; this flight itself was to be merely an official demonstration of what was in his own mind an already proven fact—namely, that a plane could take off, fly, and land on instruments alone. After he was in the cockpit, Guggenheim climbed up on the wing and pulled the canvas cover over the top of it. It was dark inside the cockpit. Doolittle heard Guggenheim's rather nervous "Good luck, Jim," and then he switched on the lights which illuminated the dials. The panel board had the standard engine and navigation instruments; tachometer, oil pressure gauge, oil temperature gauge, ammeter, voltmeter, compass, bank and turn indicator, air speed indicator, altimeter, and rate of climb indicator. But in addition, it had the beautiful Kollsman barometric altimeter (with a range of twenty thousand feet, graduated in ten-foot intervals); the Sperry artificial horizon and the Sperry directional gyroscope. The sensitive Kollsman altimeter would be kept in adjustment through two-way radio communication between ground and plane, with Brown giving Doolittle any barometric variations. The airplane had been equipped with a radio frequency laboratory standard aircraft receiver, and vibrating reed indicator. This permitted the reception of signals from the oral type beacon, from the visual type beacon and from voice.

Jo, Guggenheim, Sperry, John McCullogh, Conger Pratt, the Mitchel Field C.O., and about fifty spectators watched as the plane began to move. Ben Kelsey, relaxed and grinning with confidence, sat in the front cockpit, his hands resting in plain view above the cowling. He had gone along because Guggenheim had insisted upon it, but he had made up his mind that unless ordered by Doolittle, he wouldn't touch the stick or let his feet near the rudder bars. The plane bumped over the turf (there was no concrete runway at Mitchel Field then), and Doolittle revved the engine. He set the altimeter at zero. He set the directional gyro to read the same as the magnetic compass, and held the motor wide open. Then he released the brakes. The plane roared down the field. Doolittle kept his eyes on the directional gyro; its indicator was absolutely vertical—he was traveling straight. He watched the horizontal horizon—his wings were level. And then he felt the plane lift easily into the fog.

Doolittle flew due west for five miles, then executed a 180-degree turn to retrace his course. The two vibrating reeds took him directly to the beacon on the field; when he veered to the right, the right reed oscillated more than the left one did. By keeping them vibrating at the same rate he knew he was aiming exactly for the beacon. He passed over the field at a few hundred feet, and those on the ground noticed through the thinning fog that Ben Kelsey's hands were still outside the cowling. The plane continued on for four more miles, banked and returned.

When he was a mile from the field he switched from the long-range beacon to pick up the runway localizer beam. Theoretically this should bring him right to the end of the runway. Doolittle throttled down to lose altitude. His amazingly sensitive altimeter showed him that he was approaching the field at four hundred feet. Now the plane went into a smooth glide... a hundred feet... fifty feet.... It was thirty feet above the ground as it cleared the edge of the field. Jo found that she was clenching her hands and biting her underlip. Guggenheim wiped the sweat from his brow. The nose of the plane lifted. The plane lost its flying speed and then touched its wheels gently only a few yards from where they had left the turf a few minutes before. The grinning Kelsey raised his hands and clasped them behind his neck. The plane came to a stop and Guggenheim rushed forward to pull back the canvas hood.

Doolittle blinked his eyes and said, "What happened to the fog?"

"It sort of rolled away while you were up there, Jim," the proud Guggenheim grinned.

The next day the *New York Times* carried a page-one headline.

BLIND PLANE FLIES
15 MILES AND LANDS;
FOG PERIL OVERCOME

The story in the *Times* began:

Man's greatest enemy in the air, fog, was conquered yesterday at Mitchel Field when Lt. James H. Doolittle took off, flew over a fifteen-mile course and landed again without seeing the ground or any part of his plane but the illuminated instrument board. The occasion marked the first instance in which a pilot negotiated a complete flight while piloting absolutely blind. The demonstration was more than an exhibition of blind flying and instrument perfection. It indicated that aviation had perhaps taken its greatest single step in safety.

The story quoted Harry Guggenheim as saying,

"This is the most important announcement the Foundation has yet made.

"The demonstration represents the successful consummation of experiments which have been conducted for nearly a year in the full-flight laboratory established by the fund at Mitchel Field. The principal factors in making possible the accomplishment are a new application of the visual radio beacon, the development of an improved instrument for indicating the longitudinal and lateral position of a plane in flight, a new directional gyroscope and a sensitive barometric altimeter so delicate as to measure its height above the ground within a few feet.

"The sensitive altimeter showed him his altitude and enabled him to calculate his landing to a distance of a few feet, while he gauged his speed by a standard airspeed indicator.

"Thus the last great hazard to airplane reliability is vanishing as this principle is developed which will make the airplane more independent of weather conditions," Mr. Guggenheim continued.

"It is significant that the achievement is realized

through the aid of only three instruments which are not already standard equipment for cross-country flight. Many individuals and organizations have participated in making the development possible. Lieutenant Doolittle has been in charge of the laboratory from the start, having been released for the work through the courtesy of the Army Air Corps. With his study at several universities and his experience as a racing pilot, he was qualified for the work as few other pilots could have been. He was aided in technical subjects by Professor William Brown of the Massachusetts Institute of Technology, and worked with the Army, Navy, and the National Advisory Committee for Aeronautics.

"The Bureau of Standards have both contributed to the work, as also have the research departments of the Pioneer Instrument Company, the Taylor Instrument Company, the Sperry Gyroscope Company, the Bell Laboratories, Radio Frequency Laboratories and the Kollsman Instrument Company.

"The new principle which has been demonstrated solves what I have considered in the past one of the two remaining fundamental problems of aviation. Its application, however, and the final perfection of the best equipment for all phases of fog flying will require time and effort on the part of commercial and military organizations. The Guggenheim Fund will tabulate all the data gathered during the experiments and publish them in a form which will open them to the entire aeronautical industry for further development."

That was the night that Admiral Land signed his bold signature on Jo Doolittle's long white damask tablecloth. So did Brown and Guggenheim and Sperry and Kelsey and all of the others who had worked on the project. Henceforth that tablecloth, representing her many friends, would be one of Jo's most prized possessions.

6

In 1930 the Shell Petroleum Corporation was an up-and-coming outfit; not quite in the same league with the giants like Standard Oil, but it had progressive, imaginative leadership. At that time the Shell organization in America had three entities: the Shell Oil Company (California); Shell Eastern Petroleum Products, Inc. (New York); and the Shell Petroleum Corporation (Saint Louis). Doolittle knew the Shell company to be interested in the progress of aviation fuel—he knew that its scientists were working hard in laboratories trying to find a fuel that would enable the engines of the day to produce more power.

In 1830, Marcus Samuel started business in London as a small Oriental importer. His firm prospered, and gradually Samuel undertook to operate and, eventually, own the ships he needed to carry his cargoes. These cargoes were as diversified as the wares of the East; but staple items were copra (coconut meat for pressing into coconut oil) and all kinds of sea shells, some of them for decoration, others for manufacture into mother-of-pearl items such as buttons and knife handles. The Samuel firm became quite noted for the number and rarity of shells it imported; and Samuel often took advantage of this favorable reputation when importing other items, such as soap and matches, giving them the brand name "Shell."

Looking around for additional items to sell, Marcus and Samuel Samuel, sons of the founder, decided early in the 1890's to take on kerosene. They made arrangements to purchase refined product from a Black Sea refinery and set about building a tanker that was extremely large and modern for its day. This tanker set sail for the Orient in the summer of 1892 via the Suez Canal, and a new oil business was launched.

Being shipping men, the Samuels paid close attention to the efficiency of their distribution and transported their product entirely in bulk, unloading it into large wharfside storage plants. This was a radical departure in the Far East, for up until then that area had received its kerosene packed in five-gallon cans shipped all the way from Philadelphia or Brooklyn as hold cargo.

The Samuel kerosene venture was successful from the start and soon dwarfed the rest of their business. In 1897, the oil part of the business was separated and incorporated as The "Shell" Transport & Trading Company, Ltd., taking its name from the brand name of the kerosene. By 1900, the Shell company was one of the world's largest oil companies, with thirty ocean-going tankers, and ocean terminals and depots all through the Orient.

At this point the path of the Shell company crossed that of the Royal Dutch Petroleum Company, a small Netherlands concern which had a prospering oil-producing and refining business in the Dutch East Indies. The Shell company was always running short of supplies, and the Royal Dutch lacked an adequate tanker fleet and sales organization. A quite natural consequence was the merger of their interests in 1907 into what has since been known as the Royal Dutch-Shell Group of companies. The combined organization henceforth used the Shell brand name because it was better known.

In the next twenty years, a world-wide group of companies grew up about this alliance. In the United States, Shell Oil Company in San Francisco, Shell Petroleum in Saint Louis, and Shell Eastern in New York were Shell affiliates, using the Shell brand name.

And in aviation it was a good brand name, too. Louis Blériot's first cross-channel flight back in 1909 had been made on Shell gasoline. Most of the Allied planes from 1914 until America got in the war in 1917 were fueled exclusively by Shell "aviation grade." As soon as the war was over, Shell in London had set up an aviation department; one of its first contracts was for the gasoline to fuel K.L.M.'s first scheduled flight in 1919.

American aviation did not develop quite so rapidly. Private flying was on a small scale until Lindbergh's famous flight in 1927 fired the popular imagination and set men, who only fifteen years ago had sold their horses to buy a Model T, to wondering: Maybe now they should sell the Model T and buy a plane. All across the country cow pastures were made into "airports" overnight to accommodate these new Sunday fliers.

It was at this point that the Shell companies in the United States decided to get in on this aviation gasoline business. During late 1929, Shell Oil in San Francisco set up an aviation department, hiring Lieutenant John A. Macready, a well-known Army flier of his day, to manage it.

But young Doolittle didn't know or care about the background of the company. All he knew about was the fact these people who ran it felt as he did about the future of flying. It was John Macready who sold Colonel Theodore Peck of the Saint Louis company the idea of hiring Doolittle. He broached it to Alexander Fraser, then executive vice-president of the Saint Louis company.

"But Doolittle is a racing pilot, not a salesman," Fraser said.

Peck said dryly, "Doolittle is a great many things. Sure he's a racing pilot. He's also a scientist who has been very close to the developments going on at Wright Field. In addition, things happen to Doolittle. Whatever he does seems to be news. If he were working for us, every time the papers mentioned his name they'd have to add, 'of the Shell Company.' Now my idea is this. . . ."

He went on to expound his idea. It was to hire Doolittle and James Haizlip, and have them compete in air races as representatives of Shell. Haizlip was a former Army pilot. They would use Shell aviation fuel; their planes would be serviced and refueled by Shell, and if they won their share of races they'd be putting Shell on the map.

"You say he's not a salesman," the persuasive Colonel Peck continued. "Doolittle knows everyone of importance in the Air Corps and in commercial aviation. They all like him and respect him. Everything else—quality, price, delivery—being equal, they'd rather buy from Doolittle than from anyone else."

"Get hold of him," Fraser said.

Fraser threw the idea to Ude B. Daly, then president of the company, and it was discussed at a board meeting. In 1930 people just weren't buying automobiles, and the oil companies, which lived by the gasoline which powered the nation's cars, were in bad shape. Business concerns all over the country were faced with two alternatives—they could weather the storm by retrenching or by gambling on new markets. The St. Louis men were too progressively minded to sit back and hope for the best—they were willing to try something new, and the idea of having men like Haizlip and Doolittle publicizing the name of their company had its attractive features. They decided to gamble.

Doolittle was just finishing up his work at Mitchel Field. The Guggenheim Foundation had supplemented his Army pay of $500 a month with an additional $500. You could live pretty comfortably on $1,000 a month in the 1920's, but even then $500 a month didn't go too far if you had two hungry kids and ailing parents. Doolittle was interested in the Shell proposition. He and Jo talked it over.

"Why not go out to St. Louis and meet the Shell people?" Jo said. "See if you like them and see if they like you."

That made sense to Jimmy. He did go to St. Louis, he did

like the Shell people, and it was quite apparent that they liked him. But Doolittle, who would try anything new in the air with a plane under him, was more conservative when it came to risking the security of his family.

"I've got two months' leave coming to me from the Army," Doolittle told them. "Let's try this together for two months and see how it works out. If by then you don't think I'm the man for this job, well, I can go back into the Army."

They agreed. He was to organize the aviation department and head the development of all Shell aviation products. He decided that the first thing the new department needed was an airplane. The company had a tri-motored Fokker piloted by Milt Girton. The commercial airline companies at that time were in their formative stages. It took you two full days to fly from New York to Los Angeles, and commercial planes only serviced a relatively few large centers of population. Doolittle would have to do a lot of traveling. The thought of spending nights on trains filled him with horror. Fraser and the other Shell officials saw his point. They told him to go and buy an airplane. Doolittle warmed up to these men. He liked the way they operated.

"How much can I spend for a plane?" he asked.

"As much as you need," Fraser said laconically. Then Doolittle said he wanted Jack Dalton to be his mechanic. Fraser agreed and Jimmy arranged for his release from the Army.

He and Jo hurried out to California and he bought a Lockheed Vega for $25,000. This was a fine airplane. It had a cabin in which four people could be seated. The pilot's cockpit was above and in front of the cabin. He flew the trim ship back to Mitchel Field with Jo as a passenger. He was very proud of his new airplane. The back of the pilot's seat was actually a swinging door held by a catch opening into the cabin. It could be opened either from the pilot's compartment or from the cabin.

"Be careful of this thing, Jo," he explained to his wife. "If you ever unloosen this door while we're in the air, I'll come tumbling right back into the cabin. Never open it without giving me warning."

January 15 was the big day when the Doolittles would move to St. Louis. Jo, Jimmy junior, age nine, and John, age seven, climbed into the cabin of the trim yellow Lockheed. The cabin was loaded with all of the smaller Doolittle possessions which hadn't been sent by freight to St. Louis. A dozen Mitchel Field officers were out on the field to wish Jimmy good luck in his new venture and to say "Bon voyage" to Jo and the youngsters. The weather wasn't good. Snowdrifts were piled high over the field, but runways had been cleared. This was no concrete runway. A blistering wind was roaring across the field. Jimmy warmed up his 425-HP engine and started to taxi down the runway. He was halfway down when the swinging door behind him snapped open and he was almost propelled into the cabin.

"I've told you never to open this door without warning me," he yelled to Jo.

"I didn't open it," she yelled back. "I think something is broken."

"Nothing's broken, and please let me fly this airplane," Jimmy shouted.

Jo shrugged her shoulders and leaned back. She knew well something was wrong. She'd heard a couple of ominous cracks, and she knew that something had loosened the door. But she always allowed Jimmy to do the flying in the family, so with a quick look to see that young Jimmy and John had their safety belts tightly fastened, she looked calmly out of the window and waited. Jo had a kind of calm religion all her own, much of it based on the philosophy of a pilot. Looking at her two youngsters she breathed a silent prayer and then because silence was not one of Jo's failings, she found herself saying aloud, "Well, dear Lord, I've fastened their safety belts and my own. Now it's up to you and Jimmy." Then she sat back calmly to await whatever might happen. It didn't matter to Jo; she was with the only three people in the world she loved, and no matter what happened it would happen to all of them. Jimmy poured on the power, and now this flying moving van was rolling fast. Then it happened. Slowly, almost gently, the wheels spread out and the landing gear collapsed. The frozen mud and the snow acted as brakes, and the little plane settled firmly on its belly, then tilted over to the right.

The officers who had been waving good-by yelled for a fire truck and started running toward the woebegone-looking plane. Nobody was hurt; they all emerged unscathed—the two kids jabbering with excitement. Jimmy, after reassuring himself that Jo and the children were all right, started to carry on a one-way conversation addressed to himself. His Army career had given him a colorful vocabulary of invective. He directed it all at himself, at his inexcusable carelessness in overloading the plane. Captain John McCulloch, who had come hurrying, listened to Jimmy and then took the two youngsters and led them away.

"You kids all right?" he asked.

"Oh, sure," Jimmy junior said. "But you should have heard how my father talked to my mother. But she wasn't flying the airplane. He was."

Meanwhile, Jimmy was surveying the damage. The propeller, the main bulkhead and the struts of the landing gear were smashed, but although the plane was suffering from a dozen other minor injuries, the accident had not been fatal. He immediately gave orders to have it crated and shipped back to Lockheed to be rebuilt. Then he was faced with the embarrassing task of phoning St. Louis to tell the executives of the company just what he had accomplished on his first day as a Shell employee. He had been working for them twelve hours now, and he had already cost them about $10,000. His warm feeling for his new employers was intensified when they brushed off his estimate of the damage to inquire after the safety of Jo and the youngsters.

"These people are wonderful, Jo," he said in amazement.

"They don't even seem to care that I washed out their airplane. And they aren't even Army people."

"Get rid of that chip on your shoulder," Jo said calmly. "Most people are pretty nice if you only give them a chance."

He looked at her thoughtfully and said, "I'm getting sick and tired of you always being right."

"Okay, Doolittle," she smiled.

The aviation department of Shell now consisted of Doolittle, Haizlip, office manager Rex Brashear and research assistant Eugene F. Zimmerman.

A month later Jack Allard came to St. Louis on a curious mission. Allard was now president of the Curtiss-Wright Export Company. The company wanted Doolittle to demonstrate its planes in Europe. Would the Shell Company please give Doolittle a four-month leave of absence?

"But he's only been with us about six weeks," Fraser protested.

"This will be a great thing for Shell," the persuasive Allard went into his act. "We want Jimmy to visit nearly every country in Europe demonstrating the new Hawk, our latest fighter. He'll meet all the local Shell men in these countries. Their prestige will be increased by their association with Doolittle—and Doolittle will be getting the feel of the European market. The experience will broaden Jimmy. It will really be a great thing for the Shell Company. And of course," Allard had as a clincher, "the planes we will demonstrate will use only Shell products."

Shell agreed to Allard's proposal. Three additional pilots, Lieutenant James E. Parker, Captain John K. Cannon (never called anything but Joe Cannon then or now) and William F. Goulding, vice-president of Curtiss-Wright Export, were to make the trip. Major Melvin Hall and Goulding were to handle the business details of the mission, and two mechanics went along to service the aircraft. Doolittle was to demonstrate the Hawk, Parker the Falcon, Cannon the Fledgling, and Goulding the Robin.

The first stop was Athens. Doolittle, Parker and Cannon were three of the best pilots in the world. At Athens they put on an air show the like of which the Greeks had never seen then—or since. Jimmy did a series of aerial acrobatics which completely captivated the onlookers.

Turkey, Bulgaria, Holland, Yugoslavia, Rumania, Czechoslovakia, Switzerland, Norway, Sweden, Hungary, Poland, Belgium, Lithuania, Germany, Latvia, Esthonia, Austria and Finland were all visited. Jimmy had two humiliating experiences. While flying over Zenda in Poland, a bearing went out and he had to cut the engine and land in a pasture. A new engine was immediately shipped from Rotterdam.

Everything was fine for a while until he found himself in a steep dive for the edification of the Lithuanians, over Kovno. In the midst of the dive his untried engine conked out, and again he had to glide to a landing. Actually, even the pursuit planes of 1930 weren't well adapted to diving. This was before the day of the constant-speed propeller. When you dove a plane, the propeller overran the engine. Doolittle could have put on a show going through the conventional loops and spins, but to sell this plane to Europe, he knew he had to make it do things that hadn't been done before. To perform the eye-catching acrobatics he felt would sell the airplane, he had to constantly over-rev his engine. The inevitable overheating followed. This was a calculated risk which he had to take, and actually he had only two mishaps during the four-month tour.

The mission had the unofficial blessing of the State Department and the U.S. Army, and wherever the barnstormers went they were feted by the American Diplomatic Corps. Doolittle and his fellow pilots found that European aircraft manufacturers were not wide-eyed innocents. The acrobatics caught the eyes of the spectators, but the military officials, engineers, designers, manufacturers and foreign pilots were more interested in high speed and calibration tests. European engineers, planes and pilots were all far better than the American airmen had anticipated. Airport maintenance, however, left something to be desired.

Doolittle was putting his Hawk through its paces during a demonstration at Stockholm when a maintenance error caused him considerable embarrassment. One stunt which always sent the spectators into ecstasies was an upside-down flight just above the ground. Jimmy was in the midst of this spectacular-looking maneuver when he suddenly became violently ill. He reached for altitude desperately. In addition to having horrible cramps, he found that he was nearly blind. Somehow he landed the airplane and staggered away, trying hard not to black out. For half an hour he was violently sick, while the rugged Swedes looked on in tolerant amusement. What kind of a pilot was this whose stomach couldn't stand a little upside-down flying? Finally Doolittle staggered back to his plane to find out what had happened. He soon discovered the trouble. The Swedish maintenance man, after filling the plane with gas, had inadvertently left off one of the gas caps. When the plane assumed its inverted position the high-test gas poured out of the tank and sprayed into the compartment into Jimmy's face. He had been swallowing and inhaling the fumes of perfectly good 82-octane gas. He pointed out the uncovered gasoline vent to the Swedes. Some of them still had traces of mocking smiles on their faces. Thoroughly annoyed, he climbed back into the airplane and put it through a series of acrobatics and close-to-the-ground inverted flying. When he landed, the tolerant smiles had been replaced by looks of enthusiastic admiration.

Weather reports left something to be desired, and while flying from Munich to Berne, Doolittle found that he was flying through nothing but thick soup. He managed to get under it to land in a large pasture near Lyss. The field was wet from heavy rains, and the airplane bogged down. Doolittle wanted to find out just where he was, and then he wanted some help to pull the plane out of the mud.

He saw a man across the field looking at him curiously.

When Doolittle beckoned to him, the man approached. He looked like the typical Swiss farmer.

Doolittle asked him in French for the location of the field, but the man just shook his head, puzzled. He tried him in German with the same result. Doolittle had only one more language left at his command—Spanish. There was no reason to believe that a Swiss farmer would know Spanish, but Doolittle tried him. Again the man shook his head in bewilderment. And then he asked casually, "Just what in hell are you trying to say?"

The gentleman identified himself as a former native of Spokane, Washington, who had now embraced the intriguing profession of a European tramp.

It was raining hard now, and Doolittle and the ex-patriot huddled under the protecting wing of the airplane. Jimmy learned exactly where he was.

"I'm going to need a lot of help pulling this plane out of that mud," Doolittle said. "Do you think we could get a farmer with a couple of oxen anywhere around here?"

"They've got a great institution here in Switzerland," the tramp smiled, "called the Boy Scouts. They take a pledge to help anyone in distress. Looks to me like your airplane is in distress. There's a village right near here full of these kids. I'll rout them up and have them back here in no time."

Within an hour the rain had stopped and a group of Boy Scouts were earnestly pushing and rocking the wings of the plane. Gradually it emerged from the morass, and they hauled it to some relatively firm ground. Doolittle thanked the Boy Scouts, said good-by to the friendly tramp, gave his engine the full gun, and the Hawk managed to lift itself out of the pasture.

Admiral Horthy, one of Hitler's junior partners, gave the flyers the full treatment when they arrived in Budapest. Burton Wright, the American Minister to Hungary, in turn reciprocated by arranging a dinner for the pilots and for Horthy. Horthy's twenty-year-old son was also a guest. At the close of the dinner he suggested that Doolittle, Cannon and Parker might like to see what Budapest offered in the way of night life. The flyers, who had had quite enough of official protocol, jumped at the idea, and young Horthy showed them that he knew his way around the city's night spots. At dawn he drove them to the banks of the Danube to show them the lovely bridges which spanned it.

"Could you fly that airplane of yours under these bridges?" young Horthy asked curiously.

"There is nothing that little plane can't do," Doolittle the salesman boasted. "If you'd like to see it fly under those bridges, let's go to the airport."

They did. Doolittle went up in his Hawk and young Horthy and the others drove back to the Danube. Doolittle streaked out of the dawn, skimmed the surface of the river and flew under the ancient bridges with a foot or two to spare. Young Horthy and a few hundred early morning spectators were duly impressed. Such flights were more than mere stunts to entertain the son of a dictator; this was Doolittle's way of dramatizing the fine qualities of the little Hawk.

The incident provided the Budapest coffeehouses with a lot of chuckles the next day. But the British Minister took a dim view of the exploit. He felt impelled to write to his American colleague, Burton Wright, suggesting that it would not do diplomatic relations any good if this madcap American pilot killed himself. He began his letter by saying, "I would do little to belittle Doolittle, but. . . ."

In Belgrade, the Curtiss-Wright agent gave a party for the mission. Doolittle and his fellow pilots, who were to give a demonstration the next day, were very leery of the slivovitz and other native firewaters that were dispensed at the party. It grew crowded, noisy and gay. Doolittle walked out on the terrace of the country club where the party was held, to inhale a little fresh air. A very personable young Yugoslav girl followed him out. She said she wanted to practice her English on him. They had been talking for a few moments when a Yugoslav officer walked out, screaming insults at the astounded

Jimmy and accusing him of stealing his girl. Doolittle looked at the girl, hoping that she would explain matters, but she was smiling, apparently enjoying the situation. Her smile infuriated the Balkan officer the more, and he took a mighty swing at Jimmy. Doolittle realized that he was in Belgrade to sell airplanes and not to fight Yugoslav air officers. He backed away, trying desperately to explain that the Yugoslav was off his beam. But the enraged officer kept swinging wild punches. There was only one thing to do. More in pity than in anger Doolittle threw a short left hook under one of the Yugoslav's wild right-hand swings. It landed squarely on his mouth. The astounded Yugoslav stood there, stunned, and with a look of bewilderment on his face he spit out four teeth. He looked at the small Doolittle with a look of complete admiration. Then he embraced him profusely and apologized for his absurd suspicions. Doolittle realized that the Balkan temperament was a little bit difficult to fathom.

Jack Allard had been right. The experience had been good for Doolittle and for Shell. He not only familiarized himself with the progress being made in the aircraft and petroleum industries in Europe; he also learned a great deal about the political climate. The trip, incidentally, did a great deal for young Captain Cannon. After his return to the Air Force he began a rapid rise. Today he is General John Cannon, head of the Tactical Air Forces.

The tour completed, the Curtiss-Wright traveling circus returned to New York. Their exploits had received considerable publicity, and Mayor Jimmy Walker gave the airmen a real old-fashioned New York welcome. Peter J. Brady, chairman of the Mayor's Advisory Committee on Aeronautics, was especially interested in hearing what the pilots had to say about foreign military strengths. Doolittle told Brady that it was quite possible that Europe would soon surpass the United States in the quality and quantity of her military planes.

"Over there, the governments support the racing programs. These aerial races are not mere stunts in Europe; they give engineers, designers and pilots an opportunity of testing new equipment and new techniques. We've got to do something to increase the speed of our own aircraft, or we'll be left far behind."

"How can we best do this, Jimmy?" Brady asked.

Doolittle shrugged. "There is no simple answer to it. We've got to improve our engines, we've got to design our planes for greater speed, and we've got to develop aviation fuel that can pull more power out of the engines."

Doolittle returned to his job at Shell in a very thoughtful mood. The Shell officials listened with great interest to his report. This was a side of Doolittle they hadn't seen before. His analysis of European progress in aviation was coldly methodical. When he suggested that the Shell company acquire a couple of really fast planes to be used for racing and experimental work, Shell gave him the green light. He bought a series of fast planes designed by Walter Beech and Matty Laird.

He began to experiment with the Travelair which Walter Beech had built for him. The newspapers gave a lot of attention to this monoplane which they called the Mystery Ship. It had two pairs of wings, one large pair for stunting and acrobatics, and a small pair for speed. He and Haizlip tested it thoroughly and were delighted with it. The motor cut out and Haizlip crashed it one day, but the plane wasn't completely destroyed. Jimmy had an idea that with some redesigning this could be about the fastest plane in the world. He decided to do this on his own. It was frankly an experiment, and he didn't want Shell to take the financial rap in case of failure.

He had Pratt and Whitney install a Wasp Jr. engine in it. He decided that the struts connecting fuselage and wing were causing too much resistance. He moved the struts closer to the fuselage and encased them within the skin. Then he did something revolutionary. To further lessen resistance he put an arc in the bottom of each wing at the wing-fuselage juncture. This presented a problem with the aileron torque tube, traditionally straight tubing. He curved the two torque tubes and was now ready to test his creation. He was very pleased with it. The engine had been souped up to 400-HP. It was a trim, streamlined, beautiful-looking plane, and he was so proud of it that he asked some friends (and son Jimmy) to come and watch it be introduced to the air. It took off like a scared cat and climbed beautifully. He came down to four hundred feet and streaked it across the field close to three hundred miles an hour, at that time an unheard-of speed. There was a severe vibration. He looked toward the right wing and he froze. The ailerons had fluttered off and the wing was disintegrating before his eyes. Engineer Doolittle knew just what was happening. He knew that the curved torque tube had caused the trouble. He knew too that within seconds the whole wing would flutter off. He pulled the nose up sharply. The gallant little ship responded. It reached five hundred feet and then he rolled it on its back. Two things happened at once. The airplane went completely out of control and Doolittle dropped out of it.

He pulled the ripcord of his parachute instantly. It opened at four hundred feet, checked his headlong descent sharply, and in a few seconds deposited him gently on the ground. It was the shortest parachute drop on record up to that time.

Jimmy stood there, completely discouraged. He wasn't thinking of what to the layman appeared to be a miraculous escape. He had calculated the risk mathematically, and he wasted no time in pondering his good luck. He could only think of the months of work that had gone into the design and manufacture of this plane.

Young Jimmy, Jr., had seen the whole thing happen. Doolittle had landed only a quarter of a mile or so from where he had been standing. The crowd, led by Jimmy, hurried to him. He looked at his father and asked, surprisingly, "Dad, how much did we have wrapped up in that airplane?"

"All we had, son, all we had," Doolittle said sadly.

Although the plane was a total loss, the experience was not without value. Doolittle felt strongly that airplanes had to be made which would be able to sustain high speeds. It seemed simple enough to construct such planes on a drawing board. However, no matter how aeronautically sound innovations seemed to be, the real test came when you built the airplane, got it into the air, and then submitted it to the terrific pressure of speed.

Doolittle knew that his theory of encasing the struts within the skin of the fuselage would streamline the plane and would lessen wind resistance. Obviously the curved torque tube was not an answer, but you couldn't know this unless you submitted it to the inexorable law of trial and error.

E. M. (Matty) Laird built his next plane for him. It was called the Laird Super Solution. Doolittle had obtained an engine with a special supercharger which gave it well over four hundred HP. After testing it he entered it in the Bendix Trophy Race. This and the Thompson Trophy were the two blue-ribbon events of racing. The Bendix race began at Los Angeles and ended at Cleveland. When Doolittle arrived at Los Angeles he announced that he was not only going to fly to Cleveland, the terminating point of the race, but that if everything went well he would proceed to New York in an attempt to break the transcontinental record held by his pal, Captain Frank Hawks, who had made the trip in twelve hours and twenty-five minutes. A Los Angeles reporter asked him rather sarcastically if he had figured out just how long it would take him to reach New York.

"Of course," Doolittle said calmly. "Eleven hours and thirty minutes. If I have tail winds on the last lap, I may cut that time by ten or fifteen minutes."

The eight fliers entered in the Bendix race were competing for $15,000 in prize money. The refueling of Doolittle's plane at Albuquerque, Kansas City and at Cleveland was under the supervision of Zimmerman and his Shell crew. Doolittle and Zimmerman had worked out a technique for refueling which cut the conventional time in half. The race began at 5:45 the morning of September 4. Doolittle's little streamlined Laird biplane climbed to 11,000 feet, leveled off and headed for

Albuquerque. The Shell men were waiting for him. It took them just seven minutes to pour 140 gallons of gasoline into his tanks, and he was off again for Kansas City, eight hundred miles away. The weather was beautiful and the engine sang a high, satisfying tune. He roared into Kansas City an hour ahead of any of the other contestants. Once again Zimmerman's crew did a smart job, and ten minutes later the Laird Solution was in the air, headed for Cleveland. The weather turned nasty now, but this didn't bother the beautiful plane Matty Laird had built.

The wheels had hardly stopped rolling on the Cleveland runway before a Shell truck, with the grinning Zimmerman standing on the running board, roared up. Jo and the youngsters were there, filled with pride, but they didn't even get a chance to say hello to Jimmy. Ephraim "Pop" Cleveland, head of the Bendix Contest Committee, shook hands with Jimmy, congratulated him, and then Jimmy was off headed for New York. He flew into a driving rain, and streaks of lightning grabbed fiendishly at the little plane. But the engine never stopped singing. The Alleghenies, graveyard of so many planes in the 1930's, were completely hidden, but Jimmy's instruments weren't. He plunged through one storm after another; then, just before arriving at New York, emerged into clear weather. The wheels touched the runway at the Floyd Bennett Airport exactly eleven hours and sixteen minutes after he had left Los Angeles. He spent a half hour at the Floyd Bennett Airport talking to reporters.

"You must be tired, Jimmy," one of them said.

Doolittle shrugged his shoulders. "I had a good sleep last night."

"How about a drink to celebrate breaking this record?" another asked.

"I'll have that one with my wife," Jimmy smiled.

"But she's in Cleveland, isn't she?" the reporter said, puzzled.

"That's right," Doolittle said, and then he climbed into the plane and headed for Cleveland. Jo and the kids were waiting for him at the airport.

He phoned the office in St. Louis and found that the boys were going to hold a celebration that night in honor of his great performance.

"It would be a much better party if you were here, Jim," Fraser said.

"Well, that's easy," Doolittle laughed. "I'll see you in a couple of hours."

He hopped into a Shell plane and arrived in St. Louis in time to join the celebration. He landed at 10:20 P.M., Central standard time. Since 5:30 that morning (Los Angeles time) he had flown some 3,500 miles, and both he and the plane were in perfect condition. The next morning he flew Fraser back to Cleveland to view the air races.

The records Doolittle was establishing which received so much newspaper publicity were more than mere stunts; they did more than sell Shell gasoline. The public thought of Doolittle as a human meteor streaking across the skies in death-defying fashion. Businessmen, commercial airlines and aeronautical engineers all looked at these flights with different eyes. Businessmen realized that behind every record-breaking flight there had been a great deal of organized planning. The skillful Shell refueling crews had devised shortcuts that enabled Doolittle's plane to get away completely refueled six or seven minutes after it landed. Businessmen realized that Doolittle never took the crazy chances the newspapers and public thought of him as taking. They realized that the safety factor was all-important in Doolittle's calculations. If he found an airport closed in, he always had two or three alternate fields where he could land and he always had fuel enough to take him to one of these. His exploits turned more attention toward the less spectacular but relatively more important commercial airlines. Doolittle, Frank Hawks and the other record breakers were making American industry air-conscious, and this interest was reflected in increased air travel. The commercial airline executives studied the various routes Doolittle flew and in many cases opened up new air lanes based on his pioneering flights. Increased business meant planes, and more planes meant that they needed more gasoline. Shell received more than its share. Aeronautical engineers, designers and manufacturers were interested in the way Doolittle's racing planes reacted to the terrific strain he was putting on them. Although he used the Laird Solution for most of his record breaking, he was also flying a Lockheed-Vega and later a Lockheed-Orion.

Doolittle never lost sight of the fact that his main job at Shell was the development and sale of aviation products. When he wasn't preparing for a race, he was constantly on the road visiting Northrup, Douglas, Curtiss, United, Pratt & Whitney, and the other companies engaged in the manufacture of airplanes and engines. He was much more than a mere salesman with an order book. When he visited these plants, he was always pounced upon eagerly by the engineering departments. What had he learned lately? What did he think of this new wing or that aileron? The engineers were the theoreticians; he combined their technical knowledge with flying experience, and both he and the engineering departments gained through the free exchange of ideas.

Because Wright Field ordered a great deal of gasoline, chiefly for use in experimentation, Doolittle made frequent visits to Dayton. He went as a salesman but remained as a scientist. He followed closely the work being done by the Army fuel development men. He grew more and more interested in their efforts to develop a more powerful fuel that eventually could be produced at a cost that would enable the Army to buy it.

Someone came up with an idea that appealed to Doolittle. In one day he would fly all of the routes covered by George Washington during his entire lifetime. This flight would begin in Maine, be routed south through Washington's Revolutionary War terrain, and then be directed west to Ohio. The United

States Postal Service, interested in expanding and popularizing air mail delivery, then in its infancy, was glad to cooperate. The entire flight was conceived by and organized under the auspices of the Aeronautical Chamber of Commerce. The one-day flight was given the grandiose name of the George Washington Bicentennial Airplane Flight. Doolittle was to drop mail pouches at thirty villages, towns and cities. It was a clever, eye-catching stunt. The publicity-minded genius in charge of it managed to locate a lineal descendant of George Washington, the charming, middle-aged Ann Madison Washington. She would re-travel by air the path once taken by her illustrious ancestor.

Doolittle used his Lockheed-Orion monoplane for this trip. He dropped his first mail pouch on the little village of Kittery, Maine, and then headed for Providence, Rhode Island. He came in low over the airport and dropped another bag of mail. He streaked over New Haven, through the haze that covered New York, and hit Morristown, New Jersey, with a third mailbag. He flew over Trenton, Camden and Valley Forge, three cities closely associated with Washington's military career. He slid in below the overcast which covered Philadelphia and dropped another mailbag. Then he headed for Washington, where he made his first stop. A few minutes later Doolittle and the delighted Ann Madison Washington were flying over Mount Vernon; they came in low over Wakefield, Virginia, Washington's birthplace (Washington was not born at Mount Vernon), headed for Yorktown, and then dropped a mailbag on the airfield at Sunbury, North Carolina. To find some of these obscure spots required pinpoint navigation of a high order. After stopping for a few moments at Pittsburgh, Jimmy headed west for Pomeroy, Ohio. He turned and flashed briefly over Fort Le Boeuf, Pennsylvania, and then headed for Rome, New York, where he dropped more mail. Crown Point and Ticonderoga were next. With darkness closing in, Doolittle headed for Albany, then streaked down the Hudson to drop mail at West Point. At 10:15 that night the wheels touched the runway at Newark. The whole flight of 2,600 miles had taken 15 hours and 40 minutes.

The remarkable part of it all was the fact that Doolittle had announced an advance schedule and he had kept to it with mathematical precision. He had found a dozen little villages which were hardly dots on the map. The flight more than any other stunt popularized the United States air mail service. Previously, anyone affixing an air mail stamp to a letter dropped it in the box with the same feeling that a sailor on board a ship might toss a sealed bottle containing a letter into the Gulf Stream. The flight made millions conscious of the fact that the United States had an air mail service that could be trusted to deliver letters just about anywhere in the country. It gave the young air mail service the lift that it needed so badly, and convinced Congressional appropriation committees that funds given to the Postal Service to develop the air mail were not being tossed into some speculative, boondoggling operation. The editorial pages of the nation gave thoughtful attention to the whole matter of air mail and commercial aviation as a result of this one-day precision flight. Its tremendous success was an affirmation of Doolittle's oft-expressed philosophy that air races and ventures like the one-day flight served a very serious purpose. They were not "mere stunts." The speed of the airplane had always been accepted by the public; Doolittle was trying to make the public accept the plane as a safe vehicle for travel, and air travel as a precise method of traveling from one place to another. To him and to serious students of aeronautics, the fact that he had flown 2,600 miles in less than 16 hours was very unimportant; the fact that he had made thirty mail deliveries right on schedule was vitally important. But Doolittle didn't have much time to accept the congratulations of Government officials and newspapers.

The Bendix Race was only a month off and he hoped to lower his 1931 record. He sent his little Laird out to Wichita with orders to replace its stationary wheels with a retractable landing gear. He also ordered a new and more powerful engine. He hurried to Wichita to check with mechanics and engineers who were readying the Laird. He was confident that he could add fifteen to twenty miles per hour by having the landing gear fold up beneath the fuselage once the plane was air-borne. The Wichita engineers had devised a landing gear control that operated by hand. Finally, satisfied with the job the Wichita crew had done, he took the Laird off. The wheels retracted smoothly beneath the plane and he could feel the little Laird, now as streamlined as a needle, leap through the air as it had never done before. After twenty minutes of putting the plane through its paces, he approached for a landing. He tried to lower the wheels but something was wrong. The controls which operated the mechanism seemed to have jammed. As Jimmy circled the field his mathematical mind considered every possibility, but he just couldn't figure what was wrong. The mechanics and engineers who had worked so hard on his plane were huddled below on the field looking up anxiously. One of them might have an idea. Doolittle scribbled a note which said: "Something wrong; landing gear. Can get 3½ turns each way; no more. If any suggestions, write them on side of a plane and come up. Otherwise I will run out of gas and stall in." He dove down to the field and dropped the note. The engineers and mechanics held a hurried conference and then they chalked a message on the side of a plane. Pilot Preston Kirk took off and brought his plane up alongside the Laird. Jimmy read: "Zoom right, zoom left, power dive." Doolittle nodded. This seemed to make sense. He went up to 6,000 feet and began to zoom alternately to the right and to the left, hoping to jar the controls loose. Then he dove the plane, but the bit of mechanism that was causing the trouble withstood the shock of abruptly coming out of a steep dive. For nearly an hour he tried every flying stunt he knew but to no avail, and then he saw that he was about out of gas. He could either bail out or attempt to make a hazardous belly-landing. The light plane designed for speed flying might completely come apart at the impact of its fuselage hitting the earth. But Doolittle was very fond of this airplane and he decided to take the long chance. He eased the plane down slowly and gradually; then as gently as possible he placed it on the runway. There was a screaming sound as that part of the undercarriage which he had managed to let down was sheared off. The plane pointed high into the air and then fell back to the runway. It slithered along for a hundred yards with little damage except to the propeller, landing gear and bottom of the fuselage. Doolittle crawled from the wreckage unhurt but sick at heart. He felt that he had let the little plane down and yet in his heart he knew that a retractable landing gear was absolutely necessary if a plane was to achieve its maximum in speed. Sadly he resigned himself to staying out of the Bendix Race, only a few days away.

The story was page one news all over the country. Within a few hours Doolittle had received offers of a dozen planes to use in the Bendix event. Among them was one from Russell Boardman. He was in a hospital recuperating from a crash. He offered Doolittle the use of his Gee Bee racer. The Gee Bee (designed and built by the Granville Brothers) had a reputation as a killer. It was speedy all right, but unstable longitudinally and directionally. It was a difficult airplane to fly. It was extremely sensitive and didn't permit you to make any mistakes or to make the tight turns which saved time when you were racing around pylons. It was too late to enter the Bendix Race, so he sent his application in for the Thompson Trophy Event, feature of the Annual Cleveland Air Show. To his delight, Jimmy Haizlip ran away with the Bendix in his Wedell Williams racer, to score another victory for Shell. Doolittle tried out the chunky little red-and-white Gee Bee. He liked its 600 horsepower. He had a lot of respect for this little plane and he handled it gently. He had no trouble making the 200 miles an hour required to qualify for the Thompson Race. He learned the temperament of the Gee Bee. It didn't like to turn sharply. The Thompson course was a triangle; three legs each of ten miles. On one of his trials he roared down the last leg of the triangle at a speed of 300.09 miles an hour, the fastest speed ever reached by an airplane at that time. But the trials only qualified you. The day before the actual race the Cleveland Air Show was marked by tragedy. Al Wilson, a veteran flyer who had been working as a Hollywood stunt pilot, was killed while flying an old 1910 Curtiss Pusher. He and John Miller flying an autogyro had been entertaining the crowd with stunts. A wing of Wilson's plane hit one of the autogyro's revolving forty-foot blades and the Curtiss crashed killing Wilson.

The day of the Thompson Race was clear with high visibility, and 60,000 spectators assembled to watch what was probably the greatest group of racing pilots ever assembled. They included Jimmy Haizlip, dapper Colonel Roscoe Turner, Jimmy Wedell, Ray Moore, Bob Hall, William Ong and Lee Gehlbach. Fate almost dealt Doolittle out of the race before it had begun. He was warming up his engine when gasoline leaked out through the cowling. The heat of the exhaust ignited it and a quick flame flared up. A fire extinguisher was standard equipment in the cockpit of every plane and before the flame had a chance to spread Doolittle had grabbed it and had smothered the fire in its stream of carbon tetrachloride. Mechanics hurriedly removed the cowl, reported that there had been no damage, replaced it, tightened it, and Doolittle was ready. The planes took off ten seconds apart. Jimmy knew that he had the speed under him to win this race but he didn't have the maneuverability that characterized some of the other racers. He decided to fly what was virtually a circle instead of the shorter triangle. Jo and the two youngsters watched the race from the grandstand. Newspaper men covering the Cleveland Air Show had played up the fact that the Gee Bee was a killer. Several photographers kept their lenses trained on Jo and the two boys during the whole race but they didn't snap their cameras. When it was all over Jo asked one of them why he hadn't taken any pictures. A bit embarrassed, he explained that he and his colleagues had been given orders to be ready to photograph her reaction if her husband crashed. But he didn't crash. He won the 100-mile event with an average speed of 252.68 miles an hour. To make it a perfect day for Shell, Jimmy Haizlip was a close second.

In 1931 and 1932, the newspaper headline "Doolittle Breaks Record" was a common sight. He had completely captured the imagination of the public, and more important to him was the fact that his flying exploits were reacting to the great advantage of Shell. Shell was not bashful about letting the gasoline-buying public know that its gasoline and lubricants were used exclusively in Doolittle's plane. During September, 1931, he broke half a dozen of Hawks' old records. Every time Doolittle broke a record it sent the delighted Shell salesmen working overtime.

Doolittle decided to establish a record between Canada and Mexico City. This would be a spectacular way of making both Canada and Mexico Shell-conscious. He took off from Ottawa in the same Laird Solution with its powerful Wasp engine still going strong. He landed at Washington, Birmingham, Alabama, Corpus Christi, Texas, and then headed for Mexico City. From the viewpoint of the pilot the flight had been routine until he reached the last lap. Flying from Tampico to Mexico City, Doolittle had to climb to 19,000 feet to clear the mountains. Suddenly and unaccountably he felt terribly sleepy. This puzzled him, because sleep had always been something that he could take or leave alone. His head was heavy, and he found he had to fight desperately against blacking out. He knew that the 19,000 feet altitude couldn't be blamed for this. He was quite at home in the rarefied air of that altitude. It must be something else.

Twice his head dropped forward, and twice he recovered himself just as the plane was getting out of control. He had no idea what was wrong. His instruments showed no engine trouble, but he knew that if he couldn't come out of this semicoma he'd soon be crashing in the mountains. He tried desperately to think of some remedy that would keep him awake, but his lids got heavier and heavier. He decided to keep asking himself a lot of questions. When he found he couldn't answer them, he'd bail out.

"What is nine times eight?" he asked. It took him half a minute to think of the right answer.

"What year did Columbus discover America?" The questions were easy. The answers were more and more difficult.

"Who is the President of the United States? On what day were Jo and I married? When is John's birthday?"

He asked the questions aloud. He found that he was shouting them. But now the plane was clearing the mountains and he could start down for his landing. The thicker air didn't help any. Sheer instinct kept him making the right moves. Finally, through a blur he saw Mexico City. He made what was almost literally a blind landing, and he staggered drunkenly from the plane.

Joyous Mexican officials rushed to embrace him. They saw his white, drawn face and the glazed look in his eyes and attributed it to fatigue.

"Brandy," he managed to gasp.

An exuberant Mexican official thought it wonderful that Doolittle wanted to celebrate the termination of his flight in true Latin style. There was no brandy in reach, but there was the fiery tequila. Doolittle took two healthy drinks of it. It would have shocked a corpse back to life. Somehow he managed to stall his way through the official reception. Then he was deathly sick—sicker even than he had been in Stockholm. It wasn't until the next morning that he felt better. He was still shaky, but he went to look over his plane. He found that the engine had a burned hole in one cylinder, but that wouldn't account for his illness. He thought it might be the result of carbon monoxide, but he started the engine and found that the exhaust was working perfectly and no monoxide had penetrated the cabin. Completely puzzled, he turned his attention to the cabin, and there he found the answer. It was the old, old question of raising the octane value of fuel which had come back to haunt him.

He always carried two cans of tetraethyl lead with him. If he had been forced to land at some obscure airport having only straight-run fuels in its pumps, he could have leaded it. The altitude and resultant reduced air pressure had burst a seam in one of the cans of tetraethyl lead. The extremely toxic fumes had filled the cabin, and his lungs, with their poison. He was learning everything there was to be learned about aviation fuel, all right, but he was learning it the hard way.

A week later he was back in St. Louis telling Fraser about his experience with the can of tetraethyl lead. He hurried to Wright Field to tell the Army experts in fuel development about it and to urge them to warn Army pilots about the danger of carrying cans of lead at high altitudes.

"This is just one more reason," Doolittle said grimly, "why the Air Force should standardize 100-octane and have it available all over."

"We're doing our best, Jimmy," Frank Klein of the Fuel Development Branch said. "It takes time."

Then Doolittle made a startling announcement. He had retired from racing and would make no more spectacular flights. He felt now that racing had served its purpose. The manufacturers of planes and engines had learned a great deal from the performances of the fast little planes, but the inevitable tragedies connected with racing were given such wide publicity that the useful purposes of these tests were minimized. Doolittle felt, with the heads of the airlines, that the time had come to sell the public safety and dependability rather than breakneck speed. Commercial and military aviation had to be developed. Doolittle decided that henceforth he would confine his efforts to developing and selling Shell aviation products.

"Sooner or later there's going to be a war," he told Fraser, and the Scotsman shook his head in rueful agreement. "This war will be won or lost in the air. Right now there isn't much difference between American and foreign planes or American and foreign engines. There isn't much difference, if any, between their pilots and ours. Everything being equal, the air force which has the best fuel will have a great advantage."

"But, Jimmy, the Army has shown no willingness to buy anything better than the standard 91-octane," he said.

"It'll come," Doolittle said confidently. "And when it does, we have to be ready. We've got to enlarge our plants and produce the components that will make a better gasoline. We've got to have plenty of octane ready when the Army smartens up."

"Laddie," Fraser said, "you know what you're asking? Right now we produce gasoline for automobile use. And business, let me remind you, is lousy. To make the iso-octane you want we'll have to cannibalize the gasoline we're producing now. It will mean we'll have to gamble a lot of our salable fuel in the hope that the Army will eventually want a better gasoline."

"That's right," Doolittle said calmly. "Frank Klein and the boys at Wright Field are doing a lot of good work. They're convinced that it won't be long before the Army will be demanding fuel of higher octane number. When they do, let's be ready."

"We hired you to sell to outsiders," Fraser growled, "and now you're selling me. Well, all right, I'll go along."

Doolittle grinned. "You won't regret it, Mr. Fraser," he said cheerfully.

In the spring of 1933 Allard again came to St. Louis to ask if Curtiss couldn't borrow Doolittle to demonstrate the Curtiss Hawk, with its fine Cyclone engine, to the Chinese. Shell was again agreeable, and Doolittle flew the Hawk in Shanghai, Nanking, Hangchow and Canton. Then he went with the Curtiss crew to the Dutch East Indies. The air force commander asked him to fly one of the Hawks powered by a Conqueror engine which his government had previously bought.

"There's nothing I can do with this airplane that your pilots can't do," Doolittle said.

"Maybe you can teach us something we don't know," the Dutch air commander said, and Doolittle took up the plane. This aircraft was considerably heavier than the Hawk Cyclone which he'd been flying, and the air at Bandoeng was thinner than it had been in China. He dove the Hawk Conqueror vertically and then started to pull out at a thousand feet. But he had misjudged the pull-out characteristics of this plane in the thin air and it didn't pull out on schedule. The plane pulled out just as it was about to go right on in; as it checked its mad dive Doolittle felt a bump, and he knew that his stationary landing wheels had actually hit the ground. But the sturdy little plane zoomed upwards again while Doolittle wiped the perspiration from his brow. You couldn't cut things finer than this. He landed to accept the congratulations of the Dutch air commander and his staff.

"That was the most delicate piece of flying I've ever seen," the Dutch officer said to Doolittle.

"No it wasn't," Doolittle said ruefully. "It was just downright stupid flying, and I was lucky not to wash out your fine airplane."

The Dutchman beamed his delight. "You're right," he said calmly. "We all knew you had misjudged the actions of this heavy plane, but we wondered how you would explain it. I congratulate you on being an honest and modest man."

Doolittle hurried back to St. Louis to press his campaign for additional facilities to produce 100-octane.

7

"The biggest gamble Doolittle ever took?" Ask any one of a hundred men in the oil business and he'll grin: "That's easy. Back in the 1930's he gambled his whole career at Shell on the very thin possibility that the War Department would make 100-octane its standard aviation fuel. He talked the company into building an expensive commercial-size plant to manufacture a fuel that the Army brass said was too expensive ever to be commercial. Jimmy really went out on a limb and the War Department damned near sawed it off."

How important was 100-octane to the war effort? Well, if you were to ask a Russian what won the war, he'd say without hesitation, "Stalingrad." An American G.I. (or infantry general) would probably say the war was won the day that Omaha Beachhead was secured. Ask a Marine the same question and he'd probably tell you of the successive invasions of Pacific islands which brought the war close enough to Japan to threaten the mainland. Ask an oil man the same question and he'll remind you that without the Air Force we wouldn't have had a chance to launch an offensive in either theater of war, and he'll go further and say that if it hadn't been for the fine 100-octane used in those aircraft engines our planes would have been outclassed by German and Jap aircraft.

In late 1941 the Honorable Geoffrey Lloyd, Member of

Parliament and Petroleum Secretary of Great Britain, arose in the House of Commons to discuss the war situation. "We could not have won the Battle of Britain without 100-octane," he declared bluntly. "This octane was thirteen points higher than the fuel used by German aircraft. That extra thirteen points ended the threat of any Nazi invasion of England."

Oil men will tell you of the historic battle to make the War Department standardize the aviation fuel that enabled RAF and American bombers to lengthen their range and our fighters to reach altitudes high enough to protect the heavies. Listening to the oil men discuss desperate efforts made by oil companies, engine manufacturers, by scientists and by the progressive Air Corps leaders to force the General Staff to adopt the then-revolutionary aviation fuel as its standard, you realize the vital importance of the battle—yet while it was going on it attracted hardly any public attention at all. Doolittle is one of the men who led the fight inside the oil industry; first he had to persuade the Shell Company to throw its resources into the production of a fuel that the Army didn't want, and then he had to help sell the War Department on the necessity of using the new fuel.

The saga of the development of present-day aviation fuel is one well worth the telling. The financial brunt of the development was for the most part borne by private enterprise as represented by the oil companies and manufacturers of aircraft engines, and some of America's finest scientific minds grappled for years with the problem of how to get more power from fuel.

You can start the story of airplane gasoline almost anywhere. We may as well start it with the ordinary engine of thirty years ago.

The engine of an aircraft (or of an automobile) is a sensitive organ that has to be nursed, coddled and given constant attention. An engine is strictly feminine in its temperament; it refuses to be ignored or slighted, and it has many ways of showing its displeasure if neglected. This is occasionally true today, even when lubricants and fuel do the pampering that the driver (or pilot) once had to do himself.

During the 1920's the engine was much more temperamental than it is today. Often, for no apparent reason, an engine developed a "knock." The "knock" was the despair of every motorist and pilot of those days. What caused the cantankerous engine to "knock" anyway? A great many brilliant scientists had been kicking that one around for many years. One of them was the late Thomas Midgley, Jr., one of the greatest creative scientists of our age. He was a scientist, an inventor, a chemist, a breaker of precedents, and an optimistic scholar, ceaselessly pursuing the elusive truth into the dim recesses of the unknown. He was also quite a human being. Dr. William Lloyd Evans of Ohio State University once said, "Midge was a master of philosophic living."

It was Midgley who created Freon, the nontoxic, noninflammable refrigerant without which refrigeration and air conditioning as we know them today would have been impossible. His researches into the chemistry of rubber were years ahead of his time.

It was back in 1916 when he was twenty-eight that Midgley went to work for the Delco Light Company, and that began his long and rather wonderful associaton with Charles F. Kettering. This continued through the years, when he worked for the Dayton Engineering Company and General Motors Research Corporation. A problem would come up and Boss Kett would toss it to Midgley. He developed a means of indicating the degree of charge of storage batteries. Then he developed mercury-cooled exhaust valves. Finally Kett gave him a real tough one.

Delco sold lighting units to farmers. When the farmers ran these lighting plants on kerosene they developed a knock. This was about the same time that the knock was appearing in automobile engines run on gasoline.

"When they use Pennsylvania kerosene, these farm lighting engines start to knock," Kett explained to Midgley. "But the damnedest thing is that when they use California kerosene the knock disappears."

"But the Pennsylvania kerosene is a much better grade than the California stuff," Midgley said, puzzled.

"That's what makes it so confusing," Kett said. "Will you look into it?"

Midgley and his assistants, T. A. Boyd and Carroll Hochwalt, did look into it for a number of years. This was essentially a problem in chemistry, a subject which Midgley (trained as a mechanical engineer) hadn't been exposed to very much up to then. But this didn't bother either Kettering or himself. Both were daringly imaginative; both so sound that they found no difficulty in switching from one branch of science to another. There are very few baseball players who can play second, shortstop, or third base equally well—but those who do are the ones who gain baseball immortality. Midgley was like one of these. His intellectual equipment was such that switching from the engineering problem of mercury-cooled exhaust valves to the chemical problem of why a really fine Pennsylvania kerosene raised hell in an engine, while a kerosene you'd hesitate to put in your lamp made the same engine purr happily, was no more drastic than that presented to Gil MacDonald of the Yankees when Manager Casey Stengel told him to switch from third base to second.

Midgley wanted to "see" the knock. He installed a window in the side of a test engine, but every time the pressure generated, the pane of glass shattered. So he switched to a window of quartz. Now for the first time an engineer could actually see combustion taking place. Midgley, Boyd and Hochwalt just watched for a long time. They noticed that when the engine was running smoothly, that is when normal combustion was taking place, the flame which resulted was a blue one. But they noticed too that when the engine began to knock the flame was a bright, blinding white. This was rather startling. Midgley had heard a beautiful theory once propounded to the effect that a dark-colored fuel would absorb more of the light during combustion. Could it be possible that darkening the fuel might have some effect on the knock? Midgley would try anything, no matter how unorthodox.

He dyed the fuel with iodine until it was deeply brown. The test motor was started, the same power used that had previously produced a knock—and there was no knock. Midgley looked at his two assistants blankly. There seemed to be no rhyme or reason for this, but it did to some extent bear out a theory which Midgley hadn't thought much of.

Well, anyhow, it seemed to work. At the moment Midge didn't know it, but he was on the road to discovering a real antiknock compound. Iodine was not the best coloring agent, he decided. First of all, it was too costly for commercial use; secondly, it had the unpleasant habit of turning an engine into a chemical factory making iodides. Iron carbonyl was just as good as iodine, but it deposited a coating of iron on the spark plugs and fouled the engine. Nickel carbonyl did the same thing. He tried dozens of other chemical compounds. None of them was satisfactory. By now Midgley knew that the color of the iodine had nothing at all to do with its effect on combustion. It was some quality in the iodine itself.

Finally, after hundreds of experiments (and at the cost of some three million dollars to General Motors), Midgley emerged with a compound he called tetraethyl lead. Tetraethyl lead was a deadly poison to anything except an engine; engines thrived on this mysterious combinaton of lead, hydrogen and carbon.

All you had to do was to add a very small quantity of the lead to ordinary fuel and the knock left your lighting engine, or your automobile. We are skipping over the vast amount of research Midgley had to do before he could produce his new compound in commercial quantities at reasonable prices. It is enough to say that he was responsible for one of the greatest technological petroleum advances ever made, and today his name is one that is revered in the whole industry.

The oil industry is a highly competitive one, but once scientific advance is made by one company, the discovery quickly becomes known to all others. Primarily Midgley's discovery belonged to Ethyl, but actually it was soon made available to the whole industry as well as to the Army and Navy research laboratories.

It isn't going too far to say that the discovery of the magic chemical that banished knock really ushered in the great era of transportation progress. It increased the power and performance of vehicles by increasing the ability of fuels to operate better engines. It promoted the conservation of petroleum by promoting its best utilization in a motor. This was no abstract scientific discovery of interest only to the ranks of esoteric laboratory workers. It wasn't long before the butcher, the baker and the candlestick maker who owned automobiles were receiving direct and economical benefits from it. It was only a matter of a few years before an engine was yielding 90 per cent more power than a comparable engine of the pre-Midgley days, and mileage per gallon had been increased by 20 per cent. Petroleum technologists are unanimous in giving their late colleague much of the credit for this advance. And yet it is a sad commentary that of the millions of automobile owners in this country who benefit so hugely from his discovery, probably not one-half of one per cent ever heard the name of Thomas Midgley, Jr.

But they remember his name in the offices of the Ethyl Corporation, and if you bring it up you'll see the eyes of the engineers and lubrication experts light up warmly, and they'll start telling stories of the man they all call Midge. And if you ask about Midge in the huge RCA Building which houses the Shell offices, you'll get the same reaction, for the whole industry is proud of this man.

Tetraethyl lead did not immediately solve the problem of airplane fuel, but it opened up avenues of research that eventually did. The Air Corps (as it was then called) in the 1920's was merely a rather annoying stepchild to the Army. It had virtually no autonomy of its own and couldn't spend a dime without an Army order. The Army had a rather remarkable theory about airplane fuel. The Army brass said in effect, "If there is a war, we will immediately need huge supplies of gasoline to fly our planes. We can only find such quantities among the low-grade gasolines. Therefore, the Air Corps must learn to operate its planes with this lowest grade gas." And so the Air Corps was flying its planes on ordinary refinery gasoline with no official Army attention being directed toward the antiknock value. Actually the aircraft fuel up to 1927 had an antiknock value of about 50-octane. Today a pilot would hesitate to pour anything like that in his pocket lighter, but Army pilots like Doolittle, Harris, MacCready, Kelly, Hegenberger, Maitland, Maughan and the others had to take their chances that it would keep their engines running. The 50-octane of the 1920's consisted of virgin naphtha, natural and cracked gasoline. But Doolittle was just a lieutenant; there was nothing he could do about it—yet.

If the rest of the Army was way behind the advances made by the scientists of the oil industry, the Air Corps was not. By chiseling a bit here, cutting a corner there, the Air Corps managed to eke enough money out of its relatively minute budget to carry on engine and fuel research, first at McCook, then at Wright Field. Much of this research was in charge of Samuel D. Heron, a British scientist with a distinguished record as the world's leader in his field. At McCook Field he developed an air-cooled cylinder that soon made every comparable liquid-cooled aircraft cylinder obsolete. Then he was put in charge of fuel and oil development at Wright Field, a move that was to have far-reaching significance. Heron found a ready-made staff waiting for him, all tickled to death at the idea of working under the giant in the field of aircraft engines and fuels. For years the dedicated men at Wright Field had been keeping research into fuel development alive. First it was Major C. W. Howard who saw to it that a significant proportion of experimental funds available at Wright was diverted to the Power Plant Branch which handled fuel development.

Then it was Captain T. E. Tillinghast who was made chief of the branch, and he kept the development of leaded fuels going. By the time Sam Heron arrived, Lieutenant E. R. Page headed the Power Plant Branch and young Lieutenant Frank Klein, three years out of M.I.T., became his assistant in the Fuel and Oil Branch.

Frank Klein had been a student at M.I.T. when Doolittle was there working for his doctor's degree. Doolittle did most of his experimental flying at what was then known as Boston Airport, where Klein, a fledgling pilot, was learning the ropes under the auspices of the M.I.T. branch of ROTC (Reserve Officers Training Corps). He met Doolittle a few times, but neither ever thought that one day they'd be on the same team playing against the big brass of the General Staff. Doolittle went out to McCook Field after getting his doctorate, and Klein, after earning both his wings and an M.I.T. diploma, went into the Army. After three years of flying duty he was assigned to Wright Field, and put on Sam Heron's team. He received this appointment with the enthusiasm of a rookie ballplayer who has been sold to the New York Yankees. When you worked under Heron you were working for the world's champion. Tall, gangling Frank Klein was right at home at Wright Field.

Heron's men were all conversant with the work done earlier by Kettering, Midgley, Boyd, and Graham Edgar of Ethyl, the first to synthesize iso-octane in his laboratory (at a cost of $4,000 a gallon). Everyone thought the development of aviation fuel to be essential to the future of national defense, and everyone was willing to spend time, money and brains to go a bit further along the road. Typical of the attitude of the oil industry in those days is the fact that Kettering sent the Delco test engine with the quartz window over to Wright Field for Heron to use. General Motors picked up the bill for that; it didn't cost Joe Taxpayer a dime.

By 1930 the Air Corps was using a 91- or 92-octane as its standard aviation fuel. It was far in advance of the 50-octane used in World War I, but it still left much to be desired. When airplane engines were ordered, the specifications were that they be suitable for the standard fuel. Klein and his associates felt that eventually a superior fuel would have to be adopted, but the War Department was not enthusiastic. Even if a practicable, higher octane was developed, that would mean reshaping the engines now in use or ordering new and expensive motors. The Wall Street crash had left the American economy a little shaky, and the General Staff can hardly be blamed for not wanting to ask Congress for more funds. Then, too, there was the question of horses.

It seems almost unbelievable now, but the inoffensive horse was always a big factor in getting Army authorities to allocate money to any new venture. Life at Army posts was dull. It was made endurable only by the horse. Army officers played polo, held horse shows and hunts. It was very difficult to get the Army to release funds for tanks or airplane gasoline. "First thing you know," ancient American equivalents of the British Colonel Blimp would grumble, "these damn fool tanks and airplanes will be using the money we need for blooded stock." Army officers seldom thought in terms of war; they thought in terms of the Army posts, and these would be unlivable without horses. "Might as well take a man's bourbon away from him as take away his horse." The fact that World War I had proved pretty conclusively that the cavalry was about as much use in combat as a group of Dennishawn dancers didn't bother these doughty exponents of laissez faire.

By now Shell had built a million-dollar plant at Wood River, Illinois, for the sole purpose of producing 100-octane. The plant did a fine job in producing the fuel, but it remained at the railroad siding near Wood River waiting to be sold. Hundred-octane was really a combination of 45 per cent commercial iso-octane, 45 per cent straight-run aviation gasoline, and 10 per cent iso-pentane. Then it was "leaded" with three to four cubic centimeters of tetraethyl per gallon. In 1934, iso-octane cost about $2.40 a gallon to produce. The

Shell technicians were trying desperately to get the price down, but they were up against the age-old economic problem of supply and demand. If there had been a big demand for the 100-octane, the production costs would immediately have dropped. But the oil industry had to wait until there was a demand before going into large-scale production.

When Doolittle dropped into the Shell office he tried to avoid the reproachful eyes of Fraser, of Tony Laeomble, of Jack Taylor, of Gene Davis and the other executives who had gone along with him on gambling that there would soon be a market for the 100-octane.

"We can't eat that stuff, laddie," Fraser would say mildly.

"Don't worry, Mr. Fraser," Doolittle would say cheerfully. "As a matter of fact, I think we ought to build another plant in Texas. When the demand comes it'll be so great . . ."

"By then we'll all be out of jobs," Fraser growled.

Shell engineers and chemists were still experimenting at the pilot plant in Emoryville, California. These brilliant men, under the leadership of Jack Taylor, were all devoted to Doolittle. He was fighting their fight and doing a good job of it. Like himself, they were all convinced that it was merely a matter of time before 100-octane would be in common use. But how long could Shell take this financial beating? The Shell directors had been fairly patient up to now, but how long would their patience last?

Doolittle spent almost as much time now at Wright Field as he did in the Shell office in St. Louis. When he and Zim sold Wright Field the first batch of chemically pure iso-octane ever sold to the United States Army, they held a mild celebration. It was only a thousand gallons, but it was the first break through the wall of Army indifference. At $2.50 a gallon the Army got quite a bargain. By now a gentleman named Hitler was Chancellor of Germany. Doolittle knew that the Germans had embarked on a huge program of aircraft and fuel production. The Reich had plenty of benzol and coal tar products. By adding this to their straight aviation gasoline they emerged with the approximation of a 92-octane without tetraethyl lead. And they had benzol and coal tar derivatives in abundance. Doolittle, Klein and other pilots had the uneasy feeling that sooner or later Herr Hitler would be using this Luftwaffe of his for purposes less decorative than the air shows the great Ernst Udet was heading in Germany.

During the next two years Doolittle helped persuade Shell to build three additional plants for the production of 100-octane. The investment was now more than two million dollars.

Commercial airlines were buying relatively small quantities of 100-octane for use in take-offs. The Army occasionally gave Shell small orders for 100-octane for use in research, but all this didn't add up to much. By now the price had been cut to 71 cents a gallon.

The Air Corps had absolutely no entity of its own. The real flying men knew that the only answer to the whole problem of developing air power was a unified service with an independent Air Force. Early in the 1930's the Baker Board was appointed to study the whole perplexing air situation. The committee, headed by Newton D. Baker, was asked to report on adequacy and efficiency of technical flying equipment and of the training courses. Doolittle, Karl Taylor Compton, Clarence Chamberlin, Edgar Gorrel and George William Lewis were the civilian members of the board. For twenty-five days the board took testimony from 105 witnesses who covered 4,283 pages with the record of their views. The Baker report strongly advised against the establishment of a separate air force. Doolittle was the only dissenter. In his separate minority report he said:

> I believe in aviation—both civil and military. I believe that the future security of our Nation is dependent upon an adequate air force. This is true at the present time and will become increasingly important as the science of aviation advances and the airplane lends itself more and more to the art of warfare. I am convinced that the required air force can be more rapidly organized, equipped and trained if it is completely separated from

the Army and developed as an entirely separate arm. If complete separation is not the desire of the committee, I recommend an air force as a part of the Army but with a separate budget, a separate promotion list and removed from the control of the General Staff. These are my sincere convictions. Failing either, I feel that the Air Corps should be developed and expanded under the direction of the General Staff as recommended above.

By now there was a man in the White House named Franklin D. Roosevelt, and he shared this view. But once an appropriation was given to the Army it was up to the discretion of the brass as to how that money be spent. In 1935 the standard 91-octane cost the Army about 15 cents a gallon. If 100-octane were made the standard, it would cost a great deal more (about 30 cents a gallon). Existing contracts with aircraft manufacturers called for an engine that would use 91-octane; changes in engine construction would have to be made, were 100-octane adopted. The Army took a dim view of the whole idea. The Army was willing to authorize huge sums for the production of more aircraft, but not for a fuel that would make these planes faster and give them greater range and larger carrying capacity. The Air Corps was headed by a nucleus of real flying men; progressive, willing to take chances; men dedicated to the idea that the sky would be the real battleground in the war which they felt to be inevitable. Major General Benny Foulois was "Chief of the Air Corps," Major General Frank Andrews was in command of what was then called General Headquarters, or GHQ, Air Force. Hap Arnold, made a temporary Brigadier General, was at Rockwell Field. He was doing all sorts of things with the 19th Bomb Group—making precision bombing a fine art instead of a hit-or-miss proposition; studying the effect of damage made by .30- and .50-caliber machine guns and a 37-mm. cannon; testing and exploring the potentialities of the B-10's and B-12's, and always agitating for the development of four-engined bombers.

The Spanish Civil War exploded. German bombers and

Italian bombers began to destroy Guernica, Barcelona, Badajoz, and the pattern of future warfare was established. Men like Foulois and Arnold had been crying that this would be the way wars would be fought, and now they were proven to be accurate prophets. The effect of the bombing on Spanish cities really woke up the public, Congress, and the Army brass. The War Department even gave the Air Corps a few of the new revolutionary B-17's, which would earn undying fame later on as the Flying Fortresses. But these were given merely on paper, and only thirteen of them actually were delivered to the Air Corps. Even Spain hadn't taught the War Department that heavy bombers should operate on their own—they believed that the B-17's might be useful "in support of ground troops."

In the late thirties Doolittle made two trips to Europe for Shell. He spent some time in Germany. Ernst Udet, greatest of all European pilots, took good care of Doolittle when he reached Berlin. Udet had flown in several of the Cleveland air races, and his exhibitions of incredibly reckless flying had endeared him to his American colleagues. Udet flew on brandy. If there was no brandy he would compromise by drinking bourbon, Scotch or practically anything else that was wet and alcoholic. Udet had a great admiration for Doolittle.

Once he told W. C. Courtney, *Collier's* war correspondent, "You Americans have two air forces—your Army Air Force and Jimmy Doolittle."

Udet, who looked a bit like Doolittle and who weighed about the same, had just received several cases of champagne from a visiting French air mission. He insisted that Doolittle stay at his apartment and help him at least make a start at demolishing the wine. Doolittle, who was genuinely fond of the gay, laughing little German pilot, was happy to oblige.

Udet in 1937 was almost a law unto himself. He was a general engaged in building an air force, but he was a free soul incapable of being regimented, and to him Hitler was a joke. Over champagne he pulled a lock of his hair down over his forehead, grabbed a small black comb for a mustache and did an imitation of Hitler. It was a hilarious bit of mimicry.

Udet had a magnificent apartment in Berlin, perhaps the only apartment in Europe with a shooting gallery. He never bragged about his flying; his real vanity was his shooting, and there are those who say that he was the greatest rifle or pistol shot of modern time. Doolittle thought that 2 A.M. was a rather unconventional time to engage in target practice, but he too liked guns and he and Udet had a wonderful time shooting at a target which was backed by a sand-packed metal box.

Then Udet brought out his favorite pistol, a huge .455 caliber. He aimed carefully, but the champagne interfered. He could have drunk a bottle of brandy or whiskey without batting an eye, but two bottles of champagne did something to his aim. He missed the target and the heavy bullet smashed into the plaster of his wall. It went through the wall and left a gaping hole into the next apartment.

"Now we're in trouble, Ernst," Jimmy said. "The people next door are sure to complain."

"But, my dear Jimmy," Udet said with honest bewilderment, "who would they complain to?"

It was true enough—no civilian could complain about anything an air force general did. Doolittle didn't do much business for Shell on this trip, but he did learn a great deal about the German air force. He was convinced that Germany was on the march. This was further confirmed when he went over again in 1939, and on his return he went right to Hap Arnold to give the Air Force Chief the benefit of his views.

Doolittle was in constant demand by scientific and aviation organizations to address them on latest technical developments. Because he had access not only to the newest developments made by the Army, but to the latest improvements in the field of engine and plane and instrument manufacturing as well as advances made in petroleum technology, his speeches to these organizations were always informative, useful, and occasionally sensational. Sometimes he spoke as a scientist;

sometimes as a pilot; sometimes as a gasoline salesman. But no matter how weighty the subject, he couldn't resist an occasional joke on his audience.

Casey Jones, one of the greatest of the original barnstorming, hell-for-leather fliers of the early days, was a kindred spirit. Casey was booked to preside at the Annual Dinner of Airline Operators. These men, the most important in the industry, had asked Doolittle to deliver a technical paper on explosives. He prepared his paper carefully and then discussed it with Jones.

"It's rather heavy," he said doubtfully.

"Well, it's what they wanted, Jim." Casey shrugged his shoulders.

"I'll give it to them all right," Doolittle said grimly, "but we ought to have a little fun too. Now listen, Case . . ."

Came the night of the dinner. Doolittle traced the history of explosives from the time the Chinese first made firecrackers. He came to the day of TNT; he explained it and obligingly showed a few samples. Then he picked up a vial which he said contained the newest and most powerful explosive known to man. He told them in technical language just what its properties were. It had been a long evening, and by now most of the guests were ready for the drinking part of the festivities.

"If I ever dropped this little vial," he said gravely, "it would not only kill everyone in this room—it would destroy the whole building. Better put it away, Casey," he added, handing it over to his accomplice. Casey reached for it and then, with a cry of horror, dropped it. As the vial hit the floor there was an explosion that deafened everyone in the room and caused the horrified diners to dive under tables and chairs. Guests leapt up and made for the exits. But Doolittle stood there calm and serene, while Casey Jones was roaring with laughter, and they realized that the old Doolittle had come back for a moment. Casey had a twelve-gauge shotgun under the table with its barrel in a tin pail. When with feigned clumsiness he had dropped the vial, he had also pulled the trigger of the gun and the resulting explosion, augmented by the tin pail, was a frightening thing to hear. Previously the guests had wanted drinks—now they needed drinks.

Occasionally Doolittle made a flight which he felt would be useful to aviation. In 1935 he took off from Los Angeles in a single-engine low-wing Vultee transport plane, and with Jo as a passenger flew nonstop to New York in eleven hours and fifty-nine minutes, to beat his friend Eddie Rickenbacker's transcontinental record of twelve hours and two minutes. The Vultee was no souped-up racer; it was an American Airlines commercial passenger plane, and Doolittle made the flight to dramatize the speed and safety of passenger travel. He couldn't have found worse flying conditions. During eight of the nearly twelve hours he was without radio communication. Due to fog, winds, sleet, and all sorts of adverse conditions he flew some three hundred miles off his course.

"The old man is slipping," he said dolefully to reporters at Floyd Bennett Field when he landed. "I should have arrived here two hours sooner."

"It was an uncomfortable flight," Jo said. "I could hardly sleep."

"Did you wear a parachute?" a reporter asked.

"Whatever for?" Jo replied, looking puzzled.

This was the kind of flight that really gave people confidence in air travel. Eddie Rickenbacker, now president of Eastern Air Lines, was tickled to death to see his record broken. He knew that a flight of this kind would help not only American but all commercial lines, and he was right.

Meanwhile, brilliant Frank Klein was making history at Wright Field. He had been experimenting with the thousand gallons of iso-octane sold to Wright Field by Doolittle. He added lead and California gasoline, the blend producing 100-octane number fuel. He tested this fuel in the Pratt and Whitney Wasp and in the Wright Cyclone engines. He found that this fuel produced between 15 and 30 per cent more power than did the conventional 91-octane made from California-type gasolines and lead.

His reports went to the War Department, were acknowledged and then ignored. Klein and his associates (including his Wright Field superiors) thought that the facts he had so incontrovertibly established should be made known to the oil industry. So the daring young Klein (Captain Klein now) wrote a little article for the authoritative *Journal of the Aeronautical Sciences*. It was called, "Aircraft Engine Performance with 100-Octane Fuel," and it covered a scant four pages in the March, 1935, issue of the publication. Publication of rather secret data is hardly an orthodox way of forcing the hand of a General Staff. But it worked. The oil companies and the engine manufacturers were delighted. Wright Aero announced that it was going ahead with plans for developing engines that would be able to take full advantage of the 100-octane. The War Department may have seemed absurdly conservative in not leaping on the 100-octane bandwagon, but it had some justification for its stand. To begin with, the General Staff was disturbed about the possibility of insufficient supply of the 100-octane in case of an all-out war. Why, if there was a war, it was conceivable that the Air Corps would need three quarters of a million gallons per day. The oil industry could never produce that much 100-octane, the Army said. (Had the General Staff been able to foresee that over twenty million gallons of 100-octane would be needed every day by our air combat forces when the war finally did come, no one knows what attitude it would have taken.)

The War Department just couldn't ignore Klein's sensational report. Nor could it ignore the enthusiasm and willingness to gamble shown by private enterprise as represented by oil and aircraft companies. And so the General Staff did what General Staffs have done since the book was written; it appointed a committee to investigate the whole question of 100-octane.

The committee met at Wright Field, Dayton, in 1936. The

civilian experts who testified before the Board were P. B. Taylor (representing the Wright Aeronautical Corporation), R. C. Alden (Phillips Petroleum Company), E. E. Aldrin (Standard Oil Development Company), E. F. Zimmerman (Shell Petroleum Corporation), L. S. Hobbs (Pratt and Whitney Aircraft Division), and C. W. Deeds (United Aircraft Corporation). Lieutenant L. C. Ekstrom, the U. S. Navy expert on fuels and lubricants, was the only service witness. The testimony given by these seven men was considered so vital that the transcript of the proceeding was immediately stamped "Confidential." The report has been hidden in the archives these many years and was only declassified at the request of the author in 1952.

The committee consisted of Lieutenant Colonel J. T. McNarney, Chairman; Lieutenant Colonel W. E. Lynd, Major E. R. Page, Major J. F. Whitely, Major B. E. Meyers, and Captain Frank Klein. These were all Air Corps officers, but it didn't follow that they were all experts on the subject of airplane fuel. Captain Klein decided to give his colleagues a brief pre-meeting course on the subject. He wrote an eleven-page dissertation on the history of Octane Number as it proceeded from its original 50 status to the prevailing 91 standardization. He compared the performances of planes using 91-octane with planes using 100-octane. It was a concise, masterly presentation which answered just about any objection the War Department might later interject. Klein knew the sentiments of the officers comprising the committee. Every one of them was for 100-octane. He knew how the seven witnesses would testify, but Klein also realized that the War Department would use the written record of the proceedings when it made its decision. He wanted every useful argument incorporated in this record, so he sent each of the witnesses a copy of his report in the hope of giving them additional ammunition.

To say that this committee was "packed" would be an understatement. But by now the Air Corps was convinced that engine development had reached its peak under the prevailing

War Department specifications. The aircraft industry was frank to say that it would only move ahead in engine development if 100-octane was adopted. If 100-octane was made the standard, then of course they could go to the expense of building lighter, more powerful engines (the research, at the expense of the various airplane companies, had already been done). What Lieutenant Colonel McNarney and his fellow board members wished to do was to make out as good a case as possible for 100-octane. If it was a strong case, the impact on the men who held the Air Corps purse strings might be powerful enough to prod them into immediate action.

Back in St. Louis there was plenty of excitement in the Aviation Department of Shell. The committee had been scheduled to meet several times, but each time the unavailability of one or more committee members had resulted in postponement. It didn't look as though the Board would meet until the winter. Doolittle went moose hunting in Canada.

On November 13 an urgent message came to Shell from Frank Klein. The committee had finally decided to meet on November 17, and wished Doolittle to be a witness. Zimmerman had a moment of panic. Jimmy was lying on his belly a thousand miles away waiting to get a moose in the sights of his pet 30-06 Springfield gun. Zim rushed to the office of the president to tell him of the latest development. Fraser said curtly, "Get Jimmy on the phone." Zimmerman didn't mention that phones hadn't as yet been installed in the Canadian woods. He phoned Jo Doolittle, who suggested that he get in touch with George Ponsford at Sault Ste. Marie. That was the jumping-off spot for Jim Doolittle and his hunters.

Within an hour he had Ponsford's office on the line. "I've got to talk to Jimmy Doolittle," he said grimly.

"Well, now," Ponsford said calmly, "that'll take some doing. I know this man when he's out after moose. If lightning hit him, if a volcano erupted, if an earthquake came—he wouldn't notice any of these things. Not when he's hunting moose."

"But this is damn important," Zimmerman yelled.

"So is moose hunting," Ponsford said calmly.

"Doolittle will never forgive you if you don't get him to this phone." Zimmerman was frantic now.

"I'll tell you, son, Jimmy is about two days away from here. Now I could send for him. I could send a man on horseback. He'd have to travel about half a day to a river. He'd pick up a canoe there and paddle another half a day. He'd have to make a couple of portages. Then he'd have to walk. . . ."

"Wait a minute." Zimmerman was sweating now. He grabbed another phone, an interoffice phone, and explained the situation to Fraser.

"Get him," Fraser said. "I have to speak to him."

Fraser finally heard Doolittle's voice. It was very calm. Could he be at the Wright Field meeting by November 17? Not a chance, Doolittle assured Fraser cheerfully, no way to get there in time. "Send Zimmerman," he added. "Zim knows as much about this as I do. We've lived with this thing for years, Zim and I. Was there anything else?"

"Nothing else," Fraser sighed. Doolittle hung up and began the two-day trip back to the happy hunting grounds. He knew that Zim would say the right things before the committee. And Zimmerman did. Chairman McNarney threw questions at him and Zimmerman put the story of 100-octane on the record where the Air Corps wanted it.

Q.—What is the present approximate capacity of your company for the production of 100-octane fuel?

A.—With the present facilities of the Shell companies, without any rearrangement, we should be able to make between 10 million and 20 million gallons per year. However, the potential capacity is much greater. A recent survey shows that we can make 823,000 barrels of iso-octane on the West Coast annually, that is 42 gallons to a barrel, or 34,440,000 gallons. We figure a 45% content of iso-octane so that would be 76,000,000 gallons of 100-octane fuel per year. That is just for the West Coast and is based on taking the entire output of the cracking plants insofar as the octanes are concerned, for conversion to iso-octane. It would take about six months to get equipment installed for that purpose. Our refining facilities are confined to the West Coast and Central area. The capacity of the Central area would be approximately the same and may be somewhat greater. I am basing that on the output of the plants at present. We have four iso-octane plants now, and the ones on the West Coast are at present supplying the 100-octane fuel now being purchased from the Shell Oil Company.

Q.—If the Air Corps should standardize on 100-octane fuel, as of July 1, 1937, could your company furnish approximately twenty million gallons per year?

A.—We could furnish between ten and fifteen million gallons per year in our present plants without any extension of our facilities.

Zimmerman might have added the fact that if 100-octane wasn't adopted, he, Doolittle and probably Fraser would be out looking for jobs.

Q.—Can you make any approximate statement as to what the cost of 100-octane fuel will be next July?

A.—No, I couldn't.

Q.—Could you make any approximate statement if you were given a contract for, say, 15 million gallons?

A.—No, I am afraid not. Generally speaking and reflecting the point of view of the company, a reduction in price is to be expected with an increase in gallonage, but we cannot at this time say what decrease in price is to be expected without a close study of the situation.

Q.—That level will not be reached, will it, until there is a much greater demand for 100-octane fuel than at present? There will be no leveling off of prices until the Army, Navy, and commercial companies start using 100-octane as standard?

A.—Yes, that is true.

Q.—Do you have any information on foreign production of 100-octane gasoline?

A.—We have had inquiries abroad for 100-octane fuel and iso-octane and have shipped a small portion which is sufficient only for test purposes.

Q.—Have you had any inquiries from domestic commercial companies?

A.—Yes, we have had an inquiry from Transcontinental and Western Air and the price quoted was rather high. They are a little bit doubtful about taking it. They have some new planes which are equipped with the 1100-HP Wright Cyclone engines, intended for 100-octane fuel, and on account of the high price they are wondering if it would not be advisable to only run the engines up to the 1000-HP rating for take-off, using 87-octane fuel. That is barely sufficient for the present 1000-HP engines. We are now supplying the American Airlines at Glendale with 93-octane, C.F.R. Motor Method, which is practically 100-octane fuel, for use in Douglas aircraft which are equipped with 1000-HP Cyclone engines.

Q.—What about Pan-American?

A.—We have offered it to them for their trans-Pacific service, but it has not been used up to the present time. I believe the engine manufacturer wishes to do a little more work before they go in for 100-octane fuel. We would be very anxious for the Army and Navy to go to 100-octane fuel because it would help us in the scheduling of production through our refineries.

Q.—What would the situation be in case of war?

A.—There is only one difficulty. The oil companies have paid for iso-octane plants out of their own pockets. They are very expensive. Our investment is in the neighborhood of two million dollars and we are not getting any real return on our investment. Consequently, we should be reluctant to increase our plants in order to realize a total potential capacity unless we are sure of a definite market. It would take some time after the outbreak of war to get plants built. We wouldn't build them in time of peace unless the government furnished the money. It would be greatly to the interests of the Army and Navy to purchase and keep on hand at all times a sufficient quantity of 100-octane fuel, if they adopt it, to last for six months, until you get all of the plants built to produce wartime requirements, because if you didn't you might experience the same thing as in the last war. We wouldn't be able to supply the demand until plants were built.

L. S. Hobbs, engineering manager of the Pratt and Whitney Aircraft Division, added some pertinent facts under the questioning of Chairman McNarney. He and other expert witnesses brought out the fact that the B-1340-27 engine which powered the P-26A fighter generated an additional 30 per cent of horsepower for take-off purposes and short periods of climb and high speed when 100-octane was used. Actually, when you raised the horsepower 25 per cent the P-26A increased its speed by 7 per cent, its rate of climb to an unbelievable 40 per cent, and it decreased the take-off distance by 20 per cent—all incalculable advantages in combat. (These improvements in performance, of course, were the result of modifications in the engine to permit it to take advantage of 100-octane.) The Board, knowing that the War Department would be more impressed by low costs than anything else, brought out the fact that a purchase of 100,000 gallons of 100-octane by the Air Corps for experimental purposes from the Shell Petroleum Corporation and from Standard Oil of Louisiana cost 51 cents per gallon. The second 100,000 gallons cost 27 cents a gallon and the current price was 22 cents. Obviously, if the 100-octane were ordered in huge quantities, the price would drop further.

From a combat viewpoint the testimony of P. B. Taylor, chief engineer of the Wright Aeronautical Corporation, made great sense. "In using engines redesigned for 100-octane we find in our laboratories a reduction of 25 per cent in fuel consumption. We also find that with 100-octane we get more horsepower per pound weight of the engine."

R. C. Alden, Director of Research for the Phillips Petroleum Company, said that his concern could if necessary furnish 150 million gallons of 100-octane a year, and that eventually the cost per gallon would approximate the current price of 91-octane. Alden said that he was attending a Phillips Company executive committee meeting when the telegram summoning him to this meeting arrived. "As a result of your wire, our committee immediately decided to stop seesawing around with our program of producing 100-octane. That wire speeded us up and we decided to throw in $800,000 to increase our production facilities."

E. E. Aldrin, manager of the Aviation Department, Standard Oil Development Company, came to the meeting loaded with information as to what foreign powers were doing about 100-octane.

> The Russians have taken out a license covering hydrogenation facilities which should be completed before 1938. This alone would provide twenty million gallons of 100-octane fuel per year. Two major oil companies in foreign countries are arranging facilities which should be ready about the same time which could produce between them thirty million gallons of 100-octane per year. One of these plants would be located at Rotterdam and the other probably at Abadan [Persia]. These will most likely be available for supplying the British interests. The British Air Ministry has been discussing with our representatives the possibility of arrangements of future supplies of 100-octane fuel, more from a standpoint of putting in a large reserve storage. The supplies would have to come from a specially built facility and would tie this up for about two years. The French have placed orders for comparatively small quantities of 100-octane fuel which we know are more than what is needed for engine test work. Part of it will be used for certain flight testing in cooperation with air defense. The Germans are taking a special interest in iso-propyl ether through the I.G. Dye Trust.

The committee, at the conclusion of the hearings, unanimously recommended "that all engines hereafter procured, except those for primary training, be designed and tested on a basis of 100-octane fuel; that 100-octane fuel be adopted as standard for the Air Corps effective January 1, 1938." The conclusions and recommendations of the committee were sent to the War Department and Jimmy Doolittle returned from

Canada, Zim reported to him, and Doolittle talked to Klein.

"It's in the bag," a confident Doolittle told Fraser. "The War Department can't ignore such a strong recommendation. Let's be ready when they ask for bids."

"How sure are you of this, Jim?" Fraser asked anxiously.

"I'd bet my job on it," Doolittle said. That was good enough for Fraser. It was a long time before there was word from the War Department; anxious days for Doolittle and Zimmerman. Even more anxious days for Fraser. By now the Army G-2 had reported that Germany was producing the equivalent of 100-octane, and that her ME-109 fighter planes were attaining great speed at great altitude. Each day Hitler seemed more menacing. It may have been the Hitler threat; it may have been the completeness of the McNarney report; it may have been the behind-the-scene influence of FDR; it may have been a combination of all three—in any case the War Department finally announced some months later that the recommendations of the McNarney Committee had been adopted. The long, long fight had finally been won, and now real air power could be developed. Bids were asked for, and with complete confidence Doolittle and Zimmerman submitted the Shell bid. They lost out. There was the beautiful Wood River plant and still no customers. But they soon came.

It was at this point that Hitler stopped talking and began to march. Hap Arnold had been made Chief of the Air Corps. It was a fortuitous coincidence that Arnold and Harry Hopkins were good friends, with a great sense of mutual trust. Hopkins was a great one for listening if the conversation was worth listening to. By combat standards we had nothing then but a token Air Corps. We had good airplanes, good pilots, but not enough of either. Arnold spent a great deal of time explaining to Hopkins just what the Air Corps needed to give the country any kind of security at all. Hopkins at that time was perhaps closer to FDR than any man alive. Arnold completely sold Hopkins on the need for immediate expansion, and Hopkins sold the President. FDR and Arnold went into a huddle, and then FDR announced an immediate objective of 7,500 combat planes with an additional 2,500 available for training. Overnight the 100-octane picture changed. It was no longer a question of the oil companies underbidding each other; it was merely a question of turning out as much fuel as possible.

Doolittle had won his big gamble, but he needed the help of a power-hungry dictator to do it.

8

In January, 1940, Doolittle was named President of the Institute of Aeronautical Science, an honor comparable to a ballplayer being elected to the Hall of Fame. By now, at the age of forty-four, he had received practically every honor that civilian aviation had in its power to bestow upon one of its own. He had been awarded the Mackay Trophy, the Harmon Trophy, the Spirit of St. Louis Medal, and a dozen lesser honors. The Army had awarded him a DSC for his experimental work at McCook, and had later added an Oak Leaf Cluster to the decoration.

But in 1940 war clouds were gathering, and Doolittle said good-by to Shell and dug up his old uniforms. They still fitted, and he reported to Hap Arnold as Major James H. Doolittle. Hap needed a trouble shooter to deal with the almost hopeless problems industry was facing in converting to a wartime status. Happily, Doolittle knew most of the automobile and aircraft manufacturers well and they knew him well. They accepted him as an engineer and as a practical scientist.

"You can make nothing but enemies in this job, Jimmy," Arnold told him, "but someone has to see that the men in Detroit do it our way."

He didn't make any enemies and he did help the manufacturers with the intricate engineering problems bound up with the horrendous job of conversion. Then Arnold sent for him again to join his staff in Washington. Doolittle was quite unconscious of the fact that the fates were conspiring to throw him once more into the limelight. It happened this way....

On April 18, 1942, sixteen small American airplanes roared over Japan to throw the fifteen million citizens of Tokyo, Yokohama, Osaka, Kobe and Nagoya into frenzied panic. The destruction wrought by the bombs dropped from the sixteen planes was relatively small, but the psychological effect upon the Japanese was devastating. Their war leaders had boasted that they would reach the western shore of the United States, march to the east and dictate terms of surrender in the White House. Intelligent exploitation of the initial assault on Pearl Harbor and subsequent early success in island warfare had convinced the people of Japan of the complete invincibility of their armed forces. What quickly became known as the Doolittle Raid destroyed this myth; it showed them the awful power of the country which lay four thousand miles across the Pacific.

The daring, almost suicidal raid on Japan gave the American people their first authentic war hero. It made Doolittle a General and earned him the Medal of Honor. It changed the destinies of the eighty officers and men who participated in it. It lost Ted Lawson his right leg; it cost the lives of eight men; it made a missionary out of Corporal Jacob deShazer, who is spreading the word of Christ now in the hills of Japan and far from Tokyo; it gave the American public a badly needed psychological shot in the arm, and it gave President Roosevelt a chance to announce solemnly that the raiders had taken off from Shangri-la.

Ask any one of the pilots or crewmen who survived what was perhaps the most daring combined operation of the whole war, who originated the idea of the Tokyo raid, and most of them will tell you it was Doolittle. Ask Doolittle and he'll look thoughtful, scratch his head and say, "Damned if I know. It was Hap Arnold who called me in on it. The idea might have originated with him." The Army brass at the Pentagon will search their memories and tell you frankly that they don't know. A pleasant but spurious legend has grown ascribing the origin and the planning of the raid to the late FDR, and high ranking Naval officers will tell you confidently that the whole operation was conceived in the brilliant mind of Ernie King.

Hap Arnold and FDR are dead, but Admiral King is very much alive. Ask Admiral King who conceived the idea of the raid and he'll smile and say, "Funny thing, no one ever asked me that question before." Then he'll tell you about his aide, the submariner Francis Low, who is Rear Admiral Low now. He'll tell you about Donald Duncan (Admiral Duncan now) who was then the air officer on King's staff, and he'll tell you about the *Vixen,* too.

The *Vixen* had once been a German yacht; now in 1942 she was serving as Admiral Ernest King's flagship. King, reserved, austere, was a completely dedicated man. An eight-hour working day to King was merely an appetizer. Besides, the first eight hours of every day were taken up with the necessary but interminable conferences with military and air leaders; with the White House and with war production chiefs.

The eight hours over, Admiral King invariably rushed to his little flagship, the *Vixen,* anchored in the Potomac. Now he began the real work of the day. Several key assistants lived aboard the *Vixen*—for them, too, the war was a twenty-four-hour business. Dinner aboard the *Vixen* was a gloomy affair the night of Saturday, January 10, 1942. The shock of Pearl Harbor had worn off, but disasters had continued to pile up. The morale of the public was miserable. It seemed apparent that the people needed to be stimulated in the form of some operational success, but the Navy, trying desperately to rebuild and repair the damage done at Pearl Harbor, couldn't do anything about it, and King knew it that Saturday night.

After dinner he retired to his study. Captain Francis Low was then one of King's aides. Stocky, square-jawed, forty-seven-year-old Low had been thinking of aircraft, and Army aircraft at that. He had decided that night to present a rather fantastic idea to Admiral King. Few outsiders were ever able to penetrate the shell of Admiral King's reserve, but he considered the members of his staff to be his family, and they alone knew that King was actually a warm and imaginative man, always receptive to new ideas—if they came from experienced professionals, and Low was a real pro.

"What is it, Low?" King looked up.

"I've been to the Norfolk yard, as you know, sir," Low talked fast, "to see the progress made on the *Hornet*. At the airfield they have marked out a strip about the size of a carrier deck, and they practice take-offs constantly."

"Well, that's a routine operation for training carrier-based pilots." King was puzzled; it wasn't like Low to state the obvious.

"If the Army has some plane that could take off in that short distance," Low went on, "I mean a plane capable of carrying a bomb load, why couldn't we put a few of them on a carrier and bomb the mainland of Japan? Might even bomb Tokyo. It would be a great morale builder, and it would be a severe blow to Japan's pride."

King leaned back in his chair. Low waited for a curt rejection. Then the Admiral looked up.

"Low," he said thoughtfully, "that might be a good idea. Discuss it with Duncan and tell him to report to me." *

Captain Donald Duncan was the air officer on King's staff. Behind him were years of experience as a Naval pilot and carrier group commander. Low immediately phoned him and they arranged to meet the following morning. It was Sunday, and even King usually allowed his staff to take Sundays off.

"This better be important," Duncan grumbled when he met Low at the Navy Building.

---

* General Doolittle and the sixty-one raiders who are still alive will learn here for the first time that the operation was conceived in the mind of Admiral Francis Low.

"How would you like to plan a carrier-based strike against Tokyo?" Low asked.

Duncan blinked. "Oh, sure. That would be a cinch. Our carriers carry planes that have a range of around six hundred miles. All we'd have to do would be to sail almost into Tokyo Harbor and . . ."

"I'm not talking about Navy planes," Low interrupted. "I'm talking about Army planes that have a long range and can carry a real load of bombs."

"It's an idea," Duncan said thoughtfully. "What aircraft have you in mind for the operation?"

"How in hell would I know?" Low shrugged his shoulders. "I'm a submarine man. Maybe some medium bomber could do it. Let's assume that the Army has such a plane; say a plane with a 2,000-mile range. How many of them could a carrier take on? How close to Japan would the carrier have to get? How much of a task force would be needed?"

"Even if such a plane could take off from a carrier, it couldn't land on one," Duncan said thoughtfully. "But when they returned they could ditch beside the carrier and we could pick up the crews . . . say, have you talked to the Old Man on this?" Duncan was getting excited about this scheme.

Low nodded. "If you think it could be done, draw up a plan and show it to the Admiral."

Duncan was a rare combination of experienced pilot and brilliant staff man. He had, of course, done most of his flying in carrier-based planes, but he had flown and was thoroughly familiar with the flying characteristics of Army aircraft as well. The only plane he thought might be able to do the job was the Army medium bomber, the B-25. Captain Duncan locked himself in his office and proceeded to write a detailed plan. He felt that the vital element in the contemplated operation would be surprise. If an inkling of the operation ever reached the ears of Japanese intelligence, a task force carrying the planes toward Tokyo could be annihilated.

He suggested that the *Hornet,* soon due to head for the

Pacific, be the "mother" ship. Her movement would occasion no comment. She should be the nucleus of a real task force of cruisers, destroyers and tankers, to minimize the danger of enemy interception. In his plan he suggested that a group of B-25 pilots be trained by carrier personnel; that the aircraft be lightened and modified to add fuel tanks and give the plane the range needed. Day and night Duncan sat developing his plan—in longhand. He wouldn't allow even the most trusted officeworkers to type it for him.

Five days after Low had broached the subject Duncan laid fifty pages of longhand writing on Admiral King's desk. King read it thoroughly and nodded with satisfaction. The next day Admiral King saw General Hap Arnold. Great mutual respect existed between these entirely dissimilar men. Arnold was a genial, smiling extrovert who was called "Hap" by most of his staff. King was reserved, quiet, but equipped with a brilliant intellect. The thing the two men had in common was professional knowledge and experience. Arnold listened as King talked. Arnold had the capacity for getting excited, and this plan began to excite him.

Henry "Hap" Arnold, General of the Air Force, was a daring, imaginative commander just as he had once been a daring, imaginative young officer. Graduated from West Point as a cavalry officer, he was assigned to the Infantry, a department of warfare he disliked intensely. Very few people in 1911 thought of the airplane as anything but a dangerous toy designed for the use of reckless dreamers or lunatics. President Theodore Roosevelt was no lunatic, but he was a restless dreamer, and the possibilities of the flying machine intrigued him to the point where he suggested to the War Department that the strange new invention might be worthy of investigation. Most Army men felt bitter about flying machines; one of their own, Lieutenant Thomas Selfridge of the Field Artillery, had been the first Army officer to meet his death flying one of the crazy heavier-than-air contraptions. But Teddy Roosevelt had actually made a flight with Arch Hoxey at St. Louis, and he had lived to communicate some of his enthusiasm to a few members of the War Department. They decided to ask for a few volunteers among Army personnel to learn how to fly. The request came to the dreary bit of flat, sun-baked, grassless earth that a careless hand had dropped into New York Harbor and which had been named Governor's Island.

Second Lieutenant Henry H. Arnold, after a short tour of duty in the Philippines, was stationed then at Governor's Island, and he hated every foot of it. Why, you couldn't even work a horse to a real gallop before you had to pull him up or he'd end up floating in the harbor. Arnold knew nothing about flying, although on a brief visit to Paris he had actually seen Blériot's cross-Channel plane on exhibition. But young Hap Arnold was a bit of a reckless dreamer, too, and when the call came for volunteers he couldn't wait. He was so deathly sick and tired of the infantry drilling and of the restricted social life at Governor's Island that he would have volunteered just as cheerfully had the Army asked for men to cross the Atlantic Ocean on skis. And in the course of a few weeks Hap Arnold and Second Lieutenant Thomas De W. Milling of the 15th Cavalry found themselves en route to Dayton, Ohio, to learn about flying from Orville and Wilbur Wright.

They found themselves in the company of the best pilots in America, imaginative men who really felt that there was a future in this hazardous profession of defying nature by making heavier-than-air machines actually fly. Arch Hoxey wasn't there—he'd been killed—but Walter Brookins, the twenty-year-old daredevil of the Wright flying group, was. So were Cliff Turpin, Al Welsh, Frank Coffyn, Phil Parmalee, Leonard Bonney, Howard Gill (killed a short time later) and Oscar Brindley, who was to meet his death too. Arnold and Milling were put into the Wright factory. Methodical Orville Wright insisted that his pupils first master the construction of a plane before flying one. Pilots in those days had no ground crews; they had to do all repair work themselves, and Wright made mechanics of them before he made them pilots. When they weren't working in the factory, Arnold and Milling sat around listening to the hair-raising stories told so casually by men like Harry Atwood and Calbraithe Rodgers and Brookins. It was Brookins who said to young Arnold out of the wisdom of his twenty years, "I would rather be the oldest pilot in America than the best."

Al Welsh finally took over Arnold's flying instruction. Hap Arnold was an apt pupil. So was Tom Milling. Within three months they had qualified as the first two pilots in the United States Army. As a matter of fact, the United States Air Force then consisted of no airplanes, Arnold and Milling. Arnold was never afterwards anything but a flying man. No idea was too new or too radical to be considered by Arnold. A devout apostle of Billy Mitchell (he jeopardized his Army career by supporting Mitchell during the court-martial of the brilliant prophet of air power), he had always been considered one of the most progressive general officers in the armed services. In 1942 he was just as eager to try anything new as he had been in 1911.

"Sounds interesting, Admiral." Arnold's imagination had been completely captured by the whole plan. For weeks the President had been urging that the war be carried to Japan proper. He had a fierce, consuming hatred for the Japanese, and the casualties suffered by the Pacific forces had fanned this hatred to a white heat. Arnold knew that Roosevelt would like this. But could a B-25 take off from a carrier? King suggested that Arnold send a few B-25's to Norfolk and allow Captain Duncan to supervise some tests. Arnold reached for his phone. . . .

King, Arnold, Low and Duncan were the only men who knew anything at all about the contemplated operation, and then Arnold and King decided to take one additional man into their confidence—President Roosevelt. Roosevelt grinned his delight at the suggestion that the war finally be brought home to the people of Japan, and gave Arnold and King his blessing.

Within twenty-four hours Captain Duncan was telling three slightly bewildered pilots that the Air Force wanted to test the take-off characteristics of a B-25. The pilots found to their surprise that they could actually take off within five hundred feet with a stripped, lightly loaded B-25. Then Duncan ordered the *Hornet* to leave its dock for some offshore trials. Captain Marc Mitscher of the *Hornet* was not a man to ask questions. If Duncan wanted some offshore trials, he was, of course, speaking for Admiral King, and had King told Mitscher to head for the China Sea and take on the whole Jap navy singlehanded, little Mitscher would have tugged at the peak of the baseball cap he always wore on board his carrier and headed for the Pacific. The *Hornet* steamed thirty miles offshore and Duncan ordered a B-25 pilot to try a take-off. The plane actually made it, to the surprise of everyone except Duncan.

Meanwhile, in Washington things were happening. Arnold had given careful thought to the question of the man who would organize this operation. He would, of course, have to be an experienced pilot; he'd also have to be an aeronautical engineer, for even if the B-25 was selected, it was obvious that many modifications would have to be made on the plane. He had the whole Air Force to pick from—he sent for Lieutenant Colonel James Harold Doolittle.

Jimmy was glad to get a few things off his chest, but he noticed that his old friend wasn't listening as attentively as he might have been. Looked as though something was on Hap's mind. Then Arnold started discussing the Army bombers.

"Do you think, Jim," he asked thoughtfully, "that we have a plane that can take off in five hundred feet, carry a pay load of two thousand pounds and fly two thousand miles?"

Doolittle blinked. Take off within five hundred feet? What in God's name could Hap be thinking of? Of course the carrier-based planes took off from a five-hundred-foot deck space . . . but . . . Doolittle smiled and he felt a flicker of excitement. Could Arnold possibly mean . . . he must be thinking in terms of a carrier take-off.

"Give me a day or two and I'll have a report for you, Hap," Doolittle said casually. He had a hunch that he knew what this was all about, but as long as Arnold wasn't disclosing his thoughts he'd keep quiet. They were old friends, but Arnold had stars on his shoulder, and if you were a lieutenant colonel you didn't ask too many questions of stars, even if they were worn by your brother.

"Make it as quick as you can, Jimmy," Arnold said, "and let's keep this to ourselves."

Doolittle left, went to his hotel room and did a little figuring. The heavy bombers, the B-17's and B-24's, were obviously out of the question. They could carry two thousand pounds of bombs two thousand miles easily enough, but these heavy planes needed at least 2,500-foot runways. The medium bombers? The B-23 had too large a wing spread to pass the "island" on a carrier. The B-26 was fast, but when you loaded it up it needed plenty of runway. That left only the B-25, designed by his old friend Dutch Kindelberger. Doolittle knew the B-25 from the bottom of its tricycle landing gear to the tip of its double rudders. Load a B-25 with two thousand pounds and she'd need at least 1,200 feet in which to take off. But maybe you could lighten this airplane. Doolittle grabbed a pencil and some paper and started to take a B-25 apart.

He came to the same conclusion that Duncan had arrived at: Only the B-25 had the potential qualities essential for this difficult job. He reported back to Arnold. Arnold had received Duncan's report that morning, and he told Doolittle to get together with Duncan and go over the whole plan.

"You'll work out the modifications on the plane," Arnold said, "and then train the B-25 crews. Duncan will coordinate the whole operation. He'll let you know when he has a task force organized and where you'll load your aircraft."

Doolittle and Duncan met the next morning. They had known each other in the early days of flying, and they talked the same language. Doolittle read Duncan's plan eagerly.

"I'm off to Pearl this afternoon," Duncan said, "to present

the plan to Admiral Nimitz and Halsey. If Nimitz picks Halsey to head the task force, and knowing Halsey I bet he insists on it, he'll probably want to see you. Maybe you could meet him on the West Coast somewhere."

"You call the shots," Doolittle grinned. It was beginning to look as though he might get into this war after all, and he had a warm feeling for Donald Duncan, whose plan had been bought not only by King but by Arnold and Roosevelt.

That afternoon Duncan took off for Pearl Harbor; Doolittle headed for Wright Field. He took Lieutenant Clare Bunch, a brilliant aeronautical engineer, with him. The Wright Field personnel had been ordered to give Doolittle any assistance he wanted. They were considerably puzzled at the strange things he and Bunch did with a B-25 during the next ten days. But the men at Wright Field, accustomed to handling top-secret projects, obeyed without question and without questioning. Doolittle and Bunch worked day and night figuring out ways to lighten the airplane. The B-25 had what pilots call "good take-off" characteristics. Modifications did not hinder its ability to take off quickly and cleanly. After a week, its own father, Dutch Kindelberger, wouldn't have known his brain child. Doolittle was satisfied now that it could do the job. When he raised it fully loaded from the ground after using five hundred feet of the runway at Wright Field, he was positive of it. He hurried back to Washington to report to Hap Arnold. Hap suggested that he use the 17th Bomb Group and the 89th Reconnaissance Squadron, which specialized in B-25's. Both the group and the squadron had recently arrived at the Columbia Air Base in South Carolina.

For one year the pilots, navigators, radio operators, maintenance men, armament specialists of the 17th Group, had been working with the B-25's. This was the first team, experienced, capable airmen, getting a bit fed up with the routine of training. They were eager for action, but they did not know how close to it they were.

One late afternoon during the first week of February, 1942,

the boys had finished their day's work. Some were in the mess hall playing red dog, others were at a movie in nearby Columbia. Lieutenant Ross Greening and Major Jack Hilger (Commander of the 89th Squadron) happened to be standing outside the mess hall when they saw a B-25 approaching for a landing. All of the group and squadron planes were on the ground; this was some visiting fireman. They gazed first with indifference, then with interest at the plane as it landed on the runway.

Hilger turned to Greening. "Damn it, with all our experience none of us can fly a B-25 like that."

Greening nodded. "Alex de Seversky is the only man I ever saw land a 25 that way. He has kind of an individual way of handling an airplane, as though he and the plane were one."

The B-25 taxied smoothly to the control tower, stopped, and out stepped a short man in the uniform of a lieutenant colonel.

"For God's sake, it's Doolittle," Greening said excitedly.

"What in hell is The Little Man doing here?" Hilger asked aloud.

The next day another B-25 arrived at Columbia. Ross Greening had an overwhelming curiosity when it came to 25's. Although he was a pilot, he was also a specialist in armament. He was brilliant working with machine guns, bombsights and the hundred and one complications arising out of their use. Greening climbed into the fuselage of the airplane and was startled to see an odd-looking rubber envelope draped over the bomb bay. He found the inquisitive Hilger already there.

"What in God's name is that?" he asked Hilger.

"An extra gas tank," Hilger said.

"Who in hell designed it—Rube Goldberg?" Greening snorted.

"Don't say that out loud," Hilger said dryly. "Doolittle designed it."

The best B-25 crews in the country were there at Columbia. Now, with the arrival of Doolittle, the boys sensed that something was on tap. Most of them thought that German subs were off the eastern coast and that the group would be assigned to hunting them. Doolittle called a conference with Group Commanding Officer Lieutenant Colonel Newt Mills and the four squadron C.O.'s (Captain Edwin J. York, Major Jack Hilger, Captain Al Rutherford, Captain Karl Baumeister).

He told them that he had been put in charge of an "interesting but dangerous mission." It would involve carrying a maximum bomb load, and the airplanes would have to take off within five hundred feet. They blinked at that.

"That's about all I can tell you about the mission now," he told them. "It's strictly a volunteer operation. And the men must volunteer in the dark. It'll take us away about six weeks, but that's all you can tell your men."

The C.O. asked for volunteers the next day, and every pilot on the base responded. They didn't know what it was all about —didn't care much—but they knew that the operation was to be headed by a practical flying man who knew more about airplanes and what they could do than any of them; that was enough for them. Within a week the twenty-four crews picked by Doolittle received orders to fly to Eglin Field, near Pensacola, Florida. This was a bit of a let-down. Eglin was hardly a hopping-off spot for hunting German subs.

Doolittle called them all into the Operations Office. About 140 pilots, radio technicians, navigators, bombardiers crowded into the room. "We're all down here for some special training," he began. "This mission you've volunteered for is the most dangerous thing you've ever attempted. Any of you who wish can drop out now. There isn't much sense wasting time and money training men who aren't going through with this thing."

He stopped, but no one said anything. It was rather difficult to think of real danger here with the Florida sun streaming through the windows. Doolittle's tone had been casual; there was nothing tense about either his attitude or his voice. Many of the men said long afterwards that they thought Doolittle was exaggerating the potential danger of the mission. It was only when they came to know him better that they learned he never exaggerated.

"Can you tell us a bit more about the mission, Colonel?" a pilot asked.

"Not a hell of a lot," he said, smiling. "But you'll begin to get an idea of what it's all about as we get into our training program. I have to emphasize one thing—secrecy. If any of you guess what we're going to do, or if you figure out from your training what targets we are going to hit, keep it to yourself. Don't discuss it with your wives; don't even gossip with each other. A lot of lives—not only ours—will depend upon the complete secrecy of our plans. Okay? First thing I want you to do is to learn the location of every auxiliary flying field around here. Then for a while you'll just practice quick take-offs."

"I noticed they got some five-hundred-foot runways chalked out here on the field?" Ross Greening asked.

"That's right," Doolittle said calmly. "That's what I mean by quick, short take-offs. With a week's practice you'll be able to take off in five hundred feet."

"What makes you so sure, Colonel?" a pilot asked.

"I've done it," Doolittle said simply. There was a startled silence for a moment. Had any chair-borne Air Force general with two stars on his shoulder told these experienced pilots that a B-25 could take off with only a run of five hundred feet, they would have laughed. But this was Doolittle. You couldn't laugh at Doolittle. Probably every man in that room thought back to some of the take-offs he'd made. The thoughts that ran through the agile mind of Ross Greening were probably typical. "Five hundred feet?" Greening thought. "Load a 25 and you need three thousand feet to get off. Still, there was that time I came in on a corn patch near Omaha. . . . I got off all right the next day. I only had about a thousand feet, too. I got off, all right . . . but then I wasn't loaded. How can you lift a 25 off a five-hundred-foot runway. . . ?" Lieutenant Ted Lawson had worked for Douglas Aircraft before joining the

Air Force, and he thought in terms of the aeronautical engineer he would be one day. "How can you develop enough speed to lift you in five hundred feet?" he asked himself. "You'd have to strip the airplane . . . get rid of the radio, the bombsight, the turrets, and then . . . well, maybe if you took off with full flaps and engine at full throttle. . . ." Lieutenant William Bower just sat back, relaxed, grinning. He knew that a lot of questions were running through the minds of the boys. Calm, slow-talking, efficient Bill Bower just yawned. Doolittle had said he'd done it. That was good enough for him. These boys kind of forgot that The Little Man was an engineer, a scientist, a mathematician who wouldn't be alive today if he'd ever made any miscalculations as to what an airplane could do. "If he says it can be done, well, you can go to sleep on that," Bower said to himself.

The next day they started practicing quick take-offs. Doolittle introduced them to a man in a Naval uniform—Lieutenant Henry L. Miller. He had come over from nearby Pensacola. Miller knew about carrier techniques. He explained to the men how they did it on carriers.

"Drop your landing flaps and pour on the coal," he said laconically.

There were twenty-four crews at Eglin, and gradually they were learning to work together. Their take-offs grew shorter and shorter. The heavy Norden bombsight was removed. Doolittle told the boys it was inevitable that some airplanes fall into enemy hands, and that the Norden sight was still top secret.

"This is a low-level bombing job," Doolittle told them. "The Norden can only be used as a fixed-angle sight. We'll remove the sight head, keep the stabilizer, and mount a new sight on it."

"What'll we go in at, Colonel?"

"Fifteen hundred feet," Doolittle said casually.

This brought home the dangerous reality of the mission to the pilots and crews, but during the daylight hours at least they were too busy to worry much about it. They began at 7:00 A.M. and kept at it until 8:00 at night.

Ross Greening had designed a new bombsight that cost the taxpayers about twenty cents each. This bombsight was about as complicated as the sight on a rifle, and for low-level bombing just about as accurate. And it only weighed two pounds. Doolittle supervised the maintenance of the airplanes with the care of a watch repairer working on a twenty-jewel Swiss timepiece. And he was getting to know and to be delighted with men like Greening and Hilger and Jones and the others.

One day he sent Ski York and Greening to Pensacola to pick up an expert from the Bendix Company to check the carburetors. These boys, who by now thought only in terms of five-hundred-foot take-offs, picked up their passenger, gunned the engines and roared away, with the white-faced civilian hanging on for dear life. This to him was just crazy flying. At Eglin the expert told Doolittle that there was really no reason to check the Bendix carburetors. They were really wonderful equipment that didn't need frequent checking. He made a short speech to Doolittle on the merits of the carburetor (all of which was true enough).

"What the hell are you," Doolittle lashed out at him angrily. "A salesman? If you're a salesman, get out of here; we have all the carburetors we want. If you're an expert, check these carburetors and check them all in the next twenty-four hours." Other civilian experts arrived to install the de-icing apparatus on the B-25's. It would take two weeks' work on each plane to do the job properly, they reported. Again Doolittle exploded. "I'll give you two weeks to equip all twenty-four planes. The job will have to be finished by then."

These experts weren't accustomed to being talked to like that by lieutenant colonels, but they had to take it. Doolittle during this period was a hard-driving, calculating dynamo, pushing himself as he was pushing everyone else. The men were beginning to realize that Doolittle was a perfectionist. Every plane had to be as mechanically perfect as human ingenuity could approach. He would walk to a plane that had just landed and ask the pilot, "How does she stack up?"

"Pretty good, Colonel," the pilot would say with satisfaction.

"Let me try it." Doolittle would climb into the cockpit and put the aircraft through its paces. He'd return an hour later with a penciled list of a dozen minor flaws for the maintenance crews to work on.

"Pretty good isn't good enough, pilot," he'd say. "For this job every plane has to be in perfect condition."

He was practically commuting between Eglin and Washington; security was so vital that he wouldn't use the telephone to discuss problems with Hap Arnold.

He told Arnold that the crews were about ready and that once the planes had a final checking, they too would be ready. Several times during his conferences with Arnold, the Air Force Chief had emphasized the fact that Doolittle was still a member of his staff. Arnold had never hinted that Doolittle would be allowed to lead the actual flight. By now Doolittle thought of this whole operation as his baby. He didn't want anyone else spoiling it.

"Hap," he said bluntly one day in March, "I've gotten to know these crews very well. They're a great bunch of boys. I think by now they have confidence in me. You've got to let me lead this flight myself."

"I need you here on the staff," Arnold started. But Doolittle interrupted to make a fervent plea that he be allowed to head the operation. Finally Arnold shrugged his shoulders and said, "If it's all right with Mif Harmon, it's all right with me."

General Millard Harmon was Arnold's Chief of Staff. His office in the Pentagon was right down the hall from Arnold's headquarters. Doolittle left Arnold, ran down the hall and burst into the office of the Chief of Staff. Harmon was alone.

"General," Doolittle said, "the planning of this Tokyo operation is all wrapped up. I've been in on it from the beginning, and I want to lead the raid. Hap Arnold says it's all right with him if it's okay with you."

Harmon looked surprised, but said, "All right, Jimmy, it's all yours."

Jimmy leaned over the desk, shook hands with General Harmon fervently and said, "Thanks, General."

Just then there was a buzz from the Dictograph on Harmon's desk, and he flipped the switch. Doolittle heard Arnold's voice, turned and headed for the door. Then he heard Harmon saying, "But Hap, Jimmy said it was all right with you, so I just gave him permission to lead the raid. I can't withdraw it now very well."

Doolittle left the Pentagon chuckling and headed back for Eglin.

On one of his trips to Washington he used a crew headed by Captain Vernon L. Stinzi, with Lieutenant Richard Cole as copilot, Lieutenant Henry Potter, navigator, Sergeant Fred Braemer, bombardier, and Sergeant Paul J. Leonard as crew chief and gunner. Subsequently Captain Stinzi had the bad luck to fall ill, and on the next trip young Dick Cole found himself piloting the plane. Doolittle liked the way this crew operated, and henceforth this was his crew and his plane. Instead of getting a new first pilot to replace Captain Stinzi, he took it over and the proud Dick Cole became Doolittle's copilot.

By now Doolittle had stripped the airplanes of bombsights, bottom turrets and liaison radios, which lessened the weight by some 1,200 pounds. He was satisfied (so was every pilot) that the B-25 could be flown from a carrier fully loaded with gas and bombs. Originally the plan had called for the planes to bomb the mainland of Japan, return to the carrier, ditch beside it and hope that the crews could be picked up by small boats from the flattop. Doolittle, Arnold and Captain Duncan had discussed this thoroughly, and they had rejected the idea as being entirely too dangerous—not only for the crews but for the carrier and its escorting ships. Once the planes took off from the carrier and arrived over the target, the Japs would have a pretty good idea where the task force was located. The carrier and its escorting ships would be sitting ducks for a large-scale air raid by land-based bombers. Obviously, once the raiding planes left the carrier the big ship had better get away from the neighborhood—but fast. And so Doolittle, Arnold and Duncan decided to bomb the targets and then head for Chinese airfields or for Vladivostok. That was the final plan, and it differed only in minor detail from the comprehensive plan originally drawn up by Duncan in January.

Arnold said that Admiral Halsey was returning from Pearl Harbor to discuss the Naval side of the operation. He suggested that Doolittle meet him in San Francisco. Doolittle flew there, checked in at his hotel and found a message from Halsey. It merely said, "Meet me at seven o'clock" and named a restaurant. Doolittle had never met Halsey, but he had to smile at this. This conference would have to be held in complete secrecy. Halsey, never one to follow the orthodox rules, had picked a public restaurant for the meeting. Doolittle arrived on time, and there sitting in a booth was Halsey. There was a big grin on Halsey's face as he shook Doolittle's hand. "Let's start off by having a drink," he said. They had a drink and ordered dinner. The booths on either side of them were empty. When dinner was finished they ordered coffee, and when Halsey waved the waiter away they got down to the serious purpose of the dinner. By now it was Bull and Jimmy. These two men thought alike.

"Hap Arnold has told me," Doolittle said, "that the Navy is to have complete charge of this operation until we leave the carrier. I want you to know that my boys and I will be happy to be under your orders until then."

Halsey nodded. "We have decided to organize a little task force of two carriers, the *Enterprise* and the *Hornet*. In addition, we will have two heavy cruisers, two light cruisers, eight destroyers and two tankers. You will be on the *Hornet*. Your B-25's will take up damn near the whole flight deck. If we are attacked by Jap aircraft or a surface fleet, the carrier will be a sitting duck until you can clear the decks of those bombers."

Doolittle nodded. "If we are attacked, I suppose we will have to push our B-25's over the side."

"Not necessarily," Halsey said. "If our task force is intercepted before we reach Japanese waters, you will probably have time to fly your planes off the deck and head for Midway. If the attack is sudden, without any advance radar notice, then you will have to shove them overboard, but that will be up to Pete Mitscher, who will be in command of the *Hornet*. Once we get near the Japanese mainland you won't be able to reach Midway in case of an attack. You will have two alternatives in that case. Suppose we are 1,500 miles off Japan and are attacked. You can either shove your planes overboard or take off with your bombs, try to reach your targets, and then hope for the best."

"That would give us about a five-hundred-mile leeway," Doolittle said thoughtfully. "Instead of jettisoning the aircraft, I'd rather take the chance of finding the targets and then ditching in the China Sea. We have rubber rafts on all the planes; we might be picked up by one of our submarines, or we might be able to reach the China coast."

"That's right," Halsey said. "But assuming that we are not attacked or intercepted, we hope to be able to take you within about four hundred miles of the coast. Will that be satisfactory?"

"That will be perfect," Doolittle grinned. "Bring us in that close and we can find our targets easy enough, and we will have plenty of gasoline left to take us to China."

"Well, I guess that's it," Halsey said. "Now, how about one for the road?"

The *Hornet* was steaming toward San Francisco now. Even now, only seven men—King, Low, Duncan, Arnold, Doolittle, Nimitz and Halsey—knew the complete plan. Not even the President had been given the details. Training had been finished at Eglin. Every pilot by now had qualified. Each one had taken off, not once but half a dozen times, in five hundred feet with a maximum load. One pilot, Lieutenant Don Smith, had actually made his take-off in 287 feet. Doolittle reported to Arnold that he was quite satisfied with all of the pilots, and he added that the copilots were adequate.

"The bombers are fair," Doolittle told Arnold. "Our navigators have had good training but little practical experience. The gunners have had virtually no experience in firing from an airplane at stationary, much less moving targets. Apparently we're so short of fifty-caliber ammo that it can't be used for training gunners. I found that not a single one of our turret guns had ever been fired since their installation. We tried them, all right, and most of them wouldn't fire at all. The longest burst we got out of any gun was five rounds—then it folded up."

"What did you do about it?"

"Got some experts down to fix them up. The guns now are as good as they'll ever be. The experts tell us the best way to keep the guns in condition is not to fire them."

Arnold just grunted. He had been plagued by this horrible ammunition shortage for months. The situation was easing now, but there still wasn't enough ammo to give gunners proper training or to really test the guns.

"Now about these lower gun turrets," Doolittle went on. "To operate the lower turret the gunner has to take an awkward, unnatural position. We just don't have time to teach the boys to use equipment which is unnatural to them. Sometimes the turrets don't even retract. It would take a boy as long to learn the operation of this turret as it would for him to learn to play the violin. We just haven't got that much time. So I've removed the lower gun turrets and replaced them with wooden guns that may fool any Jap fighters. We've saved weight, cut down drag and gained fifteen miles an hour."

"You've given these airplanes quite a beating down at Eglin," Arnold said. "What do you want in the way of an overhaul before you leave?"

"New propellers," Doolittle said promptly. "They've all been marred and scratched to some extent. I put a new prop on one airplane and found that this increased its speed several miles per hour."

"Okay, take your men to McClelland Field, Sacramento, for the new propellers and whatever else you need," Arnold said. "I'll give you an order authorizing you to have the green light out there."

Doolittle returned to Eglin to supervise final preparations. He took with him a sealed crate that weighed 1,200 pounds. It contained maps, charts, target folders and target data to be used in the selection of targets and to enable the planes to reach the targets. He turned it over to Jack Hilger, told him what the crate contained and said, "Put this in the grave."

Hilger locked it away in the closely guarded bombsight vault at the field. This material wouldn't be opened until the whole expedition was at sea.

By now the extra gasoline tanks had all been installed. Each airplane carried 646 gallons in its main wing tank; 225 gallons in the bomb bay tank; 160 gallons in a rubber tank manufactured by the United States Rubber Company and tucked in the crawlway above the bomb bay; 60 gallons in the rubber leakproof tank which had been installed in the place from which the lower turret had been removed. This made a total of 1,091 gallons, of which at least 1,050 could be used (not all of the gasoline could be drained from the rubber tanks).

De-icers and anti-icers had been installed on all the airplanes. These would not be needed for landing in China, but the State Department was negotiating with Russia in hope of getting permission for the planes to land at Vladivostok. Vladivostok was only about six hundred miles from Tokyo. The State Department had suggested to the Kremlin that Russia might like to have sixteen fully equipped B-25's. If they would accept these as part of Lend-Lease, the American Air Force would be very happy to fly them to Vladivostok, via Japan. If the Kremlin had agreed to this proposal, the evidence (later assembled) indicated that all of the planes would have accomplished their missions and proceeded to Vladivostok without the loss of one aircraft or crewman. Negotations were still going on with the Kremlin as Doolittle finished training at Eglin.

Duncan had remained at Pearl Harbor, working out the complex problem of coordination. The task force which would escort the *Hornet* had to be assembled carefully, and the ships which would rendezvous with the big carrier would have to proceed singly and casually—the Japs were pretty good at spotting any move by a concentrated force. Finally Duncan had everything lined up. He sent a prearranged message to Captain Low. It was a message that might well have baffled any Jap code breakers who intercepted it. It merely read, "Tell Jimmy to get on his horse."

Low told Arnold and he shot the message down to Eglin Field. Doolittle knew what it meant. It meant that everything was ready and that he should order his men to McClelland Field, Sacramento, California. He gave the order. Jack Hilger turned over the crate containing the precious maps and charts to Dave Jones, and when Jones arrived at McClelland he immediately locked them in the bombsight vault—always the most closely guarded spot on any airfield. The Norden sight was never allowed to remain on a plane at night; it was always locked up away from prying eyes.

The maintenance men at McClelland Field were fighting a paper war, and they couldn't understand the sense of urgency which seemed to dominate Doolittle and his crews. They went ahead in their leisurely way checking instruments and engines. Doolittle stood two days of this and exploded. He picked up a phone in the office of the McClelland Field C.O. and asked for General Arnold.

"I hate to bother you with a relatively unimportant thing like this," he said, "but things are going too slowly here."

Arnold listened for five minutes. Then he said quietly, "I gave you a letter. Use it." The order Arnold had given Doolittle read, "You have the highest priority in the Air Force." That actually gave the lieutenant colonel more power than that held by any Air Force officer alive. It meant he could commandeer airplanes, crews, equipment—anything he wished, for Arnold's word was supreme in Air Force circles and his power absolute.

Work proceeded more quickly after that, but because none of the officers or maintenance men at McClelland knew what Doolittle's group was up to, they felt that they were working in the dark. They looked in understandable bewilderment at the stripped B-25's, with the funny-looking twenty-cent bombsight, with the wooden guns in the tail, with the rubber envelope for extra gasoline. They'd never seen B-25's in this shape, and when they asked Jack Hilger, Ski York, Dave Jones or Ted Lawson what it was all about, they only received a curt, "Mind your own business." The pilots were in the position of athletes who were just finishing a hard training grind; they were lean and hard and apt to be testy and intolerant of slow-moving maintenance men. Some of them by now were pretty sure of what the mission was going to be—some of them, figuring it a suicide raid, had mentally written themselves off.

Doolittle had concocted a story for them to pass on to their families. They were going to deliver some B-25 planes under the Lend-Lease Agreement. On the way to delivering these planes to an unnamed ally, they might possibly get a chance to drop a few bombs over enemy territory. This story was good enough to satisfy the families of most of the pilots and crewmen. It also had to satisfy even high-ranking officers who dropped in at McClelland Field. But beyond this bare statement, the pilots maintained the strictest secrecy.

They didn't fraternize with the officers or men at McClelland; a careless word might violate the security that Doolittle had emphasized at every chance. They were reluctant to drink more than a beer or two at the Officers' Club, and the McClelland Field officers thought them to be a snobbish lot. Inevitably they talked to no one but each other, and inevitably crews stuck together with little regard for rank. They flew together, drank together, and worked together on their planes.

The *Hornet* arrived in San Diego, and Duncan flew in from Pearl to tell Captain Marc Mitscher what it was all about. Duncan's mind was an electric brain; he refused to trust details to paper, but by now he knew to the moment what time the *Hornet* would leave, what time and what latitude and longitude her escort would pick her up. He told Mitscher to go up to the Alameda Naval Station outside San Francisco and pick up Doolittle's lads. He had a plan all worked out as to how the B-25's would be placed on deck. Carrier-based planes, of course, have folding wings which permit them to be lowered below decks—the B-25's would have to be lashed to the decks. Duncan had arranged for the extra gasoline for Doolittle's planes to be taken aboard.

Jo Doolittle was in Los Angeles. Her father was ill and she had flown west to see him. One evening she received a phone call from Jimmy saying he'd be in San Francisco for a day or two—perhaps she could join him. He spent some time on the *Hornet* going over a thousand and one last-minute details with Mitscher. Then he received the final word from Duncan and went after his boys.

Doolittle and his men were glad to leave Sacramento. Just before they were to take off, the operations officer handed Doolittle a long report which he asked him to fill out. It went into details on the work which had been done on the B-25's by the mechanics at McClelland Field, and asked for an opinion as to how creditably the work had been performed.

Doolittle took a look at the report and snapped, "I haven't got time to read all this."

"But it's our standard procedure, Colonel," the base operations officer said earnestly. "You must report on how the work was done."

Doolittle grabbed the report, picked up a heavy black pencil and wrote one word across it—"lousy."

The horrified officer protested. "This won't do, Colonel. You will have to give us a detailed report."

"I haven't got the time," Doolittle said curtly.

"In that case, I won't sign your clearance," the officer snapped.

Doolittle turned his back on him and strode to his plane. He climbed into it, started his engines, and taxied out to the runway.

The infuriated operations officer turned to Jack Hilger, who was standing there with a broad grin on his face. "I can tell you one thing," he said angrily, "that Colonel of yours is heading for a lot of trouble."

"He sure is," Jack Hilger drawled. "He sure is."

Doolittle took off first. He wheeled his B-25 around and buzzed the field at 300 miles an hour. Each succeeding pilot did the same thing. This was against every Air Force regulation. Flying low over a field is dangerous to the field personnel, but this was their way of showing their appreciation for the maintenance boys and their officers at McClelland. Then they were off to San Francisco.

Jimmy, with a casual "I may be out of the country for a few weeks," said good-by to Jo, and knowing from the very casualness of his good-by that something big was afoot, she bit back the questions and tried to be just as casual as he was.

Doolittle, after long conferences with Mitscher, had decided to take fifteen planes on the *Hornet*. This was the maximum that could be stored on the flight deck. As an afterthought he suggested that a sixteenth B-25 be put on the flight deck. This would be carried until the *Hornet* was five hundred miles out, and then it would take off and fly back to San Francisco.

"None of the boys have actually taken off from a flattop," he told Mitscher. "It'll give them a lot of confidence to see a B-25 really do it."

"Sure, Jimmy, sure," little Mitscher, with the wizened face and the light blue eyes, grinned.

The *Hornet* left San Francisco on April 1, less than three months from the evening Captain Low blurted out his "fantastic" suggestion to Admiral King.

During the final days of preparation Doolittle had become

obsessed with the notion that he might be dragged out of the operation by Arnold or Marshall. Doolittle knew that Arnold didn't like the idea of a forty-five-year-old man leading a hazardous operational flight. But now the *Hornet,* with its strange cargo of Army medium bombers on its flight deck, had left the dock and Doolittle felt a fierce and wonderful thrill of exaltation. The *Hornet* was five minutes away from the dock when a fast-moving gig left the dock from which they had just cast off to catch up with the carrier. Doolittle was wanted back on shore. General Marshall was on the phone from Washington.

Doolittle's heart sank. This then was the end of what had promised to be such a glorious venture. He shut his lips tightly and stepped into the gig. He picked up the phone. It was indeed General Marshall.

"Doolittle?" Marshall has never been able to form the habit of addressing officers by other than their last names. He never, for instance, called the Supreme Commander of the Allied Forces in Europe anything but "Eisenhower."

"Yes, General," Doolittle said bitterly.

"I couldn't let you leave without wishing you the best of luck," Marshall said warmly. "Our hearts will be with you and our prayers will be with you. Good-by, and good luck and come back safely."

"Thank you . . . thank you," is all that Doolittle could answer.

9

The big *Hornet* was twenty-four hours out of San Francisco when Doolittle gathered his men in an empty ward room to brief them on the mission.

At least ten thousand men had in one way or another contributed to the whole organization of this project. High-ranking Naval and Air Force officers, air field personnel at Wright Field, at Eglin and at Sacramento had helped prepare the planes. Naval commanders of the escorting ships and their crews had all been part of the huge jigsaw which Duncan had so skillfully assembled, yet at this moment only eight men knew the complete details of the operation—King, Duncan, Low, Arnold, Nimitz, Halsey, Mitscher, and Doolittle. Now the time had come to reveal everything to the pilots and crews of the B-25's.

Doolittle looked at these men with satisfaction. They could do things with this medium bomber that the designer of the airplane had never envisioned. Each man in this group had demonstrated his capability during the training at Eglin. It was a magnificent group, Doolittle felt. He had gotten to know many of them well by now, and those he wasn't close to, Jack Hilger vouched for.

Hilger was proving himself to be a magnificent executive officer. Like Doolittle, his approach to the difficulties of the operation was completely cerebral. He was calm, quiet, and like Doolittle, had the knack of inspiring great confidence in the other men.

"Well, here it is," Doolittle said to them when they were assembled. "For the benefit of those of you who don't know, here are your targets. We're going to bomb Tokyo, Yokohama, Osaka, Kobe and Nagoya. The Navy is going to take us in as close as possible, and then we'll take off from the deck. It's going to be a tight squeeze, but it's all been worked out. The Chinese government will cooperate with us. After we hit our targets we'll land at small Chinese airports not far inland and tank up there—the gas is waiting for us. Then we'll fly to Chungking. We're going to be on this carrier a long time, but we've got plenty of work to do. Above all, keep your planes in perfect condition. Any questions?" There were none. Then Doolittle continued.

"We've just got some unexpected news. We had hoped to be able to go on to Vladivostok after leaving our targets, but the Russians have turned us down flat. They are not at war with the Japs and they figure that if we went on to one of their Russian bases after bombing Japan, it might be construed as an unfriendly gesture. So Vladivostok is out. Let me repeat. Under no circumstances are you to head for Vladivostok. One more thing, and this is important. At all costs, avoid hitting the Temple of Heaven."

"What in hell is that?" one of the pilots asked, puzzled.

"That's the Emperor's palace; stay clear of it."

He explained that the present plans called for the take-off to be in the late afternoon of April 18, unless the task force was previously intercepted; then take-off would be immediate.

There were still no questions. Everyone felt great; the speculation, the uncertainty of the past weeks was gone. Now they were face to face with a tangible flying problem. Once brought out into the open it lost some of its terrifying aspects. Now it was a question of rechecking gas consumption and of how to meet the various emergencies that might arise. This is what they'd been trained for. Now they could study the operational problems involved, and best of all, they could discuss them openly. There was no need for further secrecy.

"No questions?" Jimmy grinned. "Okay. There's just one thing more. When we get to Chungking, I'm going to throw the biggest damned party you guys ever saw."

The Navy's preliminary organizing had been so complete that they even had two Naval officers on board who were familiar with the location of Japanese factories, machine shops, ammunition centers, shipyards and other prospective targets. They were Lieutenant Commander Stephen Jurika and Commander Appolo Soucek. The two Naval officers knew Japan thoroughly, and they not only gave the men a pretty good idea of how to recognize their targets but they supplemented this with a few lessons in Chinese. They made the raiders repeat again and again the all-important phrase, *"Lushu hoo megwa fugi"* (I am an American), which would be useful in case crews had to bail out over Chinese territory—a contingency far from remote. Doolittle put Davey Jones in charge of a map room, and pilots and navigators spent hours each day studying the targets.

In the midst of these preparations Doolittle found time to chuckle over a note he had sent to his old friend Roscoe Turner, the great speed flyer. Turner had written to Doolittle suggesting that he and a group of the famous racing pilots be organized into a special combat group. "After all," Turner had said, quite truthfully, "we have all forgotten more about flying than these kids will ever know. All they have is youth. We have the experience." Doolittle, then on the eve of leaving for Sacramento, had written, "Dear Roscoe, let's face it—you and I are too old for combat flying. Leave that to the kids, old-timer." Now he, Doolittle, was to lead one of the most hazardous combat raids ever attempted. When the news came out, Roscoe Turner would explode.

The *Hornet* was five hundred miles out of San Francisco

when Doolittle said to Mitscher, "I guess it's time we sent that sixteenth plane back to San Francisco."

"I guess it is," the skipper said.

"Seems an awful waste of a good airplane," Doolittle said dolefully. "Pity we can't take it along and aim it at Tokyo."

Mitscher looked at Doolittle and sighed. "Okay, Jim, okay. Take it along."

Mitscher turned the *Hornet* flag headquarters over to Doolittle, and every night Jack Hilger, Dave Jones, Major Harry Johnson, the administrative officer, Ski York and Ross Greening had dinner together. They discussed nothing but the technical aspects of the raid.

By now Doolittle had impressed upon them all the fact that the Navy was boss until they were air-borne. If the task force was attacked or even spotted, Pete Mitscher (he was known as Marc Mitscher only in the Naval records) would be the complete boss. The one eventuality they all hoped would not arise would be to be spotted before closing in within range of Japan. Doolittle had convinced Hilger, Jones, York and Greening that this was no suicide operation; his calculations gave everyone a fifty-fifty chance of survival. The word had been passed along. A fifty-fifty chance sounded good to the men. By now they knew their Doolittle. He didn't play guessing games. When he said "fifty-fifty," that figure had come off a drawing board. It had been the result of cold, hard calculation.

"Hell," calm Bill Bower smiled, "you take a fifty-fifty chance every time you cross Market Street in San Francisco."

The fifty-fifty chance, however, did not apply if the desperate alternative of having to take off fifteen hundred miles from their targets eventualized. The pilots tried not to think of that. But occasionally they discussed it among themselves. Jack Hilger brought this up with Doolittle one night at dinner.

"Some of the boys feel they would be better off going right on in," he said, "instead of risking capture by the Japs. How do you feel about that, Colonel?"

"I'm an old man," Doolittle grinned. "I'll be damned if I am going to spend the rest of my life in some Jap jail. But tell the men to get any ideas like that out of their heads. They are all young, they are all healthy, and even if they are captured or forced down in the China Sea they still have a chance."

The task force steamed on steadily. Doolittle kept the men busy. He knew that this was no time for them to be brooding. The *Hornet* let out kites behind the ship to give the crews some badly needed shooting practice. The crew of the *Hornet* and the Navy pilots aboard had great respect for the men whom they now called Doolittle's Raiders. Everyone from Pete Mitscher down to the galley boys did everything possible to make life pleasant for these sea-borne Air Force crews.

It was inevitable that the Army pilots should become friendly with the Naval pilots aboard. Doolittle's men spent a lot of time with the pilots and crews of Torpedo Squadron Eight. (A month later, in the Battle of Midway, this whole squadron, with the exception of Ensign Gay, would be wiped out attempting to torpedo Jap carriers.)

One day a rumor spread through the ship that Tokyo had been bombed by four-engined land-based American planes. It was a disheartening shock to the men who had been so intent about getting there first. Because radio silence was now the rule on the *Hornet* and her sister ships, it was impossible to radio for details. But then came the happy news that the rumor was merely a garbled version of the raid General Royce had made on the Philippines.

Doolittle had worked out every detail of the strike. He decided that he would take off about four in the afternoon of April 18, carrying four clusters of incendiary bombs. That would bring him over Tokyo just before nightfall. The two thousand pounds of incendiaries could be expected to start some beautiful fires. After setting his fires he would head for the coast, cross the China Sea and try to find a Chinese airfield called Chu Chow, and land there in darkness. The other fifteen planes would take off from the *Hornet* just before dusk. They would reach Tokyo during the night. The fires set by his incendiaries should act as beacons to guide them to their targets.

Doolittle felt that the safety factor could be immeasurably increased if the other fifteen planes could hit their targets at night. To begin with, it had been established that as yet the Jap air force had virtually no night fighters. If the B-25's went in at fifteen hundred feet, they would be above effective machine-gun and small-arms fire range, and below the altitude where the heavier antiaircraft guns operated most efficiently. In addition, they would have the great advantage of approaching the China coast around dawn and being able to locate Chinese airfields in daylight. He felt that he himself and his crew would probably have to bail out unless they were favored with really good weather, but that was a calculated risk that must be taken.

"I have something that may amuse your boys," Mitscher told Doolittle one afternoon, producing a handful of Japanese medals. They had been presented to Mitscher and other officers some years before on a visit to Japan.

"It's time we sent these medals back where they came from," he grinned. "Suppose we tie them to the bombs you are going to drop."

Mitscher and Doolittle made quite a ceremony out of it. The task force plunged deeper and deeper into Japanese-controlled waters. Tension mounted among the crew as the *Hornet,* bucking strong winds and heavy seas, roared into the home stretch at full speed. The eight destroyers and two tankers were left far behind.

Not one of these men had ever been in combat. They didn't know then what nearly every combat man eventually learns; fear is something that usually creeps into a man's heart before the danger has been encountered, leaves, and then returns when the danger is past. During the last week most of them were haunted by dreams, and at night many found themselves lying tensely in bed wide-awake with sweat on their foreheads. Fear is the enemy of sleep. They were to leap off into the unknown, and none knew what awaited them. Doolittle had dreams of a different nature. He, Hilger, Greening and Jones were men who thought rather than felt. Their dreams were filled with the hundred and one technical aspects of the operation. The very take-off haunted them. The weather was turning rough. Their take-off calculations had been predicated on the fact that the planes would be able to take off from a level flight deck. Could they take off from a carrier that was rolling dizzily and pitching horribly? These four just had no time for fear and very little capacity for feeling it. Doolittle was the engineer, thinking in terms of the mechanical and navigational problems involved; Hilger, the executive, had the burden of caring for every minute detail; Greening was constantly testing his guns and his bombsights; Davey Jones spent most of his time going over his maps with the pilots and navigators.

At 6:30 A.M. Saturday, April 18, the siren gave the signal "General Quarters," which meant that there was trouble afoot. Doolittle hurried to the bridge to stand behind the grim-faced Mitscher. Almost on the horizon Doolittle could see what looked like a tiny ship, and then it was hidden in dark, black smoke.

A Japanese patrol ship had been spotted and the cruiser *Northampton* had been ordered to destroy it. Now it was up to Halsey. The task force was 823 miles off the Japanese coast. If it could stay on its present course another nine or ten hours, Doolittle felt that the hazards of the raid would not be exceptional. But if Halsey insisted that they take off now, the risks would be increased enormously. A man on the bridge of the *Enterprise* began wigwagging furiously. A signal officer standing close to Captain Mitscher wrote down the message and handed it to him. Halsey had decided. Mitscher turned to Doolittle and shrugged his shoulders.

"You know the score, Jimmy," he said quietly.

Doolittle nodded. That small Japanese ship had seen the task force long before it had been spotted itself. If it had radio or wireless on board, by now Tokyo knew that a group of

American ships was headed for the Japanese coast. Within a matter of minutes Japanese airfields with airplanes ready and pilots eager might have been alerted.

"We'll get off as soon as possible, Pete," he said, and then gave the signal that called all of his crews into the briefing room. He walked in with Mitscher. The *Hornet* was rolling slightly but pitching heavily.

"This is it, men," Doolittle told his crews. "You all know exactly what to do. We have to take off about twelve hours ahead of schedule. This task force has to get the hell out of here fast. I have got just three additional things to tell you. The pitching of this ship presents a problem which we will solve this way. Watch the way I take off and do exactly as I do. If we take off when the bow of the ship is at the height of its pitch, it means we will be taking off uphill, and we may not have enough power to clear the deck. If we take off when the flight deck has its nose in the sea, we will end up in the drink. Here's how we'll do it. As the bow, after reaching its lowest point, begins to come up, give it the gun. You'll have the advantage of traveling for two seconds downhill. By the time you reach the end of the flight deck the nose of the ship should be just ship level and your take-off should be easy. This way we will be able to take advantage of the pitching of the ship. Any questions?"

The men sat there quietly, listening intently to his crisp but still rather casual voice. There were no questions.

"We will have to travel a little further than we figured on," Doolittle continued. "I've had ten additional five-gallon cans of gasoline put in each aircraft. As soon as the gas tanks back by the rear gun mount start to empty, crew chiefs will refuel them from the five-gallon cans. Don't jettison the cans as you use them or we'll leave a perfect trail for the Japs back to the task force. Wait until you empty all of the cans and then dump them all at once.

"One thing more." Doolittle turned to Pete Mitscher. "Captain, you have been wonderful to us. So was your whole crew.

I have got to ask you just one more favor. After we have taken off, can you maintain a straight course for a few moments?"

Mitscher nodded.

"All the metal on this ship has affected some of our compasses. We all know you are headed exactly due west now. As each plane takes off it will circle and then fly directly over the length of the *Hornet*. In that way each of us can get an exact compass check. If there are no questions, let's get going. But fast." Then Doolittle added, "One more word—watch those suicide fighters of theirs. They'll be glad to swap one pilot and a forty-thousand-dollar Zero for five of us and a two-hundred-thousand-dollar bomber."

During the brief time that had elapsed between the sighting of the Jap ship and Doolittle's briefing, the *Hornet* crew had pulled the B-25's into position. Lieutenant White, the medical officer, had prescribed one pint of whiskey for each man, and those were put into the planes. Quickly, efficiently, without a bit of lost motion, crewmen "topped" the gas tanks of each B-25. The gauges already read full, but this was to take care of any evaporation or spillage that might have taken place. The wind had increased now to gale proportions (27 knots). Doolittle walked to his plane. There were no dramatics. He didn't go from plane to plane wishing the pilots and crews luck. That was for amateurs—these were professionals. Every minute counted now. Doolittle climbed into the pilot seat, warmed, then idled his engines. A Navy flight officer stood at the bow of the ship to the left with a checkered flag in his hand. Doolittle and his pilots had learned the carrier customs well. When the man with the flag started swinging it in a circle faster and faster, Doolittle knew it meant to give your engine more throttle. Doolittle turned toward Dick Cole with a question in his eyes. Cole had gone through his check list.

"Everything okay, Colonel," he said laconically.

Doolittle called through his intercom to crew chief Sergeant Paul Leonard sitting in the back of the plane. "Everything all right, Paul?" he asked, and "Everything okay, Colonel," came the calm answer.

Doolittle turned his eyes back to the man with the checkered flag. He gave the engine more throttle. The flag dropped, he released the brakes, and 31,000 pounds of airplane, bombs and men began to roar down the flight deck. With full flaps and engines roaring at full throttle, the plane lunged down the deck into the teeth of the gale. Every other pilot was watching the take-off. If Doolittle couldn't do it, they couldn't. Just as the *Hornet* lifted itself to a level position, Doolittle took off with a hundred feet to spare. He hung the ship almost straight up on its props, leveled off, and came around in a tight circle. He had made it look incredibly easy, and every pilot now felt better. Doolittle completed his turn and watched the number two ship take off. Travis Hoover was the pilot. The *Hornet's* deck came up after its pitch unexpectedly fast, and Hoover's plane had to scramble uphill. It took off and dropped abruptly, and Doolittle, watching, tried to pray it up. Just before the wheels were about to hit the water, Hoover managed to lift its nose up. Brick Holstrom's plane, Bob Gray's plane, Davey Jones' plane, Dean Hallmark's plane, Ted Lawson's plane, all took off beautifully. But by now Doolittle was headed for Tokyo. He kept the plane almost on the deck, less than two hundred feet above the sea. Two hours out, he turned the controls over to Cole and checked with navigator Henry Potter. Everything appeared to be going on schedule, although strong head winds meant added fuel consumption. Doolittle took over the controls again. About five hours after they had left the *Hornet* they saw the Japanese coast.

Doolittle turned to Potter. "We're either fifty miles north of Tokyo or fifty miles south of it, that's the way I figure it."

"I think we're about thirty miles north," Potter said calmly.

Doolittle nodded.

"We've got company, Colonel," Cole laughed, and Doolittle, looking out to the left, saw a B-25 dipping its wings in a friendly gesture. This was Travis Hoover's plane—right on schedule. They would go in together.

Now they were over the land, and to his left Doolittle saw a large lake. Potter had been right. The map said that this was just about thirty miles north of Tokyo. He turned south, flying at almost treetop level, and then suddenly, dead ahead of him but a thousand feet above, were five Jap fighters. Doolittle wasn't sure that the fighters had spotted him. There was only one way to find out. He turned to the left, and the five Jap planes turned also. It seemed obvious now to Doolittle that the ship which had intercepted them had carried a radio and had sent out a warning. The whole operation promised to be more difficult than he had anticipated, and the fifty-fifty chances of survival he had announced with such confidence didn't look so good now. In a few moments, Doolittle felt, the Jap planes would peel off and dive at him. He had to think and act quickly.

He straightened out, heading toward Tokyo again, and the five fighters followed suit. Then to the left he saw two hills. He might be able to play hide-and-seek with these Jap fighters. He made another sharp left turn to streak along the valley formed by the hills. The Jap planes turned too, but not quite fast enough. He was through the valley, and a sharp right turn brought him back on his course toward Tokyo. The hill had hidden him from the five fighters for a matter of a few seconds, but that was enough. Evidently thinking that he had continued on his course paralleling the valley, they shot off to the east. All of Doolittle's B-25's had been camouflaged, and the olive drab of the wings melted beautifully into the green of the Japanese countryside.

Doolittle kept his eyes straight ahead, and there suddenly was Tokyo. His target was a munitions factory.

Doolittle lifted the plane to fifteen hundred feet. "Approaching target," he told Sergeant Fred Braemer, the bombardier.

And Braemer called back cheerfully, "All ready, Colonel."

The bomb bay was opened and Doolittle made his run. It

was up to bombardier Braemer now. A small red light blinked on the instrument board and Doolittle knew that the first five-hundred-pound incendiary cluster had gone. In quick succession the red light blinked three more times, and the airplane, relieved of two thousand pounds, seemed to leap into the air. Up to now he had been too intent upon finding the target to notice whether the antiaircraft guns had been firing. He swung the plane toward the coast. Now, looking around, he saw that the sky was pockmarked with black puffs. Through the intercom he called to Sergeant Leonard, "Everything okay back there, Paul?"

"Everything fine," Leonard said cheerfully.

"They're missing us a mile, Paul," Doolittle told him.

Just then a blast rocked the ship and peppered it with bomb fragments. A shell had burst some hundred feet to the left.

"Colonel, that was no mile," Paul Leonard laughed.

"We're getting out of here," Doolittle said, giving the engines full throttle and shooting down to the relative safety of a hundred feet. Ahead Jimmy saw an aircraft factory with some thirty brand-new Jap training planes standing temptingly on line. Sergeant Braemer saw it too.

"Colonel, can't we burn up some of those Jap planes?" he yelled through his intercom.

Doolittle resisted the temptation. "No, Fred," he said sadly. "It would only alert them down there, and this would give them a chance to raise hell with any of the boys coming after us."

At full speed the ship approached the coast. Doolittle was flying directly over what appeared to be a fine concrete highway.

The alert Braemer called, "Colonel, there is either a tank or armored car up ahead. Can't I let it have a burst?"

"Relax, Fred," Doolittle called back. "They probably think we are a friendly aircraft. Let them keep on thinking that. And knocking off one tank isn't going to win this war."

They crossed the coast and headed southwest, skirting Shikoku and Kyushu. The weather had been fine on this stretch, with a twenty-five-mile tail wind helping. They passed Yaku Shima. Potter was doing a beautiful job of navigation. Now they were over the East China Sea and the weather changed. It became overcast and presently a heavy rain began to fall. The wind changed and Doolittle, calculating the distance left to go against the remaining gasoline supply, came to the unhappy conclusion that he couldn't make the China coast. He told the crew to be prepared to ditch.

"See that the raft is ready, Fred," he called to Braemer. He then told Leonard to make certain of hanging on to the emergency rations.

"We'll keep going until we're dry," he added.

Then, unaccountably, the wind died down and the rain stopped. Doolittle, checking his fuel again, decided he might make the coast after all.

Every member of the crew had his eyes glued straight ahead, hoping to catch sight of land. Now a favoring tail wind appeared. Land, even if it was occupied by the Japs, seemed more inviting than did the cold East China Sea beneath them.

"There it is," Paul Leonard yelled. "Damned if I don't feel like Columbus." He had seen a small offshore island. The islands and the hills in back of the coast were shrouded with low clouds. Darkness was falling. China did not look very hospitable, but then Doolittle hadn't expected China to welcome him with open arms. He knew that when the State Department had informed Chiang Kai-shek of the raid, the Generalissimo had protested vigorously. He feared that if Tokyo were bombed the Japs would retaliate viciously against his own forces. When his discouraging refusal of cooperation had arrived, Hap Arnold told him that it was too late to do anything about it; the task force which carried the raiders was already in Japanese waters and radio silence was being observed. Admiral Halsey had relayed all this information to Doolittle on the *Hornet*.

Actually, the only cooperation Doolittle had wanted from the Chinese was radio help in reaching Chinese airfields. Arnold had sent a message to Doolittle saying that a "Homer" would be flown from Chungking to Chu Chow by an American crew, and that this should give Doolittle and his men a radio fix that should make it possible for them to find the Chinese field. But there was one thing that Doolittle did not know. He did not know that the plane flying the radio equipment from Chungking to Chu Chow had crashed in the hills surrounding the Chinese airfield. The crew had been killed and all of the radio equipment destroyed.

Doolittle learned afterwards that Chinese airfields had picked up his frantic plea for a "fix," but they had thought the message had been sent by Jap planes and had ordered an immediate radio blackout. A few hours before, Chungking had sent a message alerting Chinese airfields to be ready for a friendly American group of planes, but the message had been garbled in transmission and not one air base commander in China knew that Doolittle and his raiders were on the way. These were risks which no amount of careful planning could foresee.

As he crossed the coast he climbed up to nine thousand feet and put the plane on automatic pilot. Then he sent out the prearranged code signal and waited for word from the Homer that would bring him to Chu Chow. There was no answer. He tried again and again, but there was nothing but complete silence. He figured he was about fifty miles from the airport, and now he knew that if he was to reach it at all it would have to be on his own instruments.

Doolittle knew that Chu Chow was in a hollow framed by a four-thousand-foot mountain range. He knew that he was close to it, but the darkness and the bad weather kept him from determining exactly where they were.

"We don't dare go down; we can't live under this stuff," he muttered to Cole, so they remained at nine thousand feet, far above the mountains. He agreed with Potter that they were approximately over Chu Chow.

"In this weather, we can't get a better fix than we've got now," he said to the crew. "If we keep on going in any direction, we'll just be getting further away from Chu Chow. I'm going to circle as long as we have any gas left. If the weather breaks, we'll go down and take a better look. If it doesn't, we'll have to jump."

Fifteen minutes later it was obvious that the overcast was not going to break. If anything it had thickened, and finally, although the engines kept roaring, the gas gauge showed empty.

"We'll have to bail out," Doolittle said calmly through his intercom. "Leonard first, then Braemer, then Potter, then Cole. Got it?"

"Got it, Colonel," Leonard called back laconically.

He circled twice more, put the plane on gyro-pilot, and then the starboard motor began to cough. "Get going," he cried, and in rapid succession Leonard, Braemer and Potter leaped from the ship.

He turned to copilot Cole. "Be seeing you in a few minutes, Dick," he said.

Cole smiled and tried to rise from his seat. Doolittle saw that the straps of his parachute somehow had become entangled with the back of the pilot's seat. He untangled them and slapped Cole on the shoulder. Cole disappeared through the escape hatch. Doolittle shut off the gasoline and dove into the black night.

His descent was smooth. He was worried only about one thing. If he landed on hard ground, it was quite possible he would re-break the two ankles which had been fractured in South America back in the 1920's. He decided that instead of making the conventional paratrooper's landing, he would try to touch the ground lightly with his feet, and with knees bent take the full shock of the landing on his rump. But he landed in one of the softest, wettest rice paddies in China. He sank to his knees, sat down to his waist and then scrambled out of the rice paddy, soaking wet and bitter cold.

He saw lights in what appeared to be a small farmhouse only a hundred yards away. He unharnessed his 'chute, dropped it and plodded through the mud of the field to the front door of the house. He banged on it and cried out the Chinese phrase all of the pilots and crewmen had learned, *"Lushu hoo megwa fugi."* (I am an American.) There was an immediate reaction to the phrase, but not the one he had anticipated. He heard a bolt rammed into place on the other side of the door, and at the same time the lights went out. Nothing he could do would arouse the people behind that door.

Giving up the farmhouse as a bad job, he wandered on. He found a narrow road, followed it half a mile and then came across a very large box placed on two sawhorses. If he could get inside that box he would at least be protected from the chill wind. The box was merely covered with planks. He removed them, climbed up on one of the sawhorses, and then hopped down into the box. He found that he had company— a very old Chinese gentleman whose hands were folded peacefully on his chest. The Chinese gentleman, however, wasn't asleep; he was dead, and Doolittle assumed, quite correctly, that he had stumbled into the local morgue. Doolittle had no prejudice against spending the night with a dead Chinese, but the box, made out of thin strips of wood, wasn't strong enough to keep out the rising wind. So Doolittle left the dead Chinese and continued up the road.

He stumbled into an old water mill. The rain had increased now, and the ramshackle mill looked like a real haven. It was relatively dry inside. But he found that the bitter cold kept him from sleeping. He went through a series of bending exercises trying to generate some warmth in his chilled body. He didn't sleep at all that night.

The morning was overcast, but the rain had stopped. He continued down the road and finally met an old Chinese farmer who looked at him curiously. The farmer spoke no English, nor did he respond to the "I am an American" phrase, but Doolittle took out a pad and drew a picture of a locomotive on it. When he added a question mark, the farmer smiled and nodded. Evidently there was a railroad somewhere near. The farmer beckoned him to follow. He led him about a mile up the road, not to a railroad but to what was obviously a local Chinese military headquarters. A major who was in charge looked very suspiciously at Doolittle, and held his hand out for Doolittle's .45-caliber gun which he had spotted in its holster. Doolittle shook his head. He found that the major understood English fairly well. He explained that he was an American who had parachuted out of an American plane during the night. He also said that he was an ally of the Chinese army and therefore he would keep his gun.

There was an uncomfortable silence for a moment while the major and three of his men, cradling tommy guns in their arms, looked at the mud-spattered American. The major hesitated for a moment, and Doolittle felt he was on the point of giving an order to have him shot immediately.

"I'll lead you to where my parachute is," he said, and the major nodded.

Doolittle led them back along the narrow road, past the mill, the morgue, and then he located the farmhouse which had received him so inhospitably the previous night. He found the rice paddy and led them to the exact spot where he had landed. But the parachute he had left there had disappeared.

The three soldiers were muttering to each other, and the major's eyes showed nothing but disbelief. Doolittle decided that the people in the farmhouse at least would remember the shouting and would remember his banging on the door. He asked the major to check with them. They walked to the farmhouse. The farmer, his wife and two children looked completely blank when the major interrogated them in rapid Chinese.

"They say they heard no noise during the night." He turned to Doolittle. "They say they heard no plane during the night. They say they saw no parachute. They say you are lying."

Doolittle was now beginning to sweat. He protested vigorously to the major that he was in fact an American officer, that he had bombed Tokyo, and that four members of his crew had bailed out with him. Nothing he said could remove the hard suspicion from the major's eyes. But then two of the soldiers who had gone into the farmhouse reappeared with broad smiles on their faces and the parachute in their arms. Obviously the farmer had thought that the parachute could be converted into something useful. The sight of the parachute completely dissipated the officer's suspicions. He shook hands with Doolittle and immediately ordered his men to get him something to eat. He ordered another to return to headquarters and send out searching parties for Doolittle's crew.

Then he suggested that he and Doolittle report to the governor of the province, whose headquarters were some eight miles away. It was a long walk, but the governor, a kind and gentle man, received Doolittle graciously, and soon he was sipping hot tea. Within a couple of hours Cole, Potter, Braemer and Leonard arrived. Braemer had been shaken up when he had landed; Cole had injured his ankle slightly, and Potter was exhausted. Sergeant Paul Leonard seemed as fresh as when the plane had taken off from the *Hornet* just twenty-four hours before. Doolittle got a message off to Hap Arnold.

Doolittle wanted to see what was left of the B-25. If the crash hadn't completely demolished it, there was personal equipment and a great deal of material on it that might be salvaged. Leonard was the most navigable, so Doolittle decided to bring him along. They found the remains of the plane halfway up a hill twelve miles away. It was a complete wreck. One engine had torn away and then rolled down the hill to smash against the rocks in the valley. Evidently the farmers of the neighborhood had investigated the crash they had heard and had done a thorough job of scavenging. There wasn't as much as a piece of ammunition left.

Doolittle sat down on a rock looking at the strewn debris of what had been a magnificent airplane. It seemed to symbolize the wreckage of the high hopes he had had for this mission. He felt now that the whole thing had been a complete failure. Where were the other fifteen crews? Probably all were either captured or dead, their planes wrecked. He held his head in his hands and for the first time in his life experienced black despair.

"It's been a failure," he muttered. "A complete flop."

Sergeant Leonard had been looking sharply at his commanding officer. Apparently he knew just what was in Doolittle's mind. He put a comforting hand on his shoulder.

"I want to ask you a favor, Colonel," he said softly. "After we get out of here, I don't know where they'll assign you, but no matter where they send you, I want to be a member of your crew."

"Damn it, Paul . . ." For the first time in many, many years Doolittle felt tears in his eyes. "They'll never give me another plane. They'll ground me from now on and I'll be lucky if they don't break me."

"Colonel," Leonard said in a confidential voice, "you're off your beam. You know what's gonna happen when we get back? They're gonna make you a general and give you the Congressional Medal of Honor."

The complete faith Paul Leonard showed in him at that moment was just what Doolittle needed. They wouldn't make him a general, he said roughly to himself, and they wouldn't give him the big medal. (He didn't know it, of course, but at that same hour General Arnold was signing an order that made Doolittle a brigadier general.) But damn it all, he had done his best, and that's all the Air Force ever asked of you.

"Thanks, Paul," he said, and the sergeant grinned back at him.

They started the long trek back to the governor's headquarters. But night overtook them before they reached it. The Chinese major found a farmhouse. It wasn't much of a farm, and sleeping quarters were completely primitive. The whole party had to sleep on the floor of the combination kitchen-dining room-bedroom. Doolittle and Leonard were thoroughly exhausted by now. Both were asleep within a minute or two.

Some time later Doolittle was awakened by strange protesting sounds. They were low, throaty sounds, and they seemed to be directed at him. He reached up to feel some sharp bristles, and then the throaty sounds changed to frightened squeals. Doolittle realized that he had usurped what was apparently the sleeping place of the family pig. He gave the unhappy pig a sharp push and went back to sleep.

Doolittle and his crew were finally brought to their original destination—Chu Chow. Doolittle found Jack Hilger, Ross Greening, Davey Jones, Bill Bower and Robert Gray there with their crews. Efficient Major Hilger had taken charge.

"Did that *'Lushu hoo megwa fugi'* work with you, Colonel?" Hilger asked.

"It didn't," Doolittle snapped. "No one knew what I was talking about."

"Same thing happened to the rest of us," Hilger grinned. "Juricka taught us pure Cantonese, but here in Chekiang Province they have a dialect all their own."

"Well, he and Soucek pinpointed our targets for us. I'll say that for them," Doolittle said.

Chu Chow Airport was not in a very secure position. The Japs had surrounded it on three sides and were submitting it to constant aerial attack. None of this had bothered Hilger. He had been far more concerned with something else. Corporal Leland D. Faktor, gunner in Lieutenant Gray's crew, had been killed. His parachute had opened all right, but in landing on the side of a steep hill, he had fractured his skull. Hilger was concerned with his proper burial. He found that this was not as simple as it appeared. There were no public burial grounds in China. A man could only be buried in a plot which legally belonged to him or to his family by purchase. Hilger was unable to buy such a plot, for the law said that no foreigner could buy land in China. Hilger had learned that there was a Methodist missionary some distance away, and he had persuaded the commanding officer at Chu Chow to send for him. He might have a solution.

Hilger had a report on the plane piloted by Lieutenant

William G. Farrow. The crew had landed on the coast south of Nanchang and had been captured by forces of the puppet Chinese government. Doolittle, upon hearing Hilger's report, requested to see the military governor of the western Chungking province. He and Hilger were taken some seventy miles away to the headquarters of General Kou Tso-tung, commander of the Third Military Zone, at Shang Jao. The General insisted upon giving a banquet for Doolittle and Hilger. But first, Doolittle told him that the important thing now was to free those members of Farrow's crew who had been captured and to organize a search for others who might still be at liberty. The General sent out orders to search the seacoast from Hangchow Bay to Wenchow Bay, and to alert all sampans and junks along the coast to keep a lookout for the crews of any other planes which might have gone down at sea. The dinner given by the General was a memorable one. Both Doolittle and Hilger were surprised to find themselves drinking Bordeaux wines, and after dinner, the brandy of Napoleon. Back at Chu Chow, plans were progressing to evacuate the Americans to Chungking. The Methodist missionary had arrived, had conducted services for Faktor and had arranged for his burial. Doolittle, tortured by the thought that Farrow's crew might even now be undergoing torture at the hands of the Chinese puppet leaders or of the Japs, continued to plead with the Chinese military commanders to attack the forces in the lake area where it was presumed the Americans were being held, but the authorities said sadly that their forces were far too weak to attack the combined Chinese-Japanese installations. Then Doolittle suggested that they try to negotiate with those who were holding his men, and ransom them.

"Pay them anything they ask," Doolittle said. "Don't haggle over the price."

Then the raiders left for Chungking. They were happy to see a C-47 with an American pilot at the Shang Jao airfield. The pilot was Captain Wayne Richardson.

"Is this crate in good condition?" Hilger asked Richardson.

"Oh, great," Richardson grinned. "She's seventy-five hours overdue for her twenty-five-hour inspection, but she may get us to Chungking."

As soon as he arrived in Chungking, Doolittle repeated his message to Arnold. He had little faith in the Chinese communication system.

"Mission to bomb Tokyo accomplished. Ran into bad weather approaching China. It is feared all planes crashed. Five crews safe."

General Clayton Bissell was there to greet Doolittle. "You'll look better with this on your shoulder," he grinned, taking a star from his pocket. "Hap cabled me to let me know he'd signed your commission as Brigadier General."

"Paul Leonard was right," Doolittle said thoughtfully.

Doolittle then saw Madame Chiang Kai-shek. She was gracious and charming, but Doolittle was in no mood to exchange compliments. He told her bluntly that the only thing that mattered now was the safety of Farrow's crew. She promised that every effort would be made to rescue or ransom the men. Meanwhile, the Chinese guerrilla grapevine was operating beautifully, and within a week Doolittle had a pretty good idea of what had happened to his sixteen planes and eighty men. Farrow had been jinxed from the very beginning. Just as he had been about to start his run from the *Hornet,* the carrier had lurched sharply and his airplane had slipped backwards. As it swerved, the moving propeller hit a crew member and took off his arm. After Farrow had hit oil storage tanks and an aircraft factory in the Osaka-Kobe area, he headed for the China coast. His men bailed out in territory which was in control of Chinese puppet troops, who immediately turned Farrow and his crew over to the Japanese. Lieutenant Farrow and Corporal C. Spatz were executed; the others were in prison camps. (Sergeant Jacob deShazer was to spend thirty-six months in solitary confinement. Jeeringly they would throw him a Bible to read. He would read it, and his hatred for his brutal captors would change to compassion.

He would survive, become a missionary and return to Japan to bring the word of God to the hills and the villages far from Tokyo.)

Ross Greening survived an attack by four Japanese Tonies. His gunner, Sergeant Melville Gardner, shot down one of the fighters and Greening, a brilliant pilot, took evasive action to lose the remaining three fighters. His copilot, Kenneth Reddy, suffered a broken kneecap, and Gardner sprained both ankles when they landed. Lieutenant Dean Hallmark bailed out over Poyang Lake. Hallmark was captured and executed. His copilot, Robert Meder, was put in a prison camp. (He later died of malnutrition and mistreatment.) Sergeant William Deiter and Corporal Donald FitzMorris landed in Poyang Lake and were drowned. Lieutenant Chase Neilson, Hallmark's navigator, was captured by the Japs. (He survived forty months of imprisonment.) Travis Hoover landed in a rice paddy near Ningpo and all of his men were now in Chungking. Lieutenant Robert Gray had lost only Corporal Faktor. Lieutenant Jacob E. Manch was Gray's copilot. "Shorty" Manch stood six-foot-six and he weighed two hundred forty-five pounds. It was always a mystery to his fellow pilots how Manch had managed to get into the Air Force in the first place. The regulations then were that no man standing more than six-foot-two or weighing more than two hundred pounds could be a pilot. But Shorty Manch was a good pilot. In addition to being a pilot, he had two hobbies; music and guns. Before leaving the *Hornet,* he had slipped his portable phonograph as well as his 25-35 carbine rifle into the plane. When he had to jump, he just couldn't leave either behind, so he had leaped into the darkness with the carbine in one hand and the portable phonograph in the other. It was a rough descent. He made a crash-landing on the side of a hill, tumbled down the slope for sixty or seventy feet before he could come to a full stop, and then found that the only memento left of his two precious possessions was the handle of his phonograph, which was still in his left hand.

Lieutenant Everett Holstrom and his men were all safe. So was Captain David Jones and his crew. Lieutenant Ted Lawson landed his plane in the water off the coast. Reports from guerrilla forces said that Lawson was being cared for, but that his right leg had been badly injured. The same grapevine reported that Donald Smith had landed not far from where Lawson had come down, and that Lieutenant T. R. White, the only medical officer on the flight, had been brought by guerrilla fighters to where Lawson was hidden, and that the medico was taking care of him. Lieutenant Harold F. Watson and his men bailed out one hundred miles south of Poyang Lake. Watson suffered a broken arm, but none of his crew members were injured. Lieutenant Richard O. Joyce had originally been assigned to take the sixteenth B-25 off the *Hornet* five hundred miles out of San Francisco. When Doolittle had talked Mitscher into letting the extra plane go along, Joyce thought himself to be the luckiest man in the world. Now back in Chungking, he was sure of it. His plane had been attacked by nine Zeros over Tokyo. An eight-inch hole was ripped in the fuselage of his ship just forward of the horizontal stabilizer, but the stabilizer itself remained intact and Joyce managed to get away from the Jap fighters. He and his men had bailed out thirty miles north of Chu Chow. Lieutenant Edgar E. McElroy and his crew had all come through safely, as had Major Hilger and his men. Lieutenant William Bower, after destroying a large warehouse and an oil refinery in Yokohama, took time out en route to China to sink a patrol boat. He and all of his men were safe in Chungking. That left only Captain Edward J. York. Ski York had dropped his bombs on Tokyo. He had headed for the coast. His gunner, Sergeant David Pohl, reported that their top gun turret was out of commission. This left the plane virtually helpless against any fighter attack from above. York also discovered that, for some unexplained reason, his rate of gasoline consumption had been far higher than anticipated. To make matters worse, he encountered strong head winds. He was faced with a difficult decision. He knew if he kept on his course, he would run out of gas somewhere in the middle of the East China Sea. This would mean certain death for the whole crew. He had only two alternatives. He could land in Japan which meant that, at best, his crew would spend the rest of the war in a prison camp, or he could fly to Vladivostok. He decided to disobey orders and save the lives of his crew. He turned north and landed forty miles north of Vladivostok. (York and his men were interned by the Russians and the plane confiscated by the Russian government.)

Doolittle received orders to return to Washington via India and the Middle East.

10

Jo Doolittle had been through an agonizing month. Her father had died and she had not received one message from her husband. She decided to stay in Los Angeles until she received word either from him or about him. Early one morning her phone rang to awake Jo out of a sound sleep. She knew this call was either from New York or from Washington. No one in either city apparently ever thought of the time differential between the East and West Coasts. It was 5:00 A.M. in Los Angeles but it was 9:00 A.M. in the East. Jo picked up the phone and heard a familiar voice. It was General Arnold.

"We've been having a hell of a time locating you, Jo," Arnold said. "I want you to come to Washington. Can you make it?"

"Of course I can, Hap."

"You don't mind flying here, do you, Jo?"

"Really, Hap," Jo laughed.

"Okay, Jo, stay near the phone. We'll make arrangements from this end and let you know."

A few hours later Jo was told to take a TWA plane which was to leave Los Angeles at 4:15 that afternoon. She wasn't given even a hint as to why Arnold wanted her in Washington. As the plane headed east, she tried to figure it all out. A few days before the newspapers had announced that Tokyo had been bombed, but very few details had been given and no names mentioned. Jo had a strong hunch that her husband had led this operation. Perhaps Arnold was going to give her full details of it. His voice on the phone had sounded cheerful so she could be reasonably certain that nothing serious had happened to Jimmy. On that reassuring note she fell asleep. The plane landed at Pittsburgh early the next morning, much to Jo's relief. This particular TWA plane had only one lavatory, and every time Jo approached it she found it occupied by some male passenger. She was the only woman on board. As the plane rolled up to the administration building at the Pittsburgh Airport, Jo sighed with relief. The stewardess said that there would be a one-hour stopover at Pittsburgh. Jo decided she would spend that hour in the rest room brushing her teeth, washing her face, fixing her hair, and she might even find a shower bath.

As she stepped from the plane, an Army officer came up, took hold of her arm and said, "We have an Army plane waiting for you, Mrs. Doolittle, to take you right to Washington."

"That's nice of you," Jo said, hesitating, "but first do you mind . . ."

"Don't worry about a thing," the young but insensitive officer smiled. "Your bags are being taken care of and you'll be in Washington in no time. There's the plane warming up."

He led her to the plane, and as soon as her bags were stowed aboard it took off. It was a fast little plane and Jo knew that it wouldn't be long before she'd be in the immaculate, white-tiled rest rooms of the Washington Airport. This was the only thing in life that mattered to her now. Finally the plane made its approach, landed nicely, and taxied to the administration building. Jo stepped out of the plane to be greeted by another young Army officer.

"We have a car waiting for you, Mrs. Doolittle," he said nervously, "but we've really got to hurry."

"I've got to hurry, too," Jo said a little impatiently. "No

matter where you want me to go, it can't be as important as the place I want to go."

The officer looked puzzled.

"But, Mrs. Doolittle, we're due at the White House in ten minutes."

"The White House?"

Jo was so startled that she completely forgot the urgency and the uncomfortable tension of the past two hours. She forgot her unwashed face, her unbrushed teeth, and her uncombed hair. Within two minutes she was in a car speeding toward the White House. The car drove up to the main entrance. An officer was waiting for her. He rushed her upstairs into a waiting room. There were three men in the room: General Marshall, General Arnold, and her husband.

"Hello, Doolittle," Jimmy grinned putting his arms around her. "How are you?"

"I'm fine, Doolittle," she said weakly. "How are you?"

"Okay, Doolittle. How are the boys?"

"All right, I hope," Jo said. "I never hear from them. Do you?"

"Nope."

"Did you get my letter?" Jimmy asked.

"No, sweetheart, I didn't," Jo said.

"Well, Doolittle, I can explain that. I never got a chance to write a letter."

Marshall and Arnold were grinning happily.

"Now you see why I wanted you to come to Washington, Jo," Arnold laughed.

"I came as fast as I could, Hap," Jo said. "But what in heaven's name are we doing at the White House?"

"The President is going to pin the Medal of Honor on Jimmy," General Marshall said gravely.

Doolittle turned to him.

"I still don't like it," he said. "General, I lost sixteen planes and eleven men. The big medal means a great deal to me and I honestly don't think I deserve it."

"You did a really great job, Doolittle," Marshall said gravely. "You deserve it all right."

"Not," Doolittle said stubbornly, "any more than some of the men who have gotten it outside of combat these past few years. Sure, they did good jobs, but you know well how everyone felt about their getting the medal."

Marshall flushed angrily.

"I know all that," he said. "I recommended that you be given the Congressional Medal of Honor in order to raise the medal back to the level where it belongs."

"Well, if that's how you feel about it, all right. I feel that I don't deserve it, but," Doolittle stared right into Marshall's eyes, "I can tell you I'll spend the rest of my life trying to earn it."

"May I ask one favor, General?" Jo turned to Marshall. "It's a very small favor. I left Los Angeles at 4:15 yesterday afternoon. May I please, just have five minutes in a White House bathroom?"

"Of course," Marshall grinned.

But just then a door was flung open and a solemn-faced attendant said, "The President will see you now."

Jo swallowed hard, sent up a silent prayer, and walked into the President's study. There was a broad grin on Roosevelt's face as he reached out to clasp Doolittle's hand.

Jack Allard was sitting in his Curtiss office on the thirty-second floor of the RCA building in New York. The radio had carried a full description of the ceremonies, and Allard felt as proud as though he had been given the coveted medal. The announcer finally concluded his colorful description and Allard switched off his portable radio. He wanted to phone Doolittle, but he felt on this of all days Doolittle would be knee-deep in the highest brass. Just then the phone rang and a familiar voice cried in the time-honored argot of the Air Force, "Hello, you broken down ulcer-ridden civilian. How are you?" It was Doolittle checking in with his old friend.

"That's no way for a Medal of Honor man to talk," Allard said reproachfully.

"Nuts," Doolittle said cheerfully. "No matter what you are doing tonight, cancel it. Call Charlie Rochester at the Lexington and wangle a room from him. I'd like to go in hiding for a couple of days, so register me over there under your name. I'll meet you there at eight o'clock."

"Okay, General," Allard said.

"Don't give me that 'General' routine," Doolittle yelled into the phone, "and have a drink and a steak waiting for me tonight."

Charlie Rochester, manager of the Lexington, for years headquarters for Army pilots, had the governor's suite available. In fact, he told Allard over the phone, "You and Jimmy can have the whole top floor if you want."

"There will just be the two of us," Allard said, "but for God's sake don't let anyone know that Jimmy will be at your place or he'll be hip-deep in reporters."

Doolittle arrived alone. These two men had been friends for twenty-four years. Allard didn't have to go into any emotional routine. He didn't have to tell Doolittle how desperately worried he'd been, or how proud he was of the blue ribbon his friend was wearing on his uniform.

Allard just asked, "Do you want water or soda, Jim?"

"You ought to know by now I like water in my Scotch."

Allard nodded gravely, made two drinks and then said simply, "Tell me all about it, Jim."

Doolittle took off his blouse, threw his tie on a chair, sat down on the comfortable divan, spread out his legs and said, "Well, Jack, it was like this. . . ."

They talked for six hours. It was the first real chance Doolittle had had of unburdening himself of all the doubts and anxieties that had beset him after he had landed in China. He told Allard of the awful moment he had had sitting there on the side of the hill, gazing at the complete wreckage of his plane.

"I'm not kidding you, Jack," he said. "I actually cried."

"If you ever saw a tear you'd kick it in the face," Allard scoffed.

"Let me tell you about Paul Leonard, my crew chief," Doolittle said, his eyes lighting up. "If it hadn't been for him, I might have gone stark raving mad. Wherever they send me now, believe me, I am going to have Paul Leonard along."

"I guess it's time I went along too, Jim," Allard said casually.

"I figured you'd want to do that," Doolittle said, just as casually. "I think they are going to give me a pretty good job. Hap Arnold intimated as much."

"Maybe if I go down and see Hap," Allard said, "he can facilitate things. Hell, he might even make me a major."

"I have already spoken to Hap," Jimmy said. "Why not come back to Washington with me Monday morning? Hap has spoken to Jim Fechet. You will be in uniform before you know what hit you."

Doolittle had a batch of mail and congratulatory telegrams which he and Allard opened. There was one from Roscoe Turner. It merely said bitterly:

> DEAR JIMMY,
> You son-of-a-bitch.
> ROSCOE

There was another from Bruce Johnson, now head of a fast-growing little company in Providence. But Bruce wanted in. He sensed that Doolittle would be given some important assignment; he was sure that Allard would wangle his way along, and he wanted to join the old team.

"I'm going to write Bruce and tell him to stay out," Doolittle said. "Why, if he joined up now he'd have kids commanding him, and that wouldn't do at all. Then he's led a pretty soft life these past few years. I'll have to tell him he's too old and too soft for this war."

"You'll break his heart," Allard said.

"It's best, though," Doolittle said. "This war is not for Brucie. Let's get that off tonight."

When Doolittle returned to Washington, Allard went along. General Fechet was waiting for him. He told Allard to dictate his application to his secretary and go out and buy some uniforms. That took five minutes. It took him an hour to be fitted to uniforms. Allard's trim figure hadn't changed over the years. The uniforms (42 long) didn't even have to be altered. He had weighed 202 pounds in 1918 when he had met Doolittle at Camp Dick. Now he weighed 204 pounds.

While he was being fitted he suddenly remembered something. He phoned General Fechet and said, "I'm getting outfitted, but damned if I know what rank I am going to have. What'll I tell them to put on the shoulders?"

"You're a lieutenant colonel for the moment," Fechet said laconically.

And Allard ordered silver leaves. At three that afternoon he went to Doolittle's office in uniform, and together they walked into Hap Arnold's office.

"You've got yourself a war, Jack," Arnold grinned. "Five hours ago you were a civilian and president of Curtiss-Wright Export. Now you are in the Air Force and Jimmy is your boss."

Arnold sent Doolittle to nearby Bolling Field with orders to organize the 4th Medium Bomber Wing. Doolittle and Allard shared an office. Both felt that this was only a stopgap; that something big was in line for Doolittle. Doolittle did not know it, but General MacArthur had cabled Arnold asking for a new airman to replace General George Brett. MacArthur and Brett hadn't been getting along too well.

Arnold cabled to MacArthur, "I would recommend either Kenny or Doolittle and will make either available."

Shortly afterwards MacArthur sent a message to Arnold, "I will take Kenny."

Doolittle was not exactly the "Army type" that would conform to MacArthur's rigid standards. MacArthur liked West

Point men who had come up the slow, hard way and who were amenable to discipline. Doolittle was a former racing pilot and stunt man. His raid had been a spectacular one that had given a great lift to the American people, but if there were any more spectacular operations to be performed in the Pacific Theater of War, MacArthur would perform them himself.

One day in July, 1942, Doolittle received an urgent summons from Arnold. When he replaced the phone he was smiling with satisfaction. "I have got a hunch this is it," he said to Allard. "Hap said to hurry over there. Sit tight and I'll phone you as soon as I hear anything."

Two hours later Allard's phone rang.

"Meet me at Benny's on Fisherman's Wharf," Doolittle said.

Doolittle, Jo and Allard had been spending a lot of time at Benny's, a place which specialized in fish. When Allard arrived Doolittle was already there.

"I've ordered drinks and the fish platter," he said.

"The hell with that," Allard said. "Tell me, where are we going?"

"It looks like England first," Doolittle said. "We're going to organize an air force to take part," he dropped his voice, "in some invasion. George Patton and I have been recommended to Eisenhower, but he has to okay us both."

A week later they were in London. Eisenhower accepted his old friend Georgie Patton immediately. He had never met Doolittle. He had respect for his courage, his flying ability and the quality he had of making men follow him. But this in the main was to be an organizational and administrative job. Eisenhower didn't like the idea of entrusting the formation of what would be known as the 12th Air Force to a former stunt pilot who had spent most of the last eleven years selling gasoline. Doolittle sensed how Eisenhower felt. He believed that his years with Shell had actually taught him more about organization and administration than he would have learned had he remained in the Army. He also believed that he had learned a great deal about people and how to judge their potentialities. Both Hap Arnold and General Marshall appreciated these qualities in him, and neither felt that his long absence from the Army was a handicap. But he knew he couldn't sell himself to Eisenhower by quoting Arnold and Marshall. He resolved to be respectful and reserved at his first meeting with the Commander of the European Forces.

Perhaps to cover his embarrassment at receiving a man whom he had already in his own mind rejected, Eisenhower greeted Doolittle effusively and then went into a rather long discussion as to the need of new air bases all over the world. He kept hammering at the point that the vital concern at the moment was more air bases, and then he asked if Doolittle didn't agree with him.

"No, General, I don't," Doolittle said bluntly, completely forgetting his good resolutions. "What good are air bases unless we have the supplies to operate them? As I understand it, we don't have sufficient transport to bring in supplies to operate the present air bases at maximum efficiency. And then as I see it, we are completely dependent on the Army for supplies. If we had our own supply ships, our own trucks, our own transport planes, then I'd say sure, let's get more bases."

Eisenhower would always listen to another man's argument. He might even nod in apparent agreement, but Eisenhower's nod, as many are finding out even today, merely means, "Go on, I'm listening." He listened to Doolittle, nodded pleasantly, and then when Doolittle left his office, cabled the Pentagon, "Am completely satisfied with Patton but do not want Doolittle. Can't I have Spaatz or Eaker?"

Arnold was a little disconcerted when he received Eisenhower's message. He knew Eisenhower well, and he felt that Doolittle would make him an excellent junior partner. He had not tried to force Doolittle on MacArthur. He knew that their temperaments and personalities were inimical. But he hated to see Eisenhower turn down a man who he felt would be a great asset to him.

He cabled back to Eisenhower, "You can have anyone you want, but I still strongly recommend Doolittle."

Eisenhower had a lot of respect for Arnold's judgment about airmen. It was Arnold who had made Tooey Spaatz head of the Eighth Air Force; who had put General F. O. (Monk) Hunter in charge of the fighters and General Ira Eaker in charge of the bombers. Spaatz, Hunter and Eaker had achieved a miracle of organization in forming the Eighth Air Force; Arnold was certainly showing a lot of faith in Jimmy Doolittle.

General Mark Clark had been named Deputy Commander in Charge of the North African Invasion (in layman's language, this meant that he was Eisenhower's representative and that orders from him had the force of orders from the Supreme Commander). When Eisenhower had about made up his mind to accept Arnold's strong recommendation, he called in Clark and explained matters to him. Clark had none of Eisenhower's reservations. He immediately called Doolittle in for a conference.

"Who do you think should handle the air end of this African operation?" he asked.

Doolittle shrugged his shoulders. "That's a tough one to answer. We have a lot of good men around."

"Do you think you're one of them?" Clark smiled.

"Well . . . since you've asked me . . . yes, I do."

"You're elected," Clark said laconically. "Get going." *

So Eisenhower, with some reluctance, decided to go along. He accepted Doolittle and told him to organize the 12th Air Force.

It was a difficult and rather delicate assignment, made possible only because of the friendship and mutual respect that existed between Doolittle and Spaatz. It was obvious that there would be no time to wait for personnel, aircraft or sup-

* *Calculated Risk* by General Mark W. Clark.

plies to arrive from the United States. The nucleus of the new 12th would have to be formed from the 8th.

"I hate to do it, Tooey," Doolittle said to Spaatz, "but I am just going to have to castrate your Eighth."

"I know it, Jimmy," Spaatz said sadly, "but the African invasion does have priority. You can have anything I've got, but for God's sake leave me as much as you can. And so help me, if you try to take Ted Curtis or Clare Welch away from me, I'll shoot you."

"I have got some good news for you," Doolittle grinned. "Hap cabled today that he is sending over Larry Norstadt to head my A-3, Max Schneider to head my A-4, and Hoyt Vandenberg to be my Chief of Staff."

Doolittle, Patton, and Allard lived at Claridge's Hotel. Allard (he was a full colonel now) was Doolittle's A-1 (in charge of personnel). They'd meet every night, discussing Doolittle's personnel needs. It was obvious that Spaatz would have to give up nearly 50 per cent of his air force. He not only had to do that but he had to continue his daily bombing operation lest the Germans get the idea that much of the American air strength was being diverted for some other operation. Sometimes, late at night, exhausted after trying to solve apparently unsolvable problems, they would let Patton take over. The incredible Patton, who seemed incapable of inspiring anything but hatred or deep affection, would stalk up and down the big living room of Doolittle's suite entertaining them all with stories. Patton's first love was probably his ridiculous pearl-handled revolver, but his second was the hunting knife he always carried with him. His constant fear was that this knife might somehow become dull. While telling the most outrageous stories of his cavalry days, or what his tanks would do once the Navy put them ashore, he would be constantly sharpening the knife on a whetstone he always kept with him. Doolittle and Spaatz were two of those who were devoted to Patton. They liked his exuberant humor, chuckled at his flamboyancy and relaxed under the stream of his colorful invective delivered in a high, squeaky voice.

Every morning the staff of planners met at Norfolk House in St. James' Square. The brains of the Allied Command contributed to the planning of the North African invasion. It was obvious that the land forces would not be able to really secure the three beachheads (Oran, Algiers and Casablanca) until airstrips had been captured and the RAF and the 12th based upon them. The planners decided that the air elements which would be part of the invasion force would be based initially at Gibraltar—and then as soon as airstrips were captured they could fly to them. Doolittle, of course, would have to be with his airplanes at Gibraltar.

"Someone has to go along with the ground force," he said to Allard and Norstadt, "to see to it that they don't forget to grab an airfield for us and to let me know at Gibraltar so I can shoot our fighters to it. I guess you two are elected."

Allard and Norstadt shuddered at the thought of a long sea voyage. To them, any means of transport other than the airplane was dangerous and unnatural, but they resigned themselves to it. And Allard especially was cheered by the fact that he'd actually get into combat in Europe before Doolittle would.

As the plans for the invasion progressed daily meetings were held, with Eisenhower usually presiding. Brilliant General Alfred Gruenther, Mark Clark, Admiral Sir Bertram Ramsey, Air Vice Marshal Sir William Lawrie Welsh, General Sir Kenneth Anderson, General John C. Lee—the brains of the Allied Command were there. Eisenhower encouraged his land and air commanders to express their views freely. Doolittle wasn't a bit backward about taking Eisenhower at his word. He had very definite ideas as to the part the 12th Air Force should play, and he was very emphatic about expressing them. Some of the older officers shook their heads sadly and muttered that Doolittle wouldn't last long. But strangely enough, his independence, instead of alienating Eisenhower, began to earn him considerable respect from the Commander in Chief. Eisenhower couldn't help but notice the smooth way Doolittle, Vandenberg and Norstadt operated. Nor could he help noticing the way men like Tooey Spaatz and Air Marshal Tedder usually agreed with Doolittle's views. Doolittle, on his part, realized that the "Boss" was displaying a quiet and unobtrusive genius for getting this team to pull together. He was beginning to be a big Eisenhower man.

The experienced RAF officers, who had been fighting since 1939 and who had seen a good portion of their command wiped out in the Battle of Britain, were inclined to look upon the newly arrived American air officers as enthusiastic but inexperienced amateurs. Many American officers, on the other hand, supremely confident that their B-17's and B-24's were much better than anything that the British had, displayed an arrogance that understandably annoyed the British. It took all of Eisenhower's skill to soothe ruffled feelings and to get the officers of both air forces working together. One small incident did more finally to cement working conditions between the American and British officers than any official directives could have done. At a meeting of staff officers an American colonel blew his top at his RAF opposite number and exploded with a "Why, you British son-of-a-bitch. . . ."

Eisenhower, hearing of the incident, immediately sent for the offending colonel, gave him a tongue-lashing and concluded with the angry order, "Call a man a son-of-a-bitch if you want, but don't call him a British son-of-a-bitch."

The story, told by a chuckling Churchill a day or two later at a cabinet meeting, swept London, and the roar of laughter started by Churchill's chuckle seemed to melt away the tensions. The term "son-of-a-bitch," never taken as lightly in England as in this country, immediately became practically a term of endearment.

Doolittle, whose work with Shell had brought him into close contact with the British businessman and aviation executives, marveled at the intuition Eisenhower displayed in recognizing and making allowances for the sensibilities the battle-weary RAF officers occasionally displayed. The high British brass recognized and appreciated this quality in Eisenhower long before his own countrymen became conscious of it. Arthur Tedder, Bomber Harris, Air Chief Marshal Charles Portal, all the RAF ranking officers became and remained devoted to Eisenhower.

Doolittle himself was in a rather difficult position. The invasion of North Africa was to be the first real full-scale joint operation against enemy-held territory. (The Dieppe raid had been merely a tentative left jab delivered to throw the German defenses a bit off balance.) There were at first both British and American officers who found it difficult to swallow the fact that Doolittle was a maverick; he didn't fit into the pattern of either American or British military tradition. Sure he was a great pilot and one hell of a combat man—but heading up an air force was something else again. Doolittle—never the one to be tortured by self-doubts himself—knew that this feeling existed, but he also knew how to cope with it. He handled it by ignoring it and turning on his charm against those he knew to be the chief doubters. Gradually the doubters began to forget the fact that Doolittle wore neither the West Point ring nor the Sandhurst tie. And they had to admit that his technical knowledge of aircraft was superior to their own. By the time plans for Operation Torch were finished they had completely accepted Doolittle as one of their own.

Four days before the invasion date, Doolittle flew to Gibraltar in a B-17 piloted by Lieutenant Summer. Off the coast of Portugal four JU-88's attacked the B-17, which was flying without escort. Summer immediately went down to the deck. A smart pilot, he knew that the JU-88's would have to pull out of their attacking dives well above the water or risk the danger of going right on in. The German planes made several passes at the low-flying B-17, but although they hit it a dozen times, the skillful, evasive tactics used by Summer prevented them from hurting any vital spots. Doolittle stood in the radio compartment just aft of the pilot's cockpit during the attack. Summer turned to him and asked him if he had any orders.

"You're the pilot of this airplane, son," Doolittle said laconically, "and you are doing a hell of a fine job."

Again the 88's dove, and this time the copilot was hit. Doolittle helped the navigator pull the wounded man from the seat. They laid him on the floor. Doolittle slipped into the seat he had vacated.

"You've got yourself a new copilot, Lieutenant," he said to Summer, "but you're in charge of this airplane."

They were getting close to Gibraltar now and the German planes, smoke trailing from one of them, left for more friendly air. Doolittle found that things were well in hand at Gibraltar. Meanwhile, the invasion fleet was approaching North Africa.

Mark Clark had previously made his dramatic submarine trip to North Africa, and after conferring with French leaders, had told Headquarters that he was confident that the invasion forces would meet with nothing but token resistance. This ruled out the conventional tactics of softening up the defenses before landing; it seemed absurd to bomb potential allies who were merely waiting to receive the invading forces and to turn over precious landing strips and supplies. The fleet crept closer, and Eisenhower paced nervously at his temporary headquarters at Gibraltar. No one knew exactly what to expect when the forces landed. There were a great many intangible elements connected with the North African landings, and there were many uneasy moments as the invasion fleet slid in close to the shores.

The attacking forces landed at one minute after midnight, November 8. Allard and Norstadt went in with a combat team whose objective was the Tafouri airfield, about fifteen miles from Oran.* The resistance, instead of being token, was fierce and stubborn. Tafouri, of course, had not been softened up,

---

* Tafouri is the anglicized form of Tafaraoui.

and the hills not far away sheltered artillery and tanks. It was eight hours before Allard and Norstadt could feel that the airfield was "reasonably" secure, and they radioed Doolittle at Gibraltar that they were ready to receive him. Doolittle immediately dispatched twenty-four Spitfires under Colonel John Hawkins to Tafouri. The Spits looked awfully good to Allard and Norstadt as they circled and then glided in to land. As the last one approached the runway, gear down, three French fighters dove out of a cloud to catch it. Three of the Spitfires were still taxiing toward the small headquarters building. They wheeled, streaked into the air, and within five minutes had destroyed the three French fighters.

That night French and German bombers came over to give the field a good going-over. Norstadt, Allard and "Shorty" Hawkins spent most of the night huddling in slit trenches.

"As soon as daylight comes we'll put a stop to this," Hawkins said grimly.

Norstadt found that the enemy planes were based at a French naval station near Sidi Bel Abbes, about fifty miles away. When daylight came, Shorty Hawkins led his Spitfires up (by some miracle not one of the Spitfires had been hit during the night) and made good his promise. They destroyed every enemy plane that was based at the French naval station. Norstadt and Allard tried to get some semblance of order so that Tafouri would be ready when Doolittle arrived. Badly needed supplies (ammunition, gasoline, oil, antiaircraft guns) were slow in arriving. The combat team was busy cannibalizing the half-dozen enemy planes which had been captured at the airport. They were removing ammunition and gasoline from the planes to supply the Spitfires when Doolittle's plane came in. He took one look around the airport and winced.

Tafouri was a complete shambles. The unexpected resistance had thrown the whole timetable of Operation Torch awry. Supplies which should have been at the airstrip were still lying on the beach at Oran. Norstadt and Allard had thrown every man who could be spared from manning a gun into the job of siphoning gasoline out of the captured planes on the airfield and of removing the ammunition. This would have to serve the Spits until the transport difficulties between beachhead and airfield were straightened out. There had been no time to establish antiaircraft defenses. The field was still under attack.

"This place is really loused up," Doolittle said grimly to his two weary aides, "and I'm going to straighten things out and do it fast."

Within a matter of hours some order began to emerge from the chaos. Colonel Tudor Gardiner, onetime governor of Maine, acted as liaison between Oran and the 12th Air Force headquarters. Gardiner bullied, cajoled, threatened, pleaded and requisitioned everything from bulldozers to chaplains; he kept supplies flowing along the twelve-mile route. It later became a legend that Gardiner never slept nor ate for forty-eight hours—that he spent at least forty of those hours roaring back and forth on a motorcycle between Tafouri and the port of Oran. When Doolittle finally plucked him off the motorcycle and insisted that he rest awhile, legend (supported by evidence from Doolittle, Norstadt and Allard) has it that he had actually become bowlegged from his long stay on the seat of the motorcycle.

Doolittle himself was all over the place. He knew men. He knew when to give barking orders; he knew when to get results with a grin and a slap on the back. Within four days Tafouri was an operational airfield bearing a load of five times its potential—and this without an all-weather runway. Eleven days after the landing, Doolittle found time to write to General Arnold. Back in Washington Arnold read:

> The American carrier-borne Navy aviation at Casablanca, and the British Fleet Arm at Oran, did the larger part of the air fighting. By the time the airports were secured, they had destroyed, either in the air or on the ground, the majority of the French aviation.
>
> Joe Cannon, at Casablanca, has done an outstanding

job. The 33rd Fighter Group gave air support and the necessary reconnaissance to General Patton's forces. Joe unloaded some 72 aircraft from the *Chenango* at Port Lyautey. The principal runway had been bombed, and was not usable. The field was soft and 70 aircraft sustained minor damage on landing. Part of these aircraft were later moved to the Casablanca airport, and some 35 more were shot off the *Archer*. [The *Archer* was a carrier.]

Joe now has, in addition to these, a half-dozen B-25's from the 310th Group, and more are coming in steadily. He also has such transports as required, of the 62nd Group.

In addition to Port Lyautey, there are good fields at Sole, Rabat and Casablanca. The field at Casablanca is large but has no prepared runways, and there are spots that will not hold a B-17. I proved this the other day by landing there and bogging down. Apparently, the small footprint and the high unit loading was more than the sod could stand. It required four tanks to pull the B-17 out so it could take off again. Joe and George Patton have the western situation well in hand and are getting along together beautifully.

The first airport was secured at Oran at noon on D-day. Twenty-four Spitfires of the 31st Group, with Hawkins in command, hopped over from Gibraltar.

I cannot speak too highly of the work done by these groups. They twice stopped mechanized columns who were attacking the airport at Tafouri from the south. The ground units had moved forward to take La Senia airport, which is closer to Oran proper. Had it not been for the prompt and efficient action of the Spitfires, Tafouri and our air units would have been lost, and the war at Oran lengthened and made more bloody. One column taken out and routed was the French Foreign Legion, moving in from its headquarters at Sidi-bel-Abbes. Our Fighters destroyed five tanks of this outfit, burned the supplies coming forward, and routed the foot soldiers. La Senia was secured, lost, and secured again.

During the process, it was bombed by our people and shelled by the French. We have finally moved to La Senia in addition to Tafouri, and are rehabilitating it.

The necessity for marrying ground and air forces on the field of battle precluded the training and study in organization necessary to secure perfect collaboration. In spite of this, the cooperation was of the highest order, and in only two instances were mistakes made. On one occasion, we were directed to attack an enemy column east of La Macta, on Arzeu Bay. By the time the message got to us, it read *west* of La Macta. The airplanes flew over the column to the west, which was actually ours. The ground forces, being light on the trigger, cut down on the airplanes. The planes, feeling, in spite of the American appearance, they must be French troops, started to strafe them. Fortunately, our tanks were not as vulnerable as the French, and no damage was done to our ground troops, but two of our planes were shot down by our own people.

As a matter of fact, an operation of this kind promptly separates the sheep from the goats, and I am happy to report that all of our people showed up well, and most of them were superior.

Two of my principal worries were the concentration of aircraft on Gibraltar, and the long flight down from the United Kingdom in the season of bad weather. Gibraltar is now pretty well cleaned out, and to date, far less difficulty than I anticipated is experienced in flying the aircraft down.

When I was last at Casablanca, there were about 4,000 air people ashore; yesterday, at Oran, we had 14,000 men and about 1,000 officers. These are stationed at Tafouri and La Senia.

The fight has moved to the eastward. In order to get the Hun out of Tunisia and occupy this area before he can, we will have made available to the Royal Air Force, to General Anderson's army, as many of our units as they can use. This arrangement, under which these airplanes are made available, is for the British to assign the missions, but we operate the airplanes.

We must keep the Straits of Gibraltar open and provide Fighter cover, and later submarine protection for our convoys along the north and west coasts of Africa.

Patton was moving now with his tanks, and finally Doolittle had a few airstrips of sorts on which to base his aircraft. The 12th Air Force had a twofold mission—it had to support ground troops and it had to harass the German supply lines. Tunis and Bizerte were the primary targets, and these two huge supply depots, fed regularly by Axis shipping, were equipped with perhaps the best antiaircraft defenses seen up to that time. The bombing by Doolittle's heavy B-17's, B-24's, medium B-25's and B-26's had to be done in daylight—the ramshackle airstrips which based the 12th were not equipped for night landing. Pilots began to hate and fear the run over either Bizerte or Tunis; if the remarkably accurate flak didn't get you, the German fighters did. Yet there was no alternative. If supplies were allowed to pile up in these two cities, the German forces might well blast the ground forces right into the Mediterranean. Doolittle was conscious of the low morale of his pilots. He went to each base to tell the men why they had to continue what to many seemed suicidal operations. He emphasized the fact that the Germans would start a big offensive in the spring—the success of that drive would depend upon how much ammo the enemy had, how much gasoline and oil for his armor and his aircraft. Only the 12th Air Force could stop him—not six weeks hence but now, before the attack began. He talked to them soberly. These were not the type of men who would respond to Patton's curses or his "inspirational" diatribes. Doolittle talked to them in his own language; the language of carefully calculated risks, the language of logistics and of military necessity. That was the only language Doolittle ever talked.

They responded not with fiery enthusiasm, but with calm

acceptance. They knew there was no alternative now. And Doolittle flew with them. He didn't choose the milk runs. Twelve days after Tafouri was secured he climbed into the cockpit of a B-17 and dropped bombs on Tunis. He went along as either observer or copilot on many raids, and the tired crews began to have a feeling of pride in their outfit and in their Old Man. He led a strike on Kaiuan and then flew a B-25 raid on the shipping at Biskra. During January and February he spent considerable time with the pilots. He'd come back from strikes against El Aouina and Palmero and report to the intelligence officer (who might be a first lieutenant) just as did the other pilots. He flew every type of airplane in his command. He went from airstrip to airstrip in his own Spitfire. He took off on missions from Algiers and Ain M'lila and Biskra and Telergama and Chateaudun and Kairouan. He heard the pilots griping about the B-26's. This plane was too hot to handle, many of them said. When it fell off, it fell off too fast, they complained. It was a flying coffin, they whispered. They pointed to its stubby wings. "It's a flying whore," they said, "no visible means of support."

The B-26 was a hot plane. Many of them had cracked up landing. Yet Doolittle knew that it was a good plane. How could he prove it to the pilots? The only way he knew how to prove it was to lead them in B-26 missions. He himself liked the plane. It was no DC-3 that allowed you to kick it all over the sky. The twin-engined light bomber was a sensitive creature, and you couldn't handle it the way you could handle a Piper Cub. You had to fly this airplane—it refused to fly itself. But if you treated it respectfully it gave you value received. And it got you home fast.

Doolittle flew in the B-26 as copilot in strikes against El Aouina and Decimomannu. When he returned from a mission the eyes of the pilots would be on his plane. Somehow when he flew that B-26 it didn't "fall off too fast." Doolittle would discuss the plane casually with them.

"When you come in," he'd say, "just be sure to maintain

plenty of flying speed. Nose her down and pull some power."

The resistance against the B-26 weakened, and eventually disappeared. Once you learned how to fly this airplane you really had something—and as the Old Man kept saying, "It brings you home fast." The sight of a grinning Doolittle, cap tilted cockily over one eye, striding into a briefing room just before take-off to announce that he'd like to go along, became a familiar one to the men of the 12th. In all, Doolittle logged twenty combat missions during this phase of the campaign. He used a Spitfire when visiting the bases. Eisenhower, who liked to keep in personal touch with his field commanders, was constantly calling for Doolittle. He'd hop into the Spit and wing his way to the Boss's headquarters at Gibraltar. All of Ike's original doubts about Doolittle had disappeared—on his recommendation Doolittle had now been made a major general. The toughest part of Doolittle's job was to say "No." He had to say it half a dozen times a day to ground force commanders who kept pleading frantically for air cover. The ground troops were being strafed by ME-110's, harried by Stukas and bombed constantly by Heinkels. To men sweating in slit trenches it appeared as if the 12th Air Force was a myth. It was hard for them to realize that Doolittle's primary job was not to provide an air umbrella for them, but to gain control of the air and to smash enemy transport and supplies behind the German lines. It was impossible for desperate, uncertain men on the ground to accept the fact that planes could be used most cconomically and to the best advantage in smashing Tunis and Bizerte, in making roads which fed the German troops too dangerous to use. The 12th Air Force had about 1,200 planes; Doolittle couldn't spread them too thin or their effectiveness would be dissipated. One day a young officer demanded air cover for a jeep that was going out to repair broken telephone lines. The lieutenant couldn't understand that it was more important to have every available plane in action five hundred miles behind the German lines than it was to insure the safety of four men in a jeep. Not only lieutenants, but divisional commanders complained bitterly that their men never saw a 12th Air Force plane. There was one man who didn't complain—the old cavalry man, George Patton. He knew exactly what Doolittle was trying to do. He knew that every time Doolittle's men put a German airfield out of commission, or sent an ammo dump or fuel supply up in flames five hundred miles in back of the lines, it meant that things would be easier for his advancing tanks. The protests of the ground forces fell on very deaf Eisenhower ears. Ike realized that Doolittle and the other air officers knew what they were doing, and they continued to follow the pattern of offensive air attack as they had conceived it.

The 12th Air Force continued to gain respect in the field where it counted most—from the enemy. Doolittle was harrying his supply line; he was inflicting tremendous damage on supply bases and on shipping. His staff was made up not only of superlative specialists but of good friends. They ate together, lived together, argued amiably among themselves, and on the rare occasions when one of them was able to produce a bottle of Scotch or bourbon (almost nonexistent during the early months of the North African campaign), they'd sit down and lift a few glasses. As the advance continued east they established new headquarters, but one thing remained unchanged; Doolittle and Allard always shared a room. The Boss needed someone he could talk to or remain silent with; someone who could forget the two stars on his shoulder. Jack Allard filled the bill.

Allard became expert in finding the paper pocket editions of mysteries which both he and Doolittle devoured. Night after night they'd slide into their beds and wordlessly grab their whodunits, and for a brief time at least Doolittle could forget the horrendous responsibility of sending young men out each dawn to die.

Doolittle's unorthodox headquarters and unorthodox personality attracted some unorthodox officers to his staff. A Georgie Patton would have been horrified at the lack of formality and the apparent lack of interest in rank displayed by members of the 12th Air Force at staff meetings, but for the most part these men were old friends of the Boss, and if one of them stormed, "Damn it, Jim, you can't do it this way," it would provoke the kind of free-for-all argument which Doolittle liked. He'd listen to the point of view expressed by everyone, accept what was good, reject what appeared to be too hazardous or unsound, and then make his decisions. Once they were made his team accepted his judgment without question. He had attended many executive meetings at Shell, and he'd watched the shrewd Scotsman, Alex Fraser, actually encourage his subordinates to question his point of view; he'd heard them oppose Fraser violently, and he'd seen the issues fought out thoroughly across the long mahogany tables. And he'd seen Fraser weigh the arguments and invariably come up with the right answer. Doolittle had learned a great deal at Shell that the Army never would have taught him. He had learned to trust the word of experienced specialists, to look with suspicion on the stand-patters and to listen carefully but guardedly to the daring theorists.

There wasn't much left of the harum-scarum Doolittle who had once been the bane of Colonel Burwell's existence at Rockwell and who had been known as the Chinese Ace. But occasionally the ghost of that younger Doolittle did manage to break through the uniform with its two stars. When he met a man like Speedy Powell, for instance, he had to respond to a kindred spirit. Group Captain Powell was the senior RAF man attached to the air staff. Powell, a bomber pilot, had played the leading part in the great documentary film, *Target for Tonight*. Powell had an English accent you could cut with a crumpet; he also had about every decoration the British awarded their combat fliers.

"I wish you'd find a mess of your own," Doolittle grumbled. "Either that, or learn to speak basic English. That accent of yours is apt to corrupt my men."

"It'll do 'em good to listen to pure English, ol' boy," the

irresistible Powell grinned. The Doolittle mess, as a matter of fact, was considerably enlivened by the smiling bomber pilot. He'd really been through the desperately fought Battle of Britain. This campaign to him was "a piece of cake," and his complete disregard for his personal safety, his unfailing good humor and his willingness to take the inevitable kidding about his accent made him a favorite not only with Doolittle but with the whole staff. The only thing he couldn't stand was inaction. When a stretch of bad weather grounded all planes and when the experts said that the weather would remain as it was for a week, he chafed under the strain of inactivity.

"Weather's jolly good west," he said to Doolittle one afternoon.

"We're not fighting anyone west of here," Doolittle said glumly.

"You are obtuse," Powell said sadly. "I'm talking of England, ol' boy . . . jolly, jolly England. We'll have to hang around here for another week or so, if you'll forgive the expression, sitting on our respective arses. But the sun is shining on Merry England. We could hop in the Wimpy and be there in no time."

Doolittle raised his head. He was tired and he knew it. There wasn't a thing he or the staff could do with runways ankle-deep in mud. A couple of days in London. . . .

"Why not, Speedy?" he grinned.

"My aircraft is fueled," the delighted Powell said.

They stepped into a jeep, roared out to the rain-soaked field and climbed into the big twin-engined Wellington (always called the Wimpy). With no bomb load and only a small supply of ammunition to hamper it the huge plane managed to tear away from the clinging mud, and a few moments later, with Speedy Powell at the controls, it was headed across the Mediterranean and aiming for occupied France. Doolittle relaxed in the bombardier's seat. He could always sleep better in an airplane than in a bed, and he dozed off while Powell roared out a lusty chorus of the unexpurgated RAF song, "All day long we haven't flown above five hundred feet . . . the weather it was blessed cold and full of blessed sleet. . . ."

An hour later Doolittle was awakened by the swinging gyrations of the plane. To his amazement the cockpit was filled with golden light. Out of the window he saw that the night was dotted with hundreds of exploding stars—all close.

"The Frogs," Powell yelled happily from his bucking pilot's seat. "Stupid beggars—don't know who we are. Their flak is really wizard, what?"

Powell managed to get clear of the flak area and Doolittle dropped off to sleep. A half-hour later he was flung from his seat. Powell was taking violent evasive action, and was first in then out of the clouds. "Now what?" Doolittle called, irritable.

"Only a Hun fighter, laddie," Powell said calmly. "Nothin' to fret about."

"It's showing a yellow light," Powell yelled at him. Doolittle saw the yellow light, but it wasn't moving. As a matter of fact, the yellow light was a million miles or so away. It was the planet Venus from which Powell had been fleeing.

They arrived unannounced and unheralded at a bomber base in southern England, and two hours later were in London. A shower and a change of uniform at Claridge's and both were ready to see the town.

"I'll tell the operator where we're going, in case Jack or Larry Norstadt want us." Doolittle reached for the phone.

"I'm glad you told headquarters we're staying here," Powell said casually. "Forgot all about letting them know myself."

"I didn't tell anyone we were leaving," Doolittle said startled. "Jack and Larry will be out of their minds. I'll send them a message where we are."

Allard, Norstadt and the whole staff back in North Africa were frantic. No one had any idea where the Boss and his RAF staff senior officer were. The message brought great relief to 12th Air Force headquarters, and Allard soothed the ruffled feelings of those who had done so much fruitless worrying.

"Don't ever try to predict what Jim will do. I learned that twenty-five years ago."

Three days later Doolittle and Powell were back in Africa. Powell, who had done most of his bombing at night, was anxious to master the technique of day operations, and Doolittle sent him off one morning on a daylight strike. The B-24 was new to Powell, so he didn't attempt to fly it—he was along merely as an observer. The plane, returning from the target, inadvertently flew over the front lines in Italy and was immediately shellacked with vicious and accurate flak. The pilot and navigator were both killed instantly. The copilot, hit badly, slumped from his seat. Powell dragged the pilot's body from the cockpit and sat in front of the unfamiliar controls. Two motors were gone, both wings were shattered, and the rudder half shot away. He fingered the controls hoping at least to find the throttle. He did and headed the broken Liberator toward the African shore, far across the Mediterranean.

Back at the 12th Air Force the plane was reported first as overdue, then as missing. It was a gloomy group which gathered at dinner. A mess attendant silently removed Powell's chair from the table. This was the thing that war never accustomed you to, and Doolittle found that he couldn't eat. He left the table with Allard and went to their office. You couldn't live with ghosts when you were a commanding general, he told himself. Doolittle tried to concentrate on the reports in front of him. He and Allard worked until midnight, and then the door opened and a battered, bruised figure of a man limped into the room. It was Powell.

He told of the flak which had killed the two flying members of the crew. He told of experimenting with the gadgets on the instrument board until he had found a few which seemed to react. By some miracle he had gained altitude, and then a third engine conked out. Half a mile from the African coast the last engine quit. Powell had managed to glide the huge plane to the beach where he had crash-landed. Then he had pulled the badly wounded copilot from the wreckage, put him on his back and stumbled a half-mile to find help. Now the wounded man was in the hospital.

"A bad show, laddie," Powell said sadly. "A bad show all around."

Doolittle recommended Speedy Powell for the American Distinguished Flying Cross for that. It arrived a month later—two days after the British officer had been killed while flying another bombing mission.

11

Eisenhower was faced with a rather difficult problem now. He needed an air officer at his headquarters to supervise and coordinate the whole British and American air strength. Many air officers thought Doolittle to be the obvious choice. But Eisenhower, apparently believing that Doolittle's real worth lay in his tremendous ability to actually lead a command in the field, sent to England for Tooey Spaatz. Henceforth Spaatz would be senior air officer in the Mediterranean, and Doolittle would head the newly formed Northwest Africa Strategic Air Force. This included both British and American heavy bombers and supporting fighters. Headquarters was established at Algiers, in the Standard Oil Building. One day Allard was sitting in his office when he heard a vaguely familiar voice saying, "Captain Johnson reporting as directed, sir." Allard looked up and his eyes opened in amazement. There was wizened-faced Bruce Johnson, their pal of Rockwell Field days, in the uniform of a captain.

"Brucie, how did you get here?" the delighted Allard cried out.

"General Doolittle sent for me," Johnson grinned.

"Like hell he did."

"Well, the brass in Washington thinks he did," Johnson said solemnly, "so for God's sake don't tell them different."

"Come in and see Jimmy."

They walked into Doolittle's office. Doolittle's jaw dropped when he saw Johnson. "I told you to stay out of this war," he growled.

"I know, General," Johnson said very formally, "too old, you said. You forgot there is just three months' difference between our ages."

Doolittle shut his door and sat down to hear Johnson's story. Johnson had managed to hoax the whole United States Army beautifully. He had begun by going to Jo Doolittle and telling her that he was off to join her husband. He'd be glad to take any mail along. Jo was delighted. She wrote to Jim, and then in another envelope enclosed some additional mail that had arrived for him. Then Johnson had gone to New London where he had Army friends and had talked them into commissioning him as a captain.

He had all of his necessary shots; he had himself fitted out in a captain's uniform, and then he reported to the Munitions Building in Washington. (The Pentagon wasn't quite finished.) He explained to the harried young officer to whom he was directed that it was necessary he be sent immediately to Algiers to join Doolittle.

"What for?" the puzzled officer asked.

"I'm not in a position to tell you that," Johnson said in crisp tones. "I can, however, show you some confidential messages I'm bringing to General Doolittle."

He handed the officer the two letters Jo had given him. They were unstamped and they were most certainly addressed to Major General James Doolittle.

"My orders from General Doolittle are around here somewhere," Johnson said coldly. "If you people here have misplaced them, don't blame me."

"Come back tomorrow. I'll have a search made," the officer said in worried tones. Orders *had* been misplaced before.

"That won't do, son," Johnson stuttered. "My orders are to report as soon as possible. They were transmitted to me verbally. I trust I won't have to go over your head to General Arnold. . . ."

"No, no," the officer broke in. "I'll have some new orders cut for you. But how shall I word them?"

"Say I am a courier and must be given highest possible priority to reach the General's headquarters as soon as possible."

"We have no transport leaving right now for North Africa," the officer said.

"Give me the orders and I'll worry about transport," Johnson said in the manner of one accustomed to having his orders obeyed. The young officer complied, and Captain Bruce Johnson went to the nearest airfield. He hitchhiked his way to Miami, to South America, to the west coast of Africa, and now he was in Doolittle's office.

"Give him something to do, Jack," Doolittle laughed.

It wasn't long before Bruce Johnson's obvious talents for "requisitioning" became apparent. He took a look at the small room Doolittle and Allard shared in the overcrowded St. George Hotel and immediately went in search of something better. No one else could find decent living conditions in Algiers, but Bruce Johnson had once wangled a piano out of the San Antonio Army post—this was child's play to him. Within a few weeks he had Doolittle and Allard set up in a beautiful five-room apartment on a hill overlooking the bay. It was complete with balcony and well-equipped kitchen. He managed to find a superlative cook and food that had no relation to the nourishing but monotonous Army rations the staff had been living on for so long. He slipped away to Gibraltar (making up travel orders of his own), and he made beneficial deals with British commissary officers. The Doolittle-Allard kitchen began to be filled with food and wines worthy of the talents of the delighted cook. It was inevitable that Johnson be made Headquarters Commandant.

Eddie Rickenbacker stopped at Algiers on his way back from a visit to Moscow, and moved right into the Doolittle apartment. As though to celebrate his arrival, the German Air Force made a furious night attack on Algiers. Rickenbacker and Doolittle stood on the small balcony off the living room, watching the almost unbelievable display of pyrotechnics. Two British battlewagons and a dozen destroyers were in the harbor, and they sent thousands of purple and golden tracer shells into the skies. The strong ack-ack defenses of Algiers were spewing their ammunition to form a protecting barrage over the city. Searchlights crisscrossed each other in bewildering patterns. Rick and Doolittle stood completely fascinated by the sight of a city fighting back against unseen bombers five miles above its streets. A sharp sound made both of them start. A piece of shrapnel as big as a man's fist had landed at Rick's feet.

"You know, Jim," Rick said seriously as he picked up the heavy piece of jagged metal, "a man could get hurt standing out here."

At that moment a bomb landed in the street below; its concussion flared toward them and knocked them through the open French windows and flat on their backs on the floor.

"I guess, Rick," Doolittle said philosophically, "this is where we should have been in the first place."

As the advance continued, Johnson always managed to be somewhere up front—not at all interested in Germans, but merely looking over the situation. His real enemies were the British, traditionally expert at finding the best billets for officers and men. If Johnson found that his British opposite number had located a ten-room house for his general, Johnson didn't rest until he'd found a twelve-room house for *his* general.

"They've been doing this sort of thing for five hundred years or so," he complained to Allard, "and they're real good at it. But hell, Jack, you know I've been wangling things and working angles all my life, so don't sell old Brucie short."

One of the minor miracles of the whole campaign were the quarters Johnson wangled at Constantine. It belonged to a wealthy and influential Frenchman. The Frenchman was too important to dispossess with a casual sticker on the front door, "Requisitioned by the Northwest African Strategic Air Force," but when Doolittle and Allard drove into the city, there was the immaculate white house waiting for them with the Frenchman and his family living contentedly in the cellar.

"How in heaven's name did you talk them out of this place, Brucie?" Doolittle asked.

"You just stick to your job and I'll take care of mine," Bruce said, ushering Doolittle into a magnificent bedroom. "This is yours," he announced.

"Get rid of that big double bed and put two single beds in here," Doolittle said.

"You're a two-star general," Johnson stormed. "You rate a bedroom by yourself."

"Who in hell could I talk to if I was in here alone?" Doolittle said. "Set up a bed in here for Jack."

Johnson shook his head. Oh, he and Jack were friends all right, but damn it all, Doolittle ought to have more dignity than to share his room with a goddamned colonel, even a colonel he'd known for most of his life. You didn't catch those British generals sharing their rooms with anybody. But Johnson knew when to treat Doolittle as a friend of twenty-five years' standing—and he knew when to treat him as a superior officer, so he went and dug up two single beds. The Doolittle-Allard-Johnson relationship survived the tensions and strains and separations of long years because it was based on real fondness and respect. If the three were in a room with the door closed, their tunics off and a bottle on the table, no stars lay on that table. Then they were just three very old friends. Each in his own way had been successful. They might spend half the night exchanging old lies and talking of new hopes on a completely equal footing, but in the morning there were no officers in Africa more meticulous in their observance of military protocol toward their commanding general than Allard and Johnson. In public, Doolittle was "Sir" to them both, and visiting officers, noting the snappiness of their salutes and the military formality of their address to Doolittle, could never have guessed that these men had been bosom friends for a quarter of a century. Friendship is a luxury few commanding generals permit themselves in combat. The commanding officer fortunate enough to have the temperament to treat men as military units is the one who suffers least when the casualty lists come in. Doolittle never did have the knack of looking upon men under him as serial numbers.

One day he and Allard hopped into a B-26 for a trip to an advance airstrip at Youks les Bains. As usual, Sergeant Paul Leonard was the crew chief. The field, only recently captured, had been under heavy attack and its runway was pockmarked with bomb craters. A jeep was waiting for Doolittle and Allard. It took them to the command post a mile away. They had no sooner reached it than a vicious German air attack began. A row of captured ammunition dumps on the perimeter of the field was hit, and thousands of shells began to explode. The enemy followed this up with a low-level strafing air attack on the field. This kept up for two hours. When there was a lull Doolittle said he wanted to get back to the field to see what damage had been done.

Colonel Tommy Blackburn, the base C.O., hopped into his jeep and they climbed in after him. He headed directly for the field. Just before they reached it another one of the ammunition huts blew up. They had to hit the dirt to escape the flying fragments of metal and machine gun bullets which had been stored in the hut. The explosions died down finally, but the hut was ablaze.

"That next hut will catch fire in about fifty seconds. Let's run for it," Doolittle shouted.

The C.O. drove furiously past the blazing ammo dump. Just as he got beyond it, Doolittle's prediction came true with a bang. The adjacent hut blew up, and again the air was filled with undisciplined and exploding ammo. But they outran it and reached the field. Many of the planes were on fire.

"As soon as it began, General, your crew chief taxied your B-26 down to the far end of the field," a grimy mechanic told Doolittle.

"Thanks. Let's get over there fast," Doolittle snapped.

"But, General . . ." the mechanic tried to tell Doolittle something, but the C.O. had already put the jeep into motion. They found the B-26 at the end of the field. It was completely covered with debris and sand. Several members of a ground crew were standing looking at the plane.

"What happened here?" Doolittle asked sharply.

"When those dive bombers came, General," one of the men said, "your crew chief and the tail gunner climbed into the plane and started shooting. They got at least one of the bastards, too, and then they ran out of ammo."

"I hope they got out of the plane and into a slit trench then," Doolittle said anxiously.

The maintenance man nodded. "Yeah, they did. They played it the way the book says. They dove into the slit trench right there."

He pointed to a jagged crater. Allard and Doolittle walked to it. Allard saw something shining in the sand. He reached down, brushed the sand away and found what was left of a hand. Hanging from the wrist were the remains of a watch. He picked it up. It fell to pieces—all but the back of the watch. He brushed the sand and blood from it and the words, "To Paul Leonard . . ." emerged.

"Paul played it right," Doolittle said softly. "He played it smart. When the ammo was gone he dove into the trench. They aimed for the plane, missed it and scored a direct bomb hit on the trench. Paul is dead because he played it right. If he'd stayed in the plane he'd have been all right, but only an insane man would have stayed in the plane."

"I'll take care of everything, General," the C.O. said. "Leave it to me."

Doolittle nodded. "He was a good friend of mine."

Allard dropped the remains of the broken watch into the

crater. Doolittle walked to the B-26. There was a lump of cold stone where his heart belonged.

"Is this airplane all right?" he asked.

"Not sure, General." The maintenance chief shrugged his shoulders. "This area was full of bomb fragments and stuff flying from that dump, and our own flak falling back. I checked the aircraft for holes; it seems all right. And I got rid of a lot of sand and debris that half-covered it. The plane ought to have a complete check before . . ."

Doolittle wasn't listening. He was climbing into the plane with Allard on his tail. He sat in the pilot's seat and reached for the ignition. The engines roared into action. He released the brakes and the plane wobbled uncertainly toward the runway. The backwash from the whirling props sent the sand and the debris flying off the nose and wings.

"She all right?" Allard asked.

"I don't know and I don't give a damn," Doolittle said tonelessly. "We'll try it, though. Leave that bomb bay open in case we have to jump."

He sent the B-26 hurtling down the runway. Mechanics, pilots, crewmen watched it with anxious eyes. Doolittle wasn't playing this smart. The book said that every vital part of this plane should be examined before allowing it to leave the ground. Doolittle himself would have been the first to condemn anyone who took this plane off without a check. But Doolittle had thrown the book away. If Paul had thrown the book away he'd be alive now, Doolittle was thinking.

If any one of twenty thin wires had been severed by a bit of shell, the controls could go haywire and the plane would crash. Doolittle had plenty of runway. He ate it up and then the plane lifted itself into the air.

"Seems okay," Allard said, knowing just how Doolittle felt.

"Yeah, she's okay," Doolittle answered laconically.

There weren't many laughs at headquarters the next week. They all knew how the Boss felt about Paul Leonard. Paul hadn't been a serial number to Doolittle. Paul had been the only man in the world who'd ever seen him cry. Paul had been with him during the most horrible moment of his life, and Paul, by choosing the right words, had made him snap out of it. But you couldn't live with ghosts. There was a war to be fought; there was an urgent message from General Arnold to be taken care of. There were a hundred and one decisions to be made. There were always human problems to be solved. He'd noticed, for instance, that Allard had been restless of late weeks. Doolittle sensed the reason. As head of A-1, Allard's job was personnel. But the personnel of this air force was presenting no problems. That aspect of the command was just about taking care of itself now that Allard had so thoroughly organized it. And Allard was eager to get into the operational end of the show.

Doolittle didn't know that Allard was suffering from what the doctors had diagnosed as thrombophlebitis, a painful and serious block in the veins. Allard had managed to keep this knowledge to himself.

"I've got a couple of jobs for you, Jack," Doolittle said one night as each lay in his respective bed reading his respective murder mystery.

"Okay, Jim," Allard said absent-mindedly, his attention occupied by the intriguing possibility that the idiot child might have been the ax-murderer.

"Hap wants a report on how things are lining up," Doolittle said. "I've got a written report, but that only states the facts. He'll have a thousand questions to ask about personnel, equipment—you know you can't anticipate these questions in a report. I'd like you to hop over to Washington, take this report to him, and give him any additional information he wants."

"Sure, Jim, sure." Allard put the book down.

"And there's another thing. Ted Lawson gets out of the hospital next Wednesday."

"Ted Lawson?"

"Ted is the boy who lost his leg on the Tokyo operation. I've been getting regular reports on him. Ted was a pretty active sort of guy, Jack. He isn't taking this easy. It's going to be tough walking out of that hospital on one leg."

"What can I do, Jim?"

"You can be there to meet him when he comes out. You get hold of your wife and Jo and Ted's wife and any of the boys who happen to be in Washington. I want you to throw the damnedest party . . ."

"That's enough, Jim," Allard smiled. "Will do."

"Lay it on good, Jack. I don't care what it costs."

"God almighty, I haven't spent a cent in six months. We'll throw this one together. When do you want me to leave for Washington?"

"Tomorrow is as good a time as any."

Allard left for Washington the next day. He spent two days with General Arnold, and when he was finished Arnold knew the exact score in North Africa. He knew what Doolittle wanted; knew his future plans. Then Allard met Ted Lawson when he left the hospital. When Allard told Hubert Blunck, proprietor of the Statler Hotel, about his plans, Blunck gave him the presidential suite. It was a good party, and then Allard headed back to North Africa and headquarters at Constantine.

He reported to Doolittle, told him everything that Arnold had said, told him of how Jo missed him, told him that Ted Lawson was taking it fine. And then he received a shock.

"I've given your old office away," he said casually. "You report to Van."

"What do you mean?" Allard was completely puzzled, shocked. Had Doolittle learned about his phlebitis? Was he easing him out this way? It wasn't like him to do it this way. Doolittle was no hatchet man. If he had to demote you he told you why. But this . . . .

"Report to Van?" Allard repeated.

"I forgot to tell you," Doolittle grinned. "You're our new Deputy Chief of Staff."

"You're a mind reader . . . a mind reader," Allard repeated, too overjoyed even to thank Doolittle for the new job.

"Deputy Chief of Staff, that's a nice title," Doolittle laughed. "Think you and Van can get along all right?"

"Are you kidding?" Allard's affection for Hoyt Vandenberg was well known around headquarters. "Who couldn't get along with Van?"

Allard was only able to enjoy his new job for a few months before the crippling phlebitis caught up with him. The Air Force medics said that Allard needed the kind of specialized hospitalization not available in North Africa. Privately they told Doolittle that they didn't think Jack had much of a chance to beat this rap. Allard, too sick to protest, was flown back to Washington, and again Doolittle had to pay the penalty of friendship. He tried to tell himself that in the future he'd look upon men on his staff impersonally—if you thought of them as serial numbers you never had to suffer when they failed or died. He'd steel himself from now on, he said, and then Vandenberg walked into the room and his resolutions died. He looked upon Van as he'd look upon a kid brother. Doolittle just wasn't the type to consider men as "expendable." Allard had once said half jokingly, "If you ever saw a tear you'd kick it in the face." But Doolittle was finding out that the toughest tears were the unshed ones—tears that dropped from your heart when a Paul Leonard was killed or a Jack Allard was sent home to die.

Every day there were major decisions to be made; the wrong decision might set the whole campaign back a month. The Germans were now being supplied from Sicily. A periodic air lift bridged the 150 miles between Sicily and the mainland. The Germans were using a new type of aerial freight carrier—the ME-323—a gigantic six-engined affair. Spaatz and his intelligence men had studied the habits of the air lift. His individual commanders could order attacks, but that would only mean the bagging of a handful of the big cargo planes. As reports came in it became apparent that the Germans were pursuing a methodical and easily anticipated schedule. Doolittle ordered his command to leave the cargo planes alone—he wanted the whole air lift to be destroyed with one smashing blow. His intelligence staff, along with Spaatz, continued to analyze the routes taken, the times of departure and the fighter escort given the air lift.

"Don't scare them off," he told Vandenberg, and the Chief of Staff sent out the word to look the other way if cargo planes were sighted.

One day Doolittle led a B-25 strike against some shipping in the Straits of Sicily. From the copilot's seat of his B-25 he caught sight of something rather strange on the eastern horizon. It looked like a horde of insects. Finally he realized that this was a mass of strange-looking cargo planes chugging along almost on the deck. With them were a dozen or so JU-52's towing gliders—all headed for the Tunisian ports and Rommel. He had five B-25's and half a dozen B-38's with him. The pilots had also seen the tempting targets below, and they were waiting orders from him to dive out of the sun to smash this aerial convoy.

Reluctantly he ordered them to turn for home. "Don't scare them off," he'd emphasized a dozen times during the past week. If he and his small group did engage this convoy, some of it would have been destroyed, but this wasn't what he was after. He wanted the whole damn German air lift. So he headed back for the base, and that night found it hard to sleep. He was like a quarterback replaying Saturday's game, wondering if he had picked the right play. Spring was approaching and the air lift had to be crippled or allow Rommel almost unlimited supplies for his anticipated spring offensive. Spaatz had decided that they'd make it a joint operation—when the time was right they'd drop the full force of the Coastal, the Strategic and the Tactical Commands on the German air lift. He kept in close touch with Doolittle and his other commanders.

Doolittle had all of his fighters alerted for the moment when he thought he could inflict a maximum of damage on the lifeline to Tunisia. Then, on the night of April 23, 1943, Tooey gave the word. By now Intelligence had given an exact schedule of the air lift operation. Methodical Germans who had sent their cargo planes off at six A.M. for nearly a month would not change now. They had taken off from the same six airfields—there was no reason to think they'd switch now; they hadn't been scared off. The fighters fell on the low-flying winged freight cars and their supporting cast of fighters with ferocious but meticulous skill. Within a few hours two hundred German aircraft, all laden with precious supplies, had been sent flaming into the blue waters of the Mediterranean. Doolittle's planes kept screaming back to their bases to refuel and to fill their empty ammunition belts, and then they were off on the hunt again. So were the American and British fighters and light bombers of the Tactical and Coastal Commands.

"Shoot at anything that moves," Doolittle had told his pilots. They cleared the sky of German planes and then went down on the deck to search out any shipping that might be headed for Rommel's ports. More than thirty surface craft followed the planes to the depths of the Mediterranean. Doolittle's fighters never let up. By day his planes, given the advantage of good weather, scoured the area, and at night the British radar-equipped Beaufighters searched out "anything that moved." Within two weeks the air lift had been completely destroyed by the combined British-American effort and Rommel's men looked in vain for food, for gasoline, for ammunition. Within a month 300,000 hungry, supplyless Germans and Italians surrendered and the war in North Africa was over. Congratulations from Hap Arnold, from George Marshall, from Eisenhower and from Spaatz poured into Doolittle's headquarters. One note, from Spaatz, read: "I would not trade you for anyone else to be in command of the Northwest African Strategic Air Force. Sincerely, Tooey."

When you go to bat every day you're sure to strike out a few times, and Doolittle had his share of failures. The one that rankled most was the mission against the Italian fleet—a mission which looked so easy and yet ended in frustration. His intelligence men had located the battlewagon *Roma,* two cruisers and a whole bevy of lesser naval vessels hiding in the harbor of Spezia. Doolittle hurriedly assembled four groups (147 airplanes) and lightheartedly gave them the assignment. It looked like a cinch. The ships were sitting ducks just waiting for the hunters. The pilots were overjoyed to be part of this mission. They liked to say that they could drop a bomb into a barrel from 20,000 feet, and some of their amazingly accurate bombing had been just about that incredible.

"I'm going to lead this one myself," Doolittle told them. "We've got a chance to wipe out their whole navy, and our reports are that the flak over Spezia isn't too tough."

The reports were right—there wasn't much flak over the inviting targets sitting so meekly there below them. The bombers made their runs, dropped their bombs and then the pilots turned to count the damage. It was hard to believe, but there was no damage. Bombs had straddled the huge *Roma,* the two cruisers had raised mountainous geysers of water, but the battlewagons stood untouched. It appeared as though some mischievous hand had nudged the bombs to one side just as they were about to smash on the decks of the *Roma* or the other naval vessels. And then 147 red-faced crews went home.

Three months later, when the *Roma* sailed to Malta to surrender under the terms of the Italian capitulation, a lone Nazi raider attacked and sunk her. His staff never allowed Doolittle to forget this one dramatic strike-out with the bases loaded— loaded with three big Italian vessels of war. But Doolittle didn't have much time to worry about the ones that got away.

He was too busy planning the destruction of the island of Pantelleria. This island, some thirty square miles of rock, lay between Sicily and North Africa. The thought of invading it by conventional means sent chills up and down the spines of the American and British land commanders. It was a little Gibraltar with only one harbor and no inviting landing beaches at all. German 88's, the gun most feared by the infantry, were embedded in its rock. Doolittle thought he might be able to do something about it. It would be impossible, he knew, to destroy most of the rock-embedded installations, no matter how heavy a bombardment you launched, but you might possibly destroy "the will to fight" of the 15,000 Italian defenders.

For two weeks Doolittle's bombers plastered the island by day and night; his fighters, flying low, kept the roads under constant attack. The incessant battering sapped the energy and vitality of the Italians, and now an invasion fleet approached the island. They were to land on June 12—on June 11 Doolittle's fliers were amazed to see a huge white cross painted on the runway of the island's airdrome. It was the first time in history that an enemy stronghold had surrendered to air power alone. Billy Mitchell must have done some celestial celebrating that day—the paralyzing force of intelligently directed air power had never been so well demonstrated. Admiral Cunningham's British fleet had helped (2 per cent of the explosive bombardment had come from his cruisers and battlewagons), and General John Cannon's tactical fliers had dropped 18 per cent of the total poundage of bombs, but this was in the main a Northwest African Strategic Air Force operation—Doolittle's men had hurled 80 per cent of the bombs which had completely destroyed the Italians' "will to fight."

No one had gotten his feet wet, not one Navy or assault trooper had been hurt, and now the planners could think in terms of invading Sicily and the mainland. The Sicily operation went according to schedule, and then Hap Arnold handed Doolittle the most delicate of all assignments—he was told to destroy the marshaling yards in Rome. Supplies from the north of Italy were channeled through these vital freight yards, and then sent south to Kesselring's army. Arnold felt that if these yards were put out of commission, all supplies would have to go by road, and he was convinced that the light bombers and fighters could dominate them easily enough. No one liked the idea of launching any air attack on Rome. President Roosevelt was against it. Tremendous pressure was put up by the Secretary of War to leave Rome alone. Churchill and Arnold were two of the few who felt that the Germans were using the cloak of the churches and of the holy shrines in the city to hide a tremendously important supply operation. Arnold and the British had complete confidence in the precision of Doolittle's day bombers; they felt that the target, which was some five miles from the Vatican, could be destroyed without hurting any of the age-old churches. Doolittle winced when he received his orders. He was told to alert the Roman populace so that civilians could flee, but he knew that he would also be alerting the German air defenses. He was told to avoid hitting Vatican City or any church "at all costs." Doolittle knew that one misdirected bomb hitting a church would give the German propaganda mill something to crow about. He didn't like it at all, but there was no alternative.

Many of the pilots were Catholics who could hardly be expected to relish this mission. Doolittle found some unexpected allies among his Catholic chaplains. They knew that hundreds of American and British land troops were dying every day because of the supplies Kesselring was receiving from these important freight yards. Some of these chaplains, who had been educated in Rome and who revered the city, were the first to approve of the raid. Doolittle said that any pilot who felt he could not in good conscience bomb the Holy City would be excused from taking part in the operation. Not one pilot took advantage of this. Never was a raid more carefully planned. Colonel Elliott Roosevelt, in charge of aerial reconnaissance, and his men took hundreds of pictures of the city; they blew up the photos, pinpointed the shrines, and every one of the pilots familiarized himself with the topography of Rome. Only the most experienced pilots were selected, and the raid took place on a clear, cloudless day.

Doolittle flew in a B-17 acting as copilot to Lieutenant Colonel Leroy A. Rainey. Rainey's group was the last one to approach the target, and his plane was in the dreaded "tail end Charlie" spot. By now the German flak had been well calibrated to the course taken by the previous groups. Flak burst all around Doolittle's B-17, but he was too busy to notice it.

He wanted to observe the damage done by the groups which had preceded this one. It wasn't easy because the smoke rising from the marshaling yards was now blotting out half of Rome. But he had to satisfy himself that neither Vatican City nor any of the other shrines had been mistakenly hit. To do this, he told Rainey to go in low. Somehow they flew through the murderous antiaircraft barrage without being hit, and when he returned he could say with the conviction of an eyewitness that the target and only the target had been hit. This was by far the greatest example of precision bombing the world had ever seen. Only one church had been hit by glancing bomb fragments and the damage to that was negligible. When the smoke cleared away Roosevelt and his men flew over Rome to bring back incontrovertible photographic evidence that the city had not been harmed. The pictures immediately released to the press were effective answers to the German radio, which, as anticipated, was now raising raucous cries against the tactics of the barbarous Yankees who had so indiscriminately bombed the Holy City. Supplies to Kesselring were immediately stopped, as Hap Arnold had foreseen, and in retrospect one can state without fear of contradiction that the destruction of the yards literally saved thousands of American lives.

Doolittle had bombed two of the three Axis capitals. This left Berlin, and above everything else he wanted to lead just one raid on the German capital to make a complete score. When Eisenhower ordered him to England to head the Eighth Air Force, which was now softening up the German mainland in preparation for the invasion, it appeared as though he might hit the jackpot.

Author's note—I have made no attempt to give a comprehensive account of the whole North African campaign. In this chapter I have merely sketched the part General Doolittle, the 12th Air Force, and the Northwest African Strategic Air Force played in the campaign. The contributions (just as valuable) made by the ground forces, the combined Naval forces, the armored divisions, etc. have been amply covered by General Eisenhower (*Crusade in Europe*), by General Mark Clark (*Calculated Risk*) and by other military authorities. There is no intention here to minimize the importance of any of the British or American service groups which played such vital parts in the winning of North Africa. This is merely the story of what one American officer and his staff contributed.

12

Just before he left to assume his new command a heartening message came from the Supreme Commander.

>DEAR JIMMY:
>When you joined me in London you had much of what it takes to exercise high command. I am not exaggerating when I tell you that in my opinion you have shown during the past year the greatest degree of improvement of any of the senior United States officers serving in my command. You are every day rendering services of inestimable value to our country.
>
>Sincerely,
>EISENHOWER

The fullness of this confidence acted on Doolittle like a shot of adrenaline on a leaky heart. He knew that he was being given a difficult assignment—the difficulties now seemed trifling. Bolstered by Eisenhower's warm confidence he plunged right into the job of reorganizing the Eighth Air Force to his own particular taste.

The Eighth Air Force, based in England, had three enemies—weather, the Luftwaffe and German flak. English weather was the despair of even the most expert British and American meteorologists. Proximity to the Gulf Stream made English climate radically different from that of the nearby European mainland. England accepted the fact that 240 of the 365 days each year would be bad. English weather invariably arrived from the west; it originated over the Atlantic and proceeded eastwards to the British Isles.

Facilities for accurate weather observations were scarce in the Atlantic Ocean, and all forecasts were subject to frequent change. At six o'clock in the morning, all of England would be bathed in sunshine, and Eighth Air Force bombers would take off for German targets. Often when they returned five hours later it was to find the whole island blanketed with fog. During 1944 and 1945, nearly four thousand heavy bombers were destroyed, or badly damaged, a large percentage of them not by enemy fire but by accidents caused by the unpredictable weather. The instruments which Doolittle had developed back in 1928 and 1929 at Mitchel Field while working under the auspices of the Guggenheim Foundation were now standard equipment on all bombing planes, and these instruments, of course, saved hundreds of aircraft and hundreds of lives. But there were still collisions in the air, still crack-ups. Planes which limped home after combat missions with navigational instruments damaged by enemy fire had little chance of finding their home bases.

Doolittle arrived in England on January 4, 1944, and on January 5 he sent his first operation against Kiel and Elberfeld, in Germany, and Tours and Bordeaux in France. It was a heavy strike, with six hundred fighters escorting five hundred heavy bombers. It was the largest single raid Doolittle had directed up to that time. An hour before dawn on that fifth of January, Doolittle was in the Operations Room at Eighth Air Force headquarters at High Wycombe, Buckinghamshire, checking the weather. His meteorologist told him that there was a nasty front approaching England, but that this front was proceeding very slowly. If it maintained its present pace, it would arrive over England in about twelve hours.

The weather experts never made recommendations; they merely presented the weather situation to the commanding officer, and it was up to him to make the decision as to whether or not a mission was feasible that day.

Doolittle studied the weather map intently. He probably knew as much about plotting the path and speed of a low-pressure area such as this as any man alive, and his experience convinced him that this front would not reach England until the planes had returned from their mission. He ordered the mission to proceed. The bombers roared into the dawn, and Doolittle sat watching the weather map. He had four direct phone lines on his desk, one to each of the division commanders whose planes were participating in the raid, and one to the Eighth Air Force Fighter Command.

Two hours passed, and now Doolittle knew that his bombers would be over enemy territory, evading German fighters, being subjected to the merciless and accurate flak thrown up at them by the excellent German antiaircraft defenses. Then his weather experts gave him a nasty shock. The slowly moving low-pressure front had suddenly begun racing madly toward England. The three division commanders, each at his own headquarters here, received the same weather reports. They awaited word from Doolittle. He had to decide which would reach England first—the storm or the eleven hundred planes which were now over France and Germany. If the storm reached it first, it might mean the destruction of half of those planes. But if he were to recall the mission now, it would mean that his first Eighth Air Force operation had been a failure; it would mean that more than a million and a half gallons of gasoline had been wasted; it would mean that the efforts of a hundred thousand ground personnel who had serviced, had bombed up and had tuned the engines of these planes, would go for naught; it would mean that more than six thousand pilots, navigators, bombardiers and gunners had taken battle chances without having had the opportunity of dropping a single bomb. He had to decide quickly.

The three division commanders all checked in, all secretly glad that the decision was not theirs to make. Every man in that Operations Room at High Wycombe watched Doolittle. Doolittle watched the map, and then he turned his head and snapped out one word: "Recall." Aides reached for the phones to relay the word to the three division commanders. Within a matter of half a minute the pilot of every one of the eleven hundred planes heard the terse message, "Recall." Some were already over their targets, others very close to theirs. But an order is an order, so the planes all turned and headed for England.

Doolittle kept watching the weather map. The low-pressure area was close now. It would cover east England in another two hours, but by then Doolittle knew all of his chickens would have come home to roost. Then, suddenly, the freakish English weather played a heartbreaking prank. As mysteriously as the front had spurted forward, it now stood still and then turned south to dilute and lose itself in the faraway regions off the African coast.

Doolittle walked out of the Operations Room. The sun was high now, smiling benignly, and there wasn't a cloud in the sky. The bombers and fighters all returned in perfect weather, their pilots wondering what manner of man their new commanding general was. Doolittle knew that he had played it by the book. He had refused to let his men accept a risk that could not be calculated.

Six days later the same situation presented itself, and once again Doolittle snapped "Recall." Division commanders who didn't know him well were free with their criticism that night. Twice within a week what they thought to be his overcautiousness had spoiled what would have been highly successful missions. Tooey Spaatz, who of course had the over-all command of the United States Strategic Air Forces in Europe, was burned up at his old friend. He had known Doolittle for twenty-five years, and this apparent indecision on the part of the new leader of the Eighth Air Force did not seem in keeping with Doolittle's character. Had Doolittle lost his nerve? That had happened before to air force leaders.

Spaatz called him to headquarters, and without any preliminary conversation said coldly, "It looks as though you haven't got the guts necessary to run a big air force."

Doolittle stood there, stunned. A reproach of this nature was invariably reserved for commanders about to be relieved in disgrace. That this reproach should come from a man whom he liked and respected as much as he did Spaatz made it the more bitter. The Doolittle of ten years ago wouldn't have taken this. He would have started swinging verbal punches against the harshness of the reproach. But this was an older and a wiser Doolittle. He knew just how Spaatz felt. Spaatz had organized this Eighth Air Force, had fathered it and had brought it to the position where it was the greatest striking air arm the world had ever known. He had always thought of the Eighth Air Force in terms of an offensive unit. To have two missions recalled within a week was to Spaatz an incomprehensible and shameful thing. Doolittle, sensing all this, excused his friend's anger.

"You may be right, General," he said quietly, "but I'd like to explain how things looked to me." He then told of the two accidents of weather which had resulted in the two recalls. He went to a map that was on the wall and pointed out just where the two fronts had been. And he told Spaatz just why he had decided, wrongly as it turned out, that both fronts would have reached England long before the returning bombers and fighters of the Eighth.

"I never take an uncalculated risk. You know that, General," he said formally, "and I refused to allow these men of the Eighth Air Force to engage in a gamble with the weather."

"That will be all," Spaatz said, a little sadly.

Doolittle left headquarters convinced that he was all finished. Several days passed, missions were planned and executed, and there was still no word from headquarters. Then suddenly Spaatz appeared one morning to tell Doolittle that he wanted to make a tour of half a dozen bases and wished Doolittle to accompany him. Spaatz had his own B-17 with him, flown by Lieutenant Colonel Robert Kimmel, an experienced combat pilot. Weather reports were excellent. As they were about to leave each base after their visit, both Spaatz and Doolittle, in the tradition of old pilots, checked the weather. At the last base they visited they received a "Weather fine, no change" report. They walked out of the Operations Room to be greeted with lowering clouds and heavy rain.

"We'd better head for home," Doolittle said.

They took off, but were only air-borne ten minutes when they found themselves in the midst of a heavy fog. Bob Kimmel, at the controls, queried a dozen air bases but found they were all closed in. The weather had completely contradicted the optimistic report of the meteorologist. Kimmel tried to go above the front. It was clear enough at 18,000 feet, but there were no airfields at 18,000 feet. He went down again, but the fog extended right to the deck.

"I can't locate a base, General," Kimmel said to Spaatz. "I'll just have to hedgehop, hoping to find a field where we can set down."

"You're flying this airplane," Spaatz snapped. Cool, skillful Kimmel, calling upon all of his experience, finally managed to sideslip the airplane blindly into a field. By sheer happy chance there were no trees, no cattle, no wires and no barn in the path of the big B-17. And finally Kimmel brought it screechingly to a stop just a few yards from a stone wall that would have completely wrecked the plane and would have lost the United States Air Forces in Europe their two highest-ranking officers.

Wordlessly, Spaatz and Doolittle climbed down from the plane. The gloom had deepened. Spaatz turned to Doolittle and said quietly, "Jim, I see what you mean now. You were absolutely right. I've changed my mind."

"I just hate uncalculated risks," Doolittle grinned. "Even," he added, "when a pilot like Bob Kimmel is at the controls.

And remember, Tooey, most of the kids flying our heavies don't have the experience of a Bob Kimmel."

A month later Doolittle received his third star, becoming the only reserve officer in the American forces to attain the rank of lieutenant general.

He received another surprise about the same time. It was a letter from Hap Arnold telling him that Jack Allard had been having a very tough time of it at Halloran Hospital. The medicos had wanted to discharge Allard from the Army, but Allard, weak as he was from the crippling effects of the dread phlebitis, had enough energy to protest. Arnold said in his letter that the doctors had told him there was a good chance that Allard could not survive. "He knows this, too," Arnold added, "but he says that if he has to die, he'd rather die over there with you and the Eighth Air Force than in a hospital. I know it's an insane thing to do, but I'm sending Jack back to you."

Allard showed up a few days after the letter had arrived. He was as cheerful as ever, although he had lost fifteen pounds. Doolittle had too much respect for his old friend to offer him some sinecure. If the doctors were right and Allard's number was up, he was the kind of man who would like to go out fighting. Doolittle pretended ignorance of Allard's real condition and promptly made him Chief of Staff of the Eighth Air Force. He piled so much work on him that Allard had no time to think of his illness.

Meanwhile, Doolittle had sent for Bruce Johnson, who had been in Italy. He was Colonel Bruce Johnson now. He arrived from Italy with a crate of oranges and a cask of fine Italian red wine. The night that Johnson arrived, Doolittle, Allard and himself sat up quite late, eating the oranges, drinking the wine and forgetting the fact that at dawn Doolittle would have to send more than a thousand planes and thousands of men over enemy territory. Bruce Johnson was given his old job of headquarters commandant, and he promptly went on what he always called a "scrounging expedition." He wasn't at all satisfied with his

General's quarters. He toured the countryside, and a few miles outside of High Wycombe saw a magnificent estate. This, Bruce felt, would be a fit habitation for the commanding general of the Eighth Air Force.

He drove into the grounds to find himself in front of a tremendous Tudor building with huge oak doors. He rang the bell with authority. The doors were opened by a butler.

"I'm very sorry," Bruce Johnson said, "but I represent General James Doolittle, Commander of the Eighth Air Force, and in his name I must requisition this home for the use of the General and his staff."

"I am very sorry, sir," the butler replied gravely, "but this is the residence of Air Chief Marshal Sir Arthur Harris, Commander in Chief of the R.A.F. Bomber Command."

Bruce Johnson stuttered an apology and retired in fairly good order. But a man who had managed to get a grand piano out of San Antonio in 1920 found it easy enough to obtain a really magnificent home at Bourne-End-on-Thames near High Wycombe for his General. Once again Doolittle, Allard, and the rest of the senior staff moved into a beautiful fifteen-bedroom mansion which had seven bathrooms.

Gradually Doolittle had been reorganizing his command. It had grown monstrously, almost to the point where it was unwieldy. He split the whole Air Force up into three composite divisions, the first in charge of Major General Bob Williams (later succeeded by Major General Howard "Slim" Turner), the second in charge of Major General James Hodges (later succeeded by Major General William Kepner), and the third in charge of Major General Curtis LeMay (later succeeded by Major General Earle Partridge). Doolittle had very little respect for the sanctity of traditionally orthodox methods; if they happened to be sound, he embraced them, but if he thought them unsound, the fact that this was the way it had always been done meant nothing at all to him. He was one of the very few commanding generals in the armed forces who had enjoyed high-level business experience, and more and more he became thankful to Alex Fraser and the other Shell executives who had taught him so much about organization. He treated his command the way the Scotsman had looked upon the Shell organization.

B-24's and B-17's had been mixed up in one of the divisions, which meant that there had to be two supply and maintenance groups to handle them, for the planes differed widely in construction and in operational characteristics. Doolittle immediately concentrated all of his B-24's—Liberators—in the second division, while the first and third divisions contained only B-17's—Flying Fortresses. Instead of having the fighters in a separate command, he assigned fighter groups to each of the divisions, and now each division had an entity of its own and could operate independently of the other two. His staff now consisted of hand-picked, experienced men. By May 1 the Eighth Air Force began to reach its long tentacles into the heart of Germany.

General Hodges was needed in Washington by Hap Arnold, and Bill Kepner, who had begun life as a private in the Marines, who had gone through World War I, and who was a tough, aggressive battler, was put in charge of the second division. Previously he had been in charge of the fighters. When Doolittle first visited his command he noticed placards on the wall with the motto, "The first duty of the Eighth Air Force fighters is to bring the bombers back alive." This was a negation of Doolittle's attitude in regard to fighters. An airplane to him was strictly an offensive weapon, and now that he had the magnificent P-47's and P-51's, he felt that they were too important to be mere nursemaids to the bombers.

"Where in hell did these signs come from?" he asked Kepner.

Kepner shrugged his shoulders in disgust. "They've been here for months. Orders from above."

"Get rid of 'em right away," Doolittle said. "Put up some new signs. Have them read, 'The first duty of our fighters is to destroy German fighters.'"

Kepner's face lit up in a smile. "Do you mean to say that at last we are going to let our fighters take the offensive?"

"Damn right I do," Doolittle said. "We'll always have a few fighters giving close cover to the bombers to take care of any attackers who get through. But order the majority of the fighters to go out looking for Huns ahead of the bombing formations. Tell them to chase them all over the sky. Tell them to chase them down to the ground. Tell them to destroy them on the ground. Before we can ever invade Europe we've got to destroy their whole fighter command."

"This," General Kepner said softly, "is what I've been waiting for."

Doolittle and Kepner had the same basic philosophy of aerial warfare, a philosophy not shared by all air force leaders. They felt that if fighter planes merely sat above the bombers waiting for German fighters to attack, the losses to American aircraft would be considerable and continuous. As a matter of fact, they were considerable. When Doolittle took over the Eighth Air Force, the average loss per mission was 6 per cent. But now the fighters began to roam the skies searching out enemy aircraft. German fighters found it difficult to get close to the bombers. (By the end of the war the loss was only six-tenths of one per cent, and many of these were "operational"—noncombat—losses.)

One day Doolittle ordered an eight-hundred-bomber raid on Hanover and Brunswick in Germany. They were escorted by five hundred fighters. That night eight hundred bombers and five hundred fighters returned. It was the first time that a big-scale air attack had been conducted without a single casualty. That meant a lot to the pilots and crewmen of the Eighth Air Force. By now their confidence in their commanding general was well established.

He did issue one order which shocked them. He had studied the flight records carefully and thought it was time for a new approach. During its early stages the Eighth Air Force had suffered severe casualties. A crew which survived twenty-five missions was relieved of further combat duties. Pilots aimed grimly for that magic number knowing that if they made it they could sit the rest of the war out in some relatively soft spot. But as the casualty rate diminished reaching the twenty-fifth mission no longer was looked upon as a miracle—more than 50 per cent of the crews were completing twenty-five missions now. And as the Eighth Air Force fighters roamed further and higher and more and more Luftwaffe Me-109's fell to their guns the bombers began to enjoy even longer life expectancy. Doolittle rescinded the order that a crew which had completed twenty-five missions would henceforth be put on milk runs. He raised the number of combat missions to thirty. It was the most unpopular order Doolittle ever issued but he was on firm ground and he knew it.

"Here is how I figure it," he told a grim-faced group of bomber pilots. "It takes a bomber crew about ten missions to learn its trade. Very few crews do accurate bombing during those first ten missions. Then a crew does a pretty good job during its next fifteen missions. By the time it's had its twenty-five missions it has really reached its peak of maximum efficiency. Then we take it off the line. That just doesn't make sense. A crew that has been through twenty-five missions knows how to take care of itself; it knows the tricks of evading flak and of getting away from German fighters. I know it was different a year ago but you men aren't flying suicide missions now. Study the charts and you'll see that most crews which have made more than twenty missions come home all right. More important, our average loss rate is dropping steadily."

They studied the charts and although they didn't like it they knew that he was right. As the casualty rate dropped further, Doolittle raised the combat requirements to thirty-five missions.

Back in Washington, Hap Arnold was well satisfied with the progress of the man who had for so many years been his protégé. Eisenhower, one of the very few military commanders in history ever to use the phrase "I was wrong," by now had thanked Arnold for virtually forcing Doolittle on him. Eisenhower was delighted by the operational success of the Eighth Air Force, and delighted too at the way Doolittle had earned not only the respect but the liking of the RAF air chiefs. Eisenhower always emphasized the necessity not of mere tolerance of each other, but of wholehearted and warm cooperation, and Doolittle was one commander whose praises were constantly being sung by men like Air Chief Marshal Harris, Air Chief Marshal Tedder, and Air Marshal Cunningham, the New Zealander whose nickname was "Maori." General George Marshall too was immensely satisfied with the Eighth Air Force and with Doolittle.

There had been many behind-the-scenes battles as to how the war would ultimately be won. There were many high-ranking British and American commanders who were advocates of immediate invasion; they talked in terms of simultaneous strikes spread over the continent from Norway all the way south to Spain. Stalin too was almost insultingly persistent in urging an immediate land invasion of the continent. From the very beginning, General Marshall had been adamant in his opposition to these plans. He believed that the only way to invade the continent was to breach the so-called inner perimeter of German defenses, that is, the western coast of France. Marshall did not believe in scattering punches; he was convinced that the only way to paralyze Germany was to throw one murderous, short punch, and that could only be thrown if the eventual invasion was made just across the Channel. However, this could never be done if the Luftwaffe enjoyed air supremacy or even air superiority. Marshall's idea was that the Eighth Air Force plus the RAF, which did most of its bombing by night, should by its constant attack eventually paralyze German production, or at least severely cripple it.

Doolittle's concept of the job of the strategic air force was simple. He felt that his bombers should constantly harry German production centers. Every time they hit a German aircraft factory it meant that a new factory would have to be built further inland. This meant not only a diversion of valuable material but of equally valuable manpower. He knew that no air force could completely destroy production, but he was sure that it could substantially reduce it. As his bombers slashed away at the big production centers he knew that more plants were thrown up hurriedly in the interior of Germany. And as he cut down German production his fighter planes were taking a dreadful toll of Luftwaffe fighters. His real job was to see to it that German fighter losses were not compensated by increased plane production, and he felt that his Eighth was doing this job. He knew you could never stop the production of German planes—but you could slow it down considerably. When his bombers were not bombing production centers they were hitting oil reserves and blowing up ammunition dumps and wrecking communication lines. Doolittle felt that this nibbling away at the German lifeline would eventually pay off in big dividends.

General Marshall, sometimes bitterly opposed even by American officers, said bluntly that there could never be an invasion until Allied planes were in a position to give the invading forces a reasonably secure umbrella. Doolittle, who had long ago recognized the military genius of George Marshall, was an enthusiastic believer in this theory. He drove the Eighth Air Force mercilessly, and he kept crying to Spaatz and Eisenhower for more long-range fighters. As the P-47's and P-51's began arriving in increasing numbers, so did the range of the Eighth Air Force strikes increase. No target in Germany was now safe from the Eighth Air Force.

Many of our Air Force generals felt that the B-17's and B-24's were self-sufficient and self-protective. There was, in fact, an influential block of Air Force officers which felt that daylight raids by the bombers could be conducted without any fighter escort at all.

Often during the North African campaign Doolittle had been forced to send his bombers out on raids virtually unescorted. But necessity had dictated that. He had never liked it. He did not think that the bombers had to be tied by an apron string to their escorting fighters, but he did believe that a certain number of fighters would increase the effectiveness of any bombing mission.

For a long while pressure had been exerted upon him to hit Berlin, but he had steadfastly refused until he had the long-range fighters available which could accompany the Liberators and Fortresses. He saw a bombing mission as more than an attempt to destroy German production. He saw it too as a means of destroying the fighter strength of the Luftwaffe.

Finally he felt that he could hit Berlin and that the casualties would be minimized. He planned this first daylight raid on the German capital carefully. He intended to lead the raid himself. Doolittle had led the attack on Tokyo, he had helped to bomb Rome, and now he wanted to hit the third Axis capital. A few days before the Berlin operation was to take place, Doolittle received very definite orders from Eisenhower that he was not under any circumstances to participate in the raid. Frustrated and angry, he pleaded with Tooey Spaatz to use his influence on the Supreme Commander.

"I agree with the Boss," Spaatz said emphatically. "We cannot allow you to go on the raid because we will not take," his eyes twinkled, "an uncalculated risk."

"We have been planning this operation for weeks, Tooey," Doolittle protested. "We've calculated every risk."

"Not the risk of pentothal."

"What in hell is pentothal, and what has it to do with hitting Berlin?"

"Pentothal, or some derivative, is being used by the Germans to make our captured airmen talk," Spaatz said. "No man has any defense against this truth serum. No one knows more than you do about the invasion. You know the time, the place, and the strength we will throw against the continent. If by any chance you were shot down over Berlin, they'd give you a shot of this drug and you would have to spill everything you knew."

Doolittle reluctantly agreed. Spaatz, of course, was a hundred per cent right.

The Berlin raid was a terrific success, and the heartbreaking loss of forty-three bombers and twelve fighters did represent a relatively low price to pay for what was gained. In addition to making the German capital a seething inferno and completely demoralizing all transport in and out of the city, the Eighth Air Force on that day destroyed ninety-two German fighters and damaged a great many more. This was merely the first of nineteen daylight operations Doolittle directed toward the German capital, but he never went on one of these operations himself, nor did he allow any of his division commanders or senior staff members to participate. They all knew too much.

The American and British war correspondents spent a great deal of time at the Eighth Air Force headquarters. Eisenhower, who trusted the correspondents implicitly, had told them in a general way of General Marshall's over-all strategy. There could be no invasion until the Luftwaffe had been made impotent. Ernie Pyle, who made a habit of avoiding anyone with a bar, an eagle or a star on his shoulder, made an exception of Doolittle. He found that Doolittle talked the language of the GI. He accompanied Doolittle on several tours around the Eighth Air Force bases, and he wrote half a dozen columns on the General. One day he wrote:

> LONDON, June 5—Here I've been gallivantin' around with lieutenant generals. If this keeps up I'm going to lose my amateur standing. This time it is Jimmy Doolittle, who is still the same magnificent guy with three stars on his shoulder that he used to be with a captain's bars.
>
> Gen. Doolittle runs the American Eighth Air Force. It is a grim and stupendous job, but he manages to keep the famous Doolittle sense of humor about it.
>
> Gen. Doolittle, as you know, is rather short and getting almost bald. Since arriving in England from Italy he has diabolically started a couple of false rumors circulating about himself.
>
> One is that his nickname used to be Curley, and he occasionally throws his head back as though tossing hair

out of his eyes. His other claim is that he used to be six feet tall but has worried himself down to his present small height in the past six months.

Jimmy Doolittle has more gifts than any one man has a right to be blessed with. He has been one of America's greatest pilots for more than 25 years. He is bold and completely fearless. Along with that he has a great technical mind and a highly perfected education in engineering.

In addition to his professional skill he is one of the most engaging humans you ever ran across. His voice is clear and keen; he talks with animation, and his tone carries a sense of quick and right decisions.

He is one of the greatest of storytellers. He is the only man I've ever known who can tell stories all evening long and never tell one you've heard before. He can tell them in any dialect, from Swedish to Chinese.

Above all he loves to tell stories on himself. Here is an example:

The other day he had his plane set up for a flight to northern England. The weather turned awful, and one of his crew suggested that they cancel the trip. As Jimmy said, he would probably have canceled it himself, but when the junior officer suggested it he sort of had to go ahead and go.

They were hanging around the operations room, getting the latest reports. The crew thought Gen. Doolittle had left the room. The junior officers were talking about the dangers of making the trip in such weather. They didn't think the General ought to take the chance. And then he overheard one of them say:

"I don't think the b—— gives a damn about the weather."

The poor officer almost died when he discovered that the General had heard this.

Other passengers said that throughout this flight this benighted fellow just sat staring at the floor and now and then shaking his head like a condemned man.

The General thinks it was wonderful. No, he didn't do

anything about it, for he was flattered by the compliment.

"But only one thing saved him," Gen. Doolittle says. "If he had used the word 'old' in front of b—— I would've had him hung."

He tells another one. He was at a Flying Fortress base one afternoon when the planes were coming back in. Many of them had been pretty badly shot up and had wounded men aboard. The General walked up to one plane from which the crew had just got out. The upper part of the tailgun turret was shot away. Gen. Doolittle said to the tailgunner:

"Were you in there when it happened?"

The gunner, a little peevishly, replied:

"Yes, sir."

As the General walked away the annoyed gunner turned to a fellow crewman and said in a loud voice:

"Where in the hell did he think I was, out buying a ham sandwich?"

A frightened junior officer, fearing the General might have overheard, said:

"My God, man, don't you know who that was?"

"Sure I know," the tailgunner snapped, "and I don't give a damn. That was a stupid question."

With which Jimmy Doolittle, the least stupid of people, fully agrees when he tells the story.

Another time the General went with his chief, Lt. Gen. Spaatz, to visit a bomber station which had been having very bad luck and heavy losses. They thought maybe their presence would pick the boys up a bit. So they visited around awhile. And when they got ready to leave a western Fortress pilot walked up to them.

"I know why you're out here," he said. "You think our morale is shot because we've been taking it on the nose. Well, I can tell you our morale is all right. There is only one thing that hurts our morale, and that's having three-star generals coming around to see what's the matter with it."

Jimmy tells these stories wonderfully, with more zest and humor than I can put into them second-handed. As he says, the heartbreaks and tragedies of war sometimes push all your gaiety down into the depths. But if a man can keep a sense of the ridiculous about himself he is all right. Jimmy Doolittle can.

—Ernie Pyle

Doolittle had two confidants during the difficult winter of 1944—Jack Allard and Jo. Every night he would discuss the day's operations and planned future operations with Allard, and Allard, knowing that Doolittle was merely thinking aloud, was content to act as an audience. He wrote to Jo as often as he could, and more than once he found himself quite unconsciously putting down his whole philosophy on paper. He felt better after he had unburdened himself in these letters. Ever since 1917, when they emerged from the Los Angeles City Hall with $20 between them, he had confided in Jo. Over the years Jo had proven herself to be a wonderful listener. Doolittle had always been an extrovert; it was against his nature to keep things bottled up within himself. But if you are wearing three stars on your shoulder, your responsibilities are such that you have to guard your tongue. A lieutenant general was not allowed even the privilege of sorrowing when men under his command were killed. He had to present an impassive countenance to his staff. He had to present at least the outward appearance of cold objectivity. This was difficult for Doolittle. Jo was four thousand miles away, but he could sit down and bring her closer by putting his innermost thoughts in a letter directed to her. One day he wrote:

> Colder weather, shorter days, and soon another year gone. How time flies—and this in spite of the constant desire to get the job done and return home to loved ones. Sometimes tired, particularly when things go wrong. Rested, refreshed and exhilarated when things are going smoothly. Responsibility! Responsibility to God, nation, superiors, contemporaries, subordinates and self.
>
> Command, regardless of its size or importance, carries with it both responsibility and opportunity. Responsibility

to superiors and subordinates. Opportunity to utilize to advantage one's attributes and ability. It is difficult but necessary to exercise command in such a way as to assure the respect and loyalty of subordinates and the confidence of superiors. To strive to avoid engendering antagonism and annoyance and establish approbation, admiration and even affection. The last objective is rarely achieved, particularly among our contemporaries.

I sometimes think that when this is all over I'd like to run a peanut stand. Would want it on a quiet street where there wouldn't be too many customers to interfere with my meditations. Actually, after about a week's rest I imagine I'd be restless and looking for work and responsibility again.

The responsibility of command was perhaps never better summed up than in this letter written just for the eyes of his wife.

If Jo was four thousand miles away, another member of his family was not. All phone calls to Doolittle went through his aide, Captain Thomas Barrineau, who had a desk just outside of Doolittle's office. One afternoon as he passed this desk the phone rang. He reached for it. A voice said, "I'd like to make an appointment to see General Doolittle."

"This is Doolittle," he answered.

"This is Captain Doolittle," the caller said. "I'd like to come in and see you."

A few days before while glancing over the roster of his pilots he had noticed the name "Captain Doolittle" and he had made a mental note to look up the pilot. As far as he knew he had no relatives bearing his name serving in the Eighth Air Force but it was an uncommon name and he had meant to call the man in and discuss the similarity of names with him. Now the pilot had taken the initiative.

"Glad you called," Doolittle said cheerfully. "I saw your name and meant to get in touch with you. I'm pretty busy these days but I'd like to see you. My aide is right here. I'll put him on and you work out a time with him when we're both free."

He was about to hand the receiver over to Captain Barrineau when the voice on the other end of the phone cried plaintively, "But Pop, it's me—Jimmy. Don't you recognize me? I just got here and I've got a package from Mom."

"Jimmy!" the delighted father shouted. "Where are you?"

"I'm a B-26 pilot in the Ninth Air Force," Jimmy said. "I'll be right over if it's all right with you."

"Get over here fast," the happy Doolittle said.

Occasionally Doolittle received a letter from one of the Tokyo raiders or from one of the pilots who had served under him in North Africa. He seldom kept copies of the various citations and commendations which came to him from Supreme Headquarters, and he never bothered to keep any of the newspaper stories which appeared about him in both the London and American press. He did, however, treasure letters he received from pilots who had served under him. One day he received a letter from Colonel Leroy A. Rainey. He had acted as Rainey's copilot on the Rome raid. He had recommended Rainey for a DSC. Rainey was now in charge of a training command in Texas. He wrote:

DEAR GENERAL DOOLITTLE:

From reports of your momentous achievements, I remotely imagine some conception both of the scope of your great responsibilities and the long hours their demands must extract from you. For this reason, I hesitated to divert your attention to the reading of this letter. However, on further consideration I concluded, from observations of other great men, that regardless of how occupied a real man becomes, he still enjoys his personal contacts which are void of requests and all objectiveness other than those of expressed personal appreciations. My letter is, therefore, an outgrowth of this consideration plus the consideration that because I no longer have the pleasure of service under you, which precludes attainment of the slightest official benefit by anything herein expressed, I am at liberty to attempt to convey to you an expression of appreciation deeply impressed in every member of my former combat command. I hope you can visualize beyond the limitations of my meagerly recorded inadequacies.

I seriously doubt that you ever realized how much we, in the field during the African, Sicilian and Italian campaigns, admired your leadership and protective foresightedness. We, on the receiving end, well know this was responsible for both our successes and actual survival. We especially admired you as one who, without having made employment of heavy bombardment his specialized career, anticipated our combat requirements and provided their solutions.

He went on to enumerate the Doolittle achievements that had most impressed him and his fellow pilots, ending up with:

I was certainly impressed by the unaffected calmness with which you accepted the AA hit we got in the nose which took out my lead navigator's oxygen system and temporarily "passed him out" for oxygen deficiency. I feel at liberty to tell you now that of all the many people I have observed under critical combat conditions you were the most composed. . . .

Please accept this in the appreciative spirit in which it was written and, also please accept my deep appreciation for the result of your effort in uncovering that buried DFC recommended citation for my bomb run formation tactics. I have just been notified it is to be awarded upon return to headquarters from my present "pedagogical" inspection trip. . . .

Most sincerely and gratefully yours,

LEROY A. RAINEY
Colonel, Air Corps
Hdqs. AAF Training Command
T & P Building
Fort Worth, Texas.*

* In 1945, Colonel Rainey, flying an Army plane, crashed into the Empire State Building during a heavy fog.

There wasn't much time for social activities during the hectic days of 1944, but occasionally Doolittle had to accept the responsibility for entertaining distinguished visitors. The Eighth Air Force had discovered that it numbered enough show people among its ranks to put on a performance, and a rowdy hodgepodge of songs, skits and dances was assembled and opened under the name of *Skirts*. It was intended for male consumption only, and Doolittle received a shock when Queen Mary "commanded" a performance at her country residence. There was one thing Doolittle knew he could not do; he couldn't censor the show or ask his men to tone it down. On the other hand, he could not refuse the royal command. He discussed the matter anxiously with Allard.

"They say the old gal is a very proper person," Allard said. "The chances are she won't get any of the off-color humor in the show."

"Well, we'll just have to take a chance," Doolittle said gloomily.

The performance, incongruously enough, was scheduled to be held in the village church. Queen Mary invited Doolittle and his staff to be her guests at a reception at Badminton, her wartime residence. The Queen Mother proved to be a most delightful hostess. She was utterly charmed with Doolittle and the suave General Allard. She had a guest book she asked Doolittle to sign. She asked him to sign on the page which bore the date of his birth. He thumbed through the book to December 14, 1896. There was one signature there already—a childish scrawl that had been put there many many years before. It was the signature of her son, who was now King George VI. The Queen Mother was highly elated. She told Doolittle that it was the first time she had ever had a guest in her home who had been born on the same day as had her son.

With the Queen Mother were the Duke and Duchess of Beaufort, the Dowager Duchess of Beaufort, and several other men and women out of Debrett. But Doolittle was very definitely the guest of honor. He was deeply impressed by the vitality, the humor, and, to his surprise, the humility of the regal mother of the royal family. There was one thing about her which impressed him even more. During the reception he grabbed Jack Allard's arm and said, "Take a look at the Queen's stockings." Allard did, and was amazed to note that they were not only made of cheap white cotton, but that they had been darned in several places.

Finally the whole party moved on to the church. The fine orchestra, which had been recruited from pilots, bombardiers and navigators, swung into the overture, and Doolittle whispered to Allard, "I wish I were dead."

The curtain finally arose. Doolittle said a quiet prayer and *Skirts* proceeded along its ribald, riotous way. Allard's hopes were doomed to disappointment, Doolittle saw with dismay. The Queen Mother caught the significance of every double-entendre. She understood the Air Force slang perfectly. But instead of resenting it, she chuckled, and when it was all over she asked Doolittle if she might have the privilege of shaking hands with every member of the cast.

Doolittle had another encounter with royalty. King George and Queen Elizabeth visited Eighth Air Force headquarters. Such visits were organized along the lines of strict protocol borrowed from the British Army. As the car drew up, the headquarters commandant was to open the door and greet the distinguished visitors on behalf of his commanding general. He should then conduct the visitors to the general. This is how it had always been done. There was only one complication—Colonel Bruce Johnson was the headquarters commandant, and Bruce Johnson stuttered. So did King George.

Doolittle called Bruce into his office and said, "Brucie, you go out and open the door of the car for the King and the Queen, bow to them, but if you open your mouth, so help me, I'll kill you. If you start stuttering, the King might think you're kidding him."

"I only stutter when I'm nervous," Bruce protested, "and meeting these two won't make me nervous."

Bruce was right—he wasn't nervous, he didn't stutter, and the visit was a great success.

Doolittle took a few hours off from directing the Eighth to participate in a celebration being held at Wood River, Illinois. It was the tenth anniversary of the sale Shell had made to the Army of 100-octane. On that day (April 30, 1934) the Wood River plant, by straining all of its resources, had managed to produce the thousand gallons the Army had ordered. Now, ten years later, the plant was producing thousands of barrels of 100-octane a week. In 1934, two thirty-foot towers housed the twin catalytic cracking units; now there were two 200-foot "cat crackers" at work.

Alexander Fraser and Secretary of War Robert Patterson spoke at the memorial anniversary celebration, and Doolittle, sitting in a room at London's B.B.C., heard them discuss the growth of 100-octane. He heard Fraser say, "In the fifteen days of the crucial Tunisian campaign, Jimmy Doolittle's air force used sixteen and a half million gallons of 100-octane; enough to keep 28,000 automobiles on the road for a year." He heard Secretary Patterson say, "Three years ago our nation was producing 40,000 barrels of high octane a day; today the petroleum industry can be proud of the fact that it is producing 400,000 barrels per day." Then Patterson, standing on a platform outside the plant in Wood River, introduced Doolittle, and his words carried by short-wave radio reached the five thousand who had gathered to help celebrate the event.

Doolittle said:

> I am happy to have this opportunity of expressing on behalf of the Eighth Air Force our appreciation to the folks back home. 100-octane is virtually the lifeblood of our bombers and fighters. It is through the use of 100-octane fuel, rather than the next lower grade, that the speed of our fighters is increased about fifty miles per hour and the bomb load of each bomber is increased

about one ton. This improvement in performance means the difference between success and failure in combat, between life and death for our pilots and our crews. Our requirements of 100-octane gas are tremendous, and as the pace of air war steps up we shall require gasoline in ever greater quantities. On our deep penetration into Germany we consume in our bomber and fighter escorts about three tons or 1,000 gallons of gasoline for each ton of bombs dropped. During April the Eighth Air Force dropped more than 24,000 tons of bombs. While carrying out these operations more than 800 enemy planes were destroyed in air combat, and more than 500 on the ground by our fighters and bombers. This is substantially more than the entire German aircraft production for the month of April. In addition to the 1,300 we destroyed there was a large number of German planes destroyed by the Russians, Royal Air Force, and the Ninth, Twelfth and Fifteenth American air forces. It is obvious that the existence of the German air force itself is being greatly depleted coincidental with Allied strategic operations. Among the targets in Germany hit in April were 28 factories producing aircraft or aircraft parts. Incomplete photographic reconnaissance, incomplete because of unfavorable weather for air photography, indicates that six of these were almost completely demolished and fifteen more were damaged to an extent which seriously curtailed or stopped them. This month we lost 358 bombers and 144 fighters. Many of the crews of those bombers and fighters will be retrieved. Nearly one-half of these fighters were lost while strafing German air fields. I am proud for our fighter pilots and bomber crews. Their magnificent performance of duty, and their heroism, will forever be a tradition to the American Air Forces. You who provide them with the means, when you produce gasoline, equipment or food, or buy war bonds, have reason to be proud of them too.

The *New York Times* took notice of the occasion by printing an editorial headed "Anniversary of Power." It read:

Ten years ago today, 1,000 gallons of 100-octane gasoline, the first ever to be produced in commercial quantities, was delivered by the Shell Oil Company to the Army Air Corps at Wright Field. The company commemorates that anniversary by opening its new twin catalytic cracking plant for the manufacture of high-octane gasoline at Wood River, Ill., and the Petroleum Administrator for War, the Army and the Navy will inaugurate tomorrow the national celebration of 100-Octane Week. There can be little question that fuel of 100-octane or better rating, set down in huge quantities for our Air Force and Navy fliers around the world, has been one of the vital underlying factors in our superiority over the enemy. The margin in speed and performance provided by such gasoline has heavily weighted the odds in our favor and saved hundreds of lives.

Many details of the wartime advances in petroleum technology, especially in relation to high-octane, must still remain on the confidential list, but it is a matter of record and a tribute to the petroleum industry that constant improvement in quality and reduction in price have accompanied the development. The first 1,000-gallon shipment delivered from California to Ohio ten years ago cost $2.40 a gallon. Today the price to the air services in bulk is less than the motorist pays for his day-by-day fuel at the roadside pump. Many companies and individuals have shared in the achievement represented by our dominance in high-octane fuel. It should not be forgotten, however, that among the many debts which American airpower owes to Lieutenant General Doolittle is his insistence a decade ago, when, as a civilian, he was in charge of the aviation development of Shell, that his company carry on energetically research in 100-octane gasoline.

During the months preceding the invasion, the Eighth Air Force hammered away constantly at German production centers. If the weather was too bad for the heavy bombers to operate, Doolittle would send his fighters out in pursuance of his policy to keep hammering away at the Luftwaffe fighter command. During the weeks preceding the invasion the Eighth Air Force worked overtime. And when June 6, 1944, dawned, Doolittle was confident that the invading ground forces would be able to operate with the assurance that attack by the German air force would not be too severe.

No invasion in history was ever planned as meticulously as the one which was called Operation Overlord. As always, the weather presented the one intangible element which was not subject to calculation. But the Air Force could make plans to cover the landings if the weather was adverse. Doolittle had a great many radar-equipped bombers. He sent them out over the French coast on dozens of tests through heavy overcast. He found out that if the bombers could get above the overcast, the radar was accurate in picking out targets below; targets visible only to the little screen on the instrument board. He and Tedder went over the results of the tests carefully.

"Weather conditions won't bother us," Doolittle said, "if we can take off and then go above the overcast. We'll have to bomb just ahead of our troops, and we'll want fighters to fly under the overcast to check on the bombing. The radar plus the fighter check should give us a margin of safety."

Doolittle kept on making tests (everywhere except in the actual invasion area) on the assumption that there would be an overcast on D-day. The assumption was correct—the weather was so bad that Eisenhower spent a few tense hours before ordering Operation Overlord to proceed as planned. There was a solid overcast, but happily it did not extend to the ground. The bombers could go above it and the fighters could fly below it to check the bombing. The margin of safety which Doolittle had insisted upon to prevent bombs falling on the invasion troops was more than adequate; not one American life was lost as the result of bombing, even though the pilots and bombardiers high above couldn't even see the ground. Actually Doolittle felt afterwards that he had erred on the side of conservatism. Just behind Omaha Beach a German division had been practicing anti-invasion maneuvers. The Eighth Air Force, wishing to allow the assault troops a generous margin, left an unsoftened strip which by sheer ill luck contained the German division. The bombs, falling too far inland, missed them entirely and gave them a chance to harass the men who landed on Omaha Beach.

Doolittle could not sit at headquarters on D-day. He took off at 4:30 that morning, flying a P-38, so that he could observe just what was going on. General Partridge, who commanded the Eighth Air Force Third Division, flew another P-38. They were constantly in touch with Eighth headquarters. The thing that delighted Doolittle above everything else was the fact that although he ranged all over the invasion area that day, he never once encountered an enemy fighter. Twenty-four hours after H-hour, the London newspapers were asking in wonderment, "Where is the Luftwaffe?" Doolittle knew where the Luftwaffe was—for a solid year he had been nibbling away at it. Today his long-term policy of seeking out the German fighters was paying off.

As the invasion forces moved steadily on, the old team of Doolittle and Patton, which had worked so effectively in North Africa, again proved its worth. Most of Patton's relations were, of course, with the Tactical Command, a branch of Hoyt Vandenberg's Ninth Air Force. But Patton was one ground general who had the imagination to appreciate the tremendous importance of strategic air power, and he and Doolittle were constantly exploring the possibilities of long-range knockout punches. Correspondence constantly sparkled between the two dynamic commanders. Neither bothered to couch his messages in formalized military language. Once, when Doolittle did send a formal message to Patton, he received an immediate reply written in Patton's usual lurid language demanding to know why they couldn't be less sticky with each other.

In a postscript to the communication Patton asked if he could watch one of Doolittle's air attacks.

Once, when a bomber crew, after hitting a target ahead of Patton's forces, had been forced to bail out near his Third Army headquarters, Patton chose the opportunity of paying Doolittle an oblique compliment. He decorated each of the airmen. He sent Doolittle a copy of the official citation, and because it was official he had to exercise unaccustomed restraint. However, with the citation was a penciled note to Doolittle which advised him not to get stuck up because he wrote to him so formally.

Sometimes Patton's armor advanced so rapidly and so far ahead of schedule that the air units giving him ground cover failed to keep up with him. One day late in December his forces were mistakenly strafed by light bombers and fighters of the Ninth and Eighth Air Forces. They had no idea that Patton had moved ahead so quickly, and had thought the armor beneath them to be German tanks. Patton's cry of rage filled the whole European theater, and Tooey Spaatz gathered Doolittle and Vandenberg and suggested they all pay Georgie a visit to soothe his understandably ruffled spirits. They flew to Patton's headquarters and gave profuse apologies. It being New Year's Eve anyway, Patton mellowed under the sincerity of the apologies and the four men spent a convivial evening together.

The next day they started back to their respective headquarters. Doolittle flew a C-45 (a twin-engined Beechcraft) with Spaatz as his passenger, while Vandenberg flew another similar aircraft. Shortly after their take-off Doolittle noticed fiery tracer shells bursting uncomfortably close to his plane. Thinking a German fighter was on his tail he dove for the deck, with Vandenberg right behind him. Both Doolittle and Van took violent evasive action, but they couldn't seem to shake the fighter or fighters off. They were almost belly down on the ground before Doolittle noticed that the tracer shells were coming from ground forces—from Patton's trigger-happy men. Both he and Vandenberg managed to hightail it out of the area. Spaatz was furious—not at the ground troops, who could be pardoned for not quickly identifying the C-47's.

"Damn it, Jimmy," he growled, "if we'd waited just one day we could have demanded that Patton apologize to us."

When they landed Spaatz got on the phone to Patton to tell him coldly what had happened. He expected, of course, that Patton would express his regret that his men had come very close to killing the top three American air generals in the ETO. Instead, the unpredictable Patton bellowed with laughter.

"You just can't stay mad at George," Spaatz chuckled to Doolittle as he hung up the phone.

When the Third Army captured Metz on the Moselle River, it was the first time that fortress had been taken by frontal assault since Attila had done it fourteen hundred years before. But the bad weather which slowed up Patton's tanks, and fuel shortages, bogged down his attempts to immediately exploit his advantage. He was very unhappy about this temporary setback and immediately wrote to Doolittle that he wanted him to throw the nastiest possible bombs at Fort Driant so that the Patton-Doolittle combination should not be humiliated before the world.

Spaatz, Doolittle, Patton and Vandenberg had worked together for so long now that they thought alike. They were all quick, imaginative and daring. Together during the last weeks of 1944 they concocted a plan which, had it been successful, might have shortened the war by months. Their idea was to get Patton and his tanks to the Rhine. They would send a thousand of the Eighth's heavy bombers plus the Ninth Air Force's medium and fighter bombers ahead of Patton and bomb and strafe for three consecutive days and nights. After this murderous around-the-clock rain of bombs and shells, the Rhine defenses theoretically should be pulverized and Patton could take off from Metz and race to the Rhine. The three-day blitz was to begin on December 19. But the great plan was contradicted by the German General Staff, which at this propitious moment had ordered the all-out attack which resulted in the historic breakthrough, and now the Battle of the Bulge became a defensive instead of an offensive operation. Everything else now was subordinated to the task of saving the ground troops who had been trapped by the brilliant German maneuver. The Germans were helped by the fact that the weather made flying virtually impossible.

At night Doolittle would huddle with his chief lieutenants, Pat Partridge, Bill Kepner and Slim Turner. The wind would be howling outside, sending swirling drifts of snow across the field.

"I can't order men to fly in this weather," Doolittle said hopelessly.

"You don't have to order them to fly, Jimmy," Partridge said calmly. "They insist upon flying."

"They know the horrible spot the infantry is in," Turner added. "They're willing to risk the weather, Jimmy, to get those kids out of that predicament."

For ten dreadful days and nights the men of the Eighth Air Force flew in weather such as no air force had ever flown through. Their operational losses were far in excess of losses by enemy action.

The Eighth Air Force flew, dropping nearly a hundred thousand tons of bombs at the supply lines which were feeding the German front. Vandenberg's Ninth Air Force flew too, giving the troops the "air-ground" support so vitally needed. Each morning through fog and sleet and rain, Doolittle's bombers lumbered off runways dimly outlined by red flares. They felt their way into the sky, they crept toward their targets and returned hours later, surviving only by the magic of the instruments Doolittle and Sperry and Kollsman had developed nearly twenty years before.

On Christmas Eve, 1944, Doolittle sent off 2,056 bombers and 1,024 fighters, the largest single mission of the war. These were grim days, and there was little laughter around Eighth Air Force headquarters. When it was all over and the Germans had been rolled back, Doolittle was able to experience the satisfaction that few Strategic Air Force commanders ever felt; he saw hundreds of German tanks, trucks and airplanes on the ground completely untouched, but which had been made unusable because the bombing of supply lines had prevented oil, gasoline and ammunition from reaching them.

It had been a beautifully coordinated attack with the Eighth, the RAF Bomber Command, the RAF Tactical Command and the American Ninth all cooperating in perfect harmony. Had not the German supplies been cut off by the strategic bombing, most military men felt that the all-important city of Antwerp could not have been saved.

By now the V-2's were being launched against London and the Eighth was given the job of ferreting out and destroying their production centers. This was one of the most difficult jobs of the war. The intelligence was good, the chief V-2 breeding spot was found. It turned out to be a hill with subterranean passages and it also proved to be absolutely impregnable to bombing. You couldn't destroy this amazing underground factory but you could harry the supply lines and at least minimize production. Before the V-2 was able to become a vital factor Berlin had been ruined and the German war effort had collapsed.

And then it was all over. Doolittle received orders to move his Eighth Air Force to the Far East and to establish headquarters at Okinawa. He sent Bruce Johnson out ahead of him, but for once the indefatigable Brucie fell down on the job. There were no magnificent Tunisian pleasure palaces to requisition on Okinawa. There were no ancient Tudor buildings. The best he could do for his General was a tent with a mud floor.

Doolittle was received with something less than enthusiasm by General MacArthur. This puzzled him, until one of MacArthur's aides showed him a clipping from a London newspaper which someone had sent the Supreme Commander in the Far East. It was written by some overzealous journalistic friend of Doolittle's, and MacArthur was understandably annoyed to see the headline, which read:

DOOLITTLE TO SHOW MACARTHUR
HOW TO WIN PACIFIC WAR

Doolittle reached Okinawa two months before two atomic bombs ushered in V-J Day. A few days later he stood on the deck of the battleship *Missouri,* watching the Japanese representatives sign the articles of surrender. But he found it difficult to keep his attention on them. He raised his eyes and looked across Tokyo Bay. It looked different now than it had three years before, when he had roared across this same bay as a lieutenant colonel.

13

Jack Allard hadn't died after all. He'd just been too busy to bother with anything like thrombophlebitis. But now it was all over and Allard no longer had a war on his hands. He received a message from Doolittle one day late in September, 1945, saying that he'd be home within twenty-four hours.

"Phone Charlie Rochester at the Lexington," the message said. Allard phoned Rochester and he phoned a few others and when Doolittle arrived the suite Rochester had for him at the Lexington was bulging. Jo was there and Tooey Spaatz, to say nothing of a dozen Shell men and twice that many pilots and Army officers. Jo's heart was full that night; the war was over and her three men were safe. Captain Jimmy Junior had returned a few days before and young John, a year too young to have enlisted, was now a West Point cadet. When Doolittle walked in he was pounced on by Allard and Bruce Johnson. Doolittle, Johnson and Allard had begun their friendship twenty-seven years before over a drink in a hotel in Dallas, Texas. Nothing had happened during those twenty-seven years to mar the friendship of these three men. Jo looked at the three of them with warm eyes. They touched glasses and grinned at each other; they didn't need words—these three.

Doolittle had the same twinkle in his eyes, the same infectious grin, the same jaunty air—he didn't have quite as much hair but otherwise Jo thought he looked about the same. Bruce Johnson didn't stutter as much, there were only a few touches of gray in his closely cropped hair; he was as wiry and lean as he had been that day at Camp Dick in 1918 when he'd said to Doolittle, "Take off your shirt and get into a pair of gym shoes." Jack Allard, his shock of gray hair contradicting the youthful lines of his face, had gained only four pounds in the past twenty-seven years; he was still as casually debonair as he'd been the day in Texas when he'd met another young pilot and he'd said, "I don't know what you're going to do, Doolittle. I'm going to get out of this hellhole and have a few drinks." These three had acquired many new loyalties over the years but none had superseded the loyalty each felt for the other.

The word spread around New York—"Doolittle is back," and men left tables at Toots Shor's and Moore's and Gallagher's to hurry to the Lexington. Rochester opened an adjoining suite to accommodate the overflow but still they came. Alex Fraser arrived to throw his arms around Doolittle. "Glad you're back, laddie," he said simply. "We've got to talk."

"Whenever you say." Doolittle grinned affectionately at his old boss.

"Right now will do as well as any time," Fraser said calmly.

"In this madhouse?" Jimmy indicated the crowded room.

Rochester had sent some of the Hawaiian singers up from his Lexington Hotel supper room and they were strumming ukuleles and singing island songs.

Fraser looked around and shrugged his shoulders helplessly. "Let's slip outside for a few minutes, Jim," he said.

He and Doolittle walked to the elevator. They went to the lobby but it too was crowded. People recognized Doolittle and surged forward. Fraser grabbed his elbow and steered him to the street. An empty cab was waiting outside the entrance. He propelled Doolittle into it. "Drive uptown," he snapped to the driver.

"Where to?" the driver asked.

"Anywhere, man, anywhere," Fraser said, and the driver shrugged his shoulders and headed uptown.

"When will you be out?" Fraser asked.

"It won't be long," Doolittle said.

"I know you've gotten a lot of offers from industry," Fraser said. "You're a lieutenant general now and I know they've all been after you. However I have an idea that might interest you. We all want you back at Shell."

"I never thought of not returning to Shell," Doolittle said in surprise.

"Well now what was I worrying about," Fraser sighed. "My idea is for you to be vice president. Not an operational vice president in charge of aviation, or of technical development—just a general vice president. You'll be a kind of trouble shooter taking care of things that do not specifically come under the other departments."

"Sounds good," Doolittle grinned. "You've hired yourself a boy. Now let's get back to the Lexington; I've hardly had a chance to see Jo."

The cab was in Central Park now. Fraser tapped on the window and told the slightly puzzled driver to go south to the Lexington.

"There's one thing though," Doolittle said slowly. "Once you are made an Air Force general, in a way you belong to the Air Force. They may have special jobs for me from time to time. I owe an awful lot to the Air Force and I'll have to go along any time they want me."

"I know, I know," the Scotsman grinned. "Your first loyalty is to the country and any time the country needs you, son, you're free as the air."

When Doolittle took off his uniform he moved to his new office high in the RCA Building, the American home of Shell. H. Frank Brown was made his assistant. Doolittle was hardly settled in the magnificent office when there were calls from Washington. There have been calls from Washington ever since.

Canny Alex Fraser and his fellow directors knew their Doolittle. They realized that Shell could take full advantage of the large scope of his talents only if he were put in a spot where they could all be utilized. Fraser never actually gave his new vice president a specific directive as to his duties but in general they were:

1. To undertake special assignments delegated by the president or Board of Directors.

2. To act as Shell's senior advisor on all aviation matters.

3. To act as a technical advisor to the president and Board of Directors.

4. To keep abreast of engineering and scientific advances in a broad sense and to evaluate their relationship to the petroleum industry and to Shell in particular.

5. To assist in the establishment of Shell public relations' policies.

6. To aid governmental agencies if requested.

That last duty was understood from the beginning. It was always Shell's policy to make its qualified experts in the petroleum or engineering fields available to the government whenever they were needed. Men like Ed Cumming and Gene Davis (vice presidents of Manufacturing), Dean Hodges (vice president, Transportation and Supplies), and Monty Spaght, the company's top research scientist, have in recent years spent as much time in Washington and working on government projects as they have in the Shell office. And inevitably Doolittle found himself doing the same thing.

In April, 1946, Jim Doolittle was elected a director of the Shell Union. At the time of his election he was not waiting outside the Directors' Room to be congratulated. He was in Bogota, Colombia, with Max Burns (who was made president of Shell two years later) and was notified there by cable. When the holding company, Shell Union, was incorporated into the primary operating company, Shell Oil, he continued on the Board of Directors and was shortly made a member of Shell Oil's Executive Committee. He is one of three Shell Oil officers who serve on the Board of Directors. In the absence of the chairman and the president, he presides at Board meetings.

Shortly after he returned to Shell someone asked how he should be addressed. His swift answer was, "Jimmy, of course. If you have to be formal, make it Mr. Doolittle—not General Doolittle. I am now out of the service and as much a civilian as anyone else. You do not go around calling ex-sergeants and ex-corporals by the military titles, so I shouldn't be called 'General.' "

He was in great demand as a speaker, and the talks which he did give were generally concerned with aviation or petroleum. He had witnessed and had been part of the growth of United States air power since 1917. From his intimate knowledge of it, he was certain in his heart and mind that the United States Air Force should be a separate and fully integrated branch of our military establishment. In many of his speeches he presented strong arguments for unification, and in some quarters was looked upon with the same jaundiced eyes Billy Mitchell had encountered so long ago. He was sure that unification was fundamentally sound; that there should be one service for land, one service for sea, and one service for air. He was convinced that this basically sound concept would save the taxpayers' money, result in a more effective military organization, and that the establishment of a strong autonomous air force would be the greatest deterrent from possible outside aggression and that, if properly used, it could maintain world peace.

The battle of unification was finally won, and a separate Air Force established. The trend of the speeches then changed toward a warning to our people that the maintenance of peace depended upon an adequate and properly equipped military establishment—an establishment sufficient in properly balanced striking power to make the thought of overt aggression against the United States intolerable, and that lasting peace could come only through the efforts of the community of nations and the achievement of a strong world organization.

In April, 1949, Jim was asked to speak in Washington before the Georgetown University Alumni Association at a banquet being given to celebrate the convocation of Father Hunter Guthrie, S. J., as President of Georgetown University, the oldest Catholic university in North America. Before he accepted he called his good friend Cardinal Spellman and said, "Cardinal, I will be more than happy to do this, but I think that your people should know that I am a Thirty-third Degree Mason."

The Cardinal laughed and told him he had been invited to speak there because he was a great American.

When Jim returned to Shell in 1946 the airlines were for the most part flying DC-3's and DC-4's which did not always reach points that Doolittle had to visit. On his recommendation, Shell bought a surplus B-25 and had it slightly modified for civilian use. It was purely a functional plane and was not fitted with any accouterments that approximated luxury. It was noisy and cold. However, it provided fast transportation, whenever and wherever he wanted to go. Nevertheless, to his mind, transportation was not enough. He began to test in this airplane Shell's aviation products, and soon it became progressively laden with thermocouples, wires, instruments and recorders to take down flight data. As this scientific research grew, it was necessary to take on an additional crewman, an engineer, to watch the dials and record the data. Pretty soon the B-25 became known as the Shell Flying Laboratory. There was an instance of one product for certain type engines which in all laboratory tests appeared to be excellent. But at Jim's insistence it was not made available to Shell's customers until it had been thoroughly tested in the B-25. This was a case where laboratory results did not coincide with actual operational results. At the end of the test period the product was withdrawn from the market. A Shell competitor who had released a similar product for sale to the airlines, allegedly paid out rather large sums of money to repair the damage it had done.

Later when the airlines got a sufficient number of Constellations and DC-6's the speed of the B-25 no longer held its attraction and Doolittle gave up the aircraft. However, the research work that he had started was so valuable to both Shell and to the military that the flight testing continued.

One of the first calls from Washington was from the late Robert Patterson, then Secretary of War. He asked Doolittle to head up the Board on Enlisted Men-Officer Relationship. This board later became known as the "Doolittle Board" or the "G. I. Gripe Board." This board, under different auspices, could have been a whitewash for some abuses and outdated customs which hampered proper officer-enlisted man relations. It was not. The board offered thirteen concrete recommendations to improve the officer-enlisted man relationship and to increase a mutual understanding between the two groups. Nine of these suggestions were acted upon immediately and were put into effect.

There were calls from the National Advisory Committee for Aeronautics. Since 1915, when this committee was organized by direction of Woodrow Wilson, it had been one of the country's most important agencies. It usually works anonymously but its contribution to the advancement of both military and civil aviation cannot be overestimated. Wilson, the scholar, had the vision to see even in 1915 the fact that one day airplanes would play a big part in the defense as well as in the economy of the country. He set up the N.A.C.A. "for the supervision and direction of the scientific study of the problems of flight." Woodrow Wilson, far ahead of his time, realized that such problems could not always be handled alone by aircraft and engine manufacturers. He felt that if a pool of the nation's best aeronautical brains could be assembled to consider all the complex problems arising out of flying and then make their information available not only to the Army and Navy but to private industry, it would result in useful progress. Wilson was right.

The original membership of twelve was hiked to fifteen in 1929 and to seventeen in 1949. Today under the chairmanship of brilliant Dr. Jerome C. Hunsaker of M.I.T., the committee does research in the esoteric realm of aerodynamics, propulsion and structures. It concerns itself with such problems as the development of practical military planes which can operate at supersonic speed. Ever since he first heard the name Hunsaker when he was at M.I.T. in 1924, Doolittle had respected the engineering genius of the scientist and over the years they had become firm friends. When Hunsaker asked him to serve on the committee in 1948 he could only say, "Of course, Jerry."

The committee is composed of scientists, engineers and military men. All civilian members of the committee serve without pay. Congress, realizing the vital importance of the work done by these seventeen men, annually appropriates fifty million dollars for its research. The committee works miracles with this money—committee members insist that twice that amount would be needed to really do the job assigned to it.

Whenever a new experimental plane crashes the N.A.C.A. wants to know why it failed. Staff members investigate and as often as not come up with the technical answer. The mortality among test pilots has decreased considerably in recent years as the result of N.A.C.A. research.

"Let's find out what's wrong with an airplane on our drawing boards," Hunsaker says, "before we risk the life of test pilots. Accidents due to structural defects can be anticipated and prevented if we find the weakness before the aircraft is flown."

Much of their work is top secret. All of it is useful and, if little known to the public, is appreciated by the Air Force and by the industry which produces engines and planes.

In 1951 came a new honor and a new responsibility. Hoyt Vandenberg was Chief of Staff of the U. S. Air Force now and he needed help. Stuart Symington, Secretary of the Air Force,

Vandenberg, and the other Air Force leaders were trying desperately to create an adequate combat force in being and at the same time give proper emphasis to the Air Force of the future. Vandenberg appointed Doolittle special assistant to the Chief of Staff and his memorandum which went to all of his deputies read:

> SUBJECT: Appointment of Lieut. General Doolittle as Special Assistant to the Chief of Staff
>
> 1. Lieut. General James H. Doolittle is acting as my special assistant to advise me in matters of mutual concern to the Air Materiel Command and the Air Research and Development Command pertaining to the establishment, organization, and operation of the Air Research and Development Command.
>
> 2. Problems in connection with this Air Force reorganization of mutual concern to the Air Materiel Command and the Air Research and Development Command which cannot be resolved by mutual agreement between the two Commands will be forwarded with a clear statement of each of the conflicting views to me for decision through General Doolittle who will study the problem and make recommendations to me. Similar action will be taken on problems arising in the Air Staff which cannot be resolved by mutual agreement between the Deputy Chief of Staff, Materiel and the Deputy Chief of Staff, Development.
>
> 3. General Doolittle will base his recommendations on the best interest of the Air Force as a whole, with due consideration to the continuing capability of both the Air Materiel Command and the Air Research and Development Command to perform their assigned functions and responsibilities.
>
> (Signed) HOYT S. VANDENBERG

Alex Fraser had retired now and youthful-looking Max Burns (another Scotsman) had assumed the presidency of Shell. Doolittle told him of the new appointment. Burns, as understanding as his predecessor had been, grinned and said, "Go to it, Jimmy, that job comes first."

Doolittle, in the language of the Army, was now wearing two hats: the hat of the Shell Company—and the hat that covered his N.A.C.A. and Air Force activities. He was changing hats constantly. He almost literally lived on planes now and Jo complained that he was so accustomed to sleeping in them that he could no longer get a decent night's sleep in his bed in their New York apartment.

Doolittle was in and out of the Pentagon constantly. Washington correspondents who saw him slipping into Vandenberg's office one day, lunching with Tooey Spaatz the next, leaving with Secretary for Air Symington at night, realized that he was busy with top-level problems, and one day one of them asked Stuart Symington just what were Doolittle's duties.

Symington grinned and said, "Whenever a problem comes to me that is really tough, I yell for Jimmy. It might be an organizational problem; it might concern the best road to take toward more efficient research and development; it might concern a method of saving money through proper integration of service missions; it might be a morale problem—it might in fact be anything at all connected with the Air Force. Van tosses the same kind of problems to Jimmy and he hasn't failed us yet. As with a few other men," Symington grew serious, "when Jimmy sings the national anthem he means every word of it. There's no job he won't undertake if he thinks it will help the country. The words 'public service' don't mean much to most men—when you ask Jimmy to perform a service for the country, he looks upon it as a sacred trust. Our only worry is that he won't be able to stand the pace. He puts in working hours that would kill an ordinary man. I guess," Symington added, "Jimmy Doolittle comes close to being my favorite American—he has brains, courage and business ability. He's got everything and he's a great guy in addition."

It was a case of shingles that finally made Doolittle slow down a bit. He returned to New York from a coast trip to find a huge rash across his stomach. The doctor said it was caused by nerves, which came as a complete shock to Doolittle. He'd never known that he had any nerves.

"Call it overwork if you wish," the doctor said. "Your system is just rebelling against the strain you're putting on it."

It was Frank Brown and Jo who talked him into going to the Lovelace Clinic in New Mexico for a complete overhaul.

"Okay, Brownie, if you'll go through it too, I'll play ball," Doolittle growled, and Brownie made the sacrifice.

Dr. Randolph Lovelace, an old friend of Doolittle's, together with Doctor Samuel White, put him through the works. They submitted him to just about every test known to medical science.

"All you need, Jim," White said, "is a good rest. Stay here for a month and absorb some sun; then you'll be as good as new."

"What's wrong with me?" Doolittle asked.

The doctor hesitated. "Organically not a thing," he said dolefully.

"In that case, I don't need a rest. Brownie, let's pack," he called.

The next day he and Brownie were back in harness.

He did take it easy for a month or so and then forgot all about his experience with shingles. His associates at Shell will wager that Doolittle puts in more working hours per week than any man in America. No one has accepted the bet.

During the winter of 1952 a series of tragic air crashes (three at Elizabeth, New Jersey) shocked the nation. Doolittle received a phone call, then a letter from the White House. It read,

THE WHITE HOUSE

February 20, 1952

DEAR JIM:

For some time now, I have been seriously concerned about airplane accidents, both commercial and military, that have occurred in the take-off and landing of aircraft, especially in heavily populated areas. I have been concerned about the loss of life and I have been concerned about the anxiety in some of our cities. I have decided to set up a temporary President's Airport Commission to look into the problem of airport location and use. I am delighted that you are willing to serve as Chairman of the Commission, and I hereby appoint you as such. Mr. Charles F. Horne, the Administrator of Civil Aeronautics, and Dr. Jerome C. Hunsaker, Head, Department of Aeronautical Engineering, Massachusetts Institute of Technology, will serve with you on the Commission.

The present location of many of our major airports was determined a number of years ago when the aviation industry was new and operations were relatively limited. Also some of the locations reflected special military requirements. Since that time both civil and military air traffic have been growing rapidly, and simultaneously our cities have been continuously spreading out toward these airports.

I feel that the Nation's policy on airport location and use should be restudied. We need a study that is both objective and realistic. That is what I want your Commission to do. In undertaking this survey, several major considerations should be kept in mind. On the one hand, provision must be made for the safety, welfare and peace of mind of the people living in close proximity to airports. On the other hand, recognition must be given both to the requirements of national defense and to the importance of a progressive and efficient aviation industry in our national economy.

Because of the urgency of the problem, I hope you will be able to give me your final recommendations within ninety days. In your work, you will have the full cooperation of all the Executive agencies whose functions and interests relate to your assignment. And you will want, of course, to keep in close touch with other groups concerned about this problem, including the Committees of Congress, local authorities and the aviation industry.

Arrangements will be made to meet the expenses of

your Commission out of the Emergency Fund for the President.

Sincerely yours,
HARRY S. TRUMAN

Mr. James H. Doolittle,
Vice President,
Shell Union Oil Corp.,
New York, New York.

Doolittle and his two associate commissioners enlisted the services of civil and military experts, and within a few days the President's Airport Commission was rolling along in high gear. They sent a questionnaire to the mayors of 102 cities which had airports; he himself visited thirty major airports to observe and check their safety regulations.

The Commission worked unremittingly for nearly three months, and before the ninetieth day Doolittle was able to hand a 116-page report to the President. Its recommendations were in large part approved. Doolittle and his associates did not suggest that any existing airports be closed; they did recommend additional safety measures. The most revolutionary was the establishment of the single, or parallel, runway system which would limit approaches and departures to two relatively narrow zones. For years it had been assumed that airplanes did not have greater cross-wind tolerance than fifteen miles per hour. The report said that this was an erroneous assumption. It stated that the faster the aircraft and the higher the wing loading, the less effect a cross wind would have on a landing or departing aircraft. Special cross-wind landing gear (as used on a Military C-54 test plane) was recommended for use in high winds. This C-54 lands successfully in a forty-mile cross wind.

The report was received with satisfaction by public, press and the knowledgeable aircraft leaders. Then Doolittle, with a letter of gratitude from President Truman, hurried back to put on his Shell hat.

Typical of his busy life is his schedule for August, 1952. He spent the first few days of the month in New York, but there was a lot of Shell business crying to be done in outlying regions; there was Air Force experimental work to be looked at; there were meetings in Washington that had to be attended. His schedule was:

August	11	New York to Washington
"	11	Washington to St. Louis
"	12	St. Louis to Idaho Falls
"	13	Idaho Falls to Richland
"	14	Richland to San Francisco
"	15	San Francisco to Livermore
"	15	Livermore to San Francisco
"	16	San Francisco to Chicago
"	17	Chicago to Denver
"	18	Denver to Rifle
"	18	Rifle to Denver
"	19	Denver to Calgary (Canada)
"	20	Calgary to McMurray
"	21	McMurray to Bitumount
"	21	Bitumount to Great Falls
"	22	Great Falls to Denver
"	23	Denver to Chicago
"	24	Chicago to Houston
"	25	Houston to Washington, D.C.
"	26	Washington to New York

A month later he and Jo were in Holland attending a meeting of the Shell technical men. One night the phone rang; it was San Diego calling Doolittle. A very old friend, Tom Lanphier, past president of the Air Force Association, was at the other end of the wire.

"Do you know that 1953 is the fiftieth anniversary of the flight of the Wright Brothers?" Lanphier demanded.

"Sure I do, Tom," the puzzled Doolittle said. "It's about six thousand miles from San Diego to the hotel here at The Hague. Don't tell me you made this phone call just to remind me of that."

"The Industry has announced a 1953 celebration to commemorate the event," Lanphier said. "It's going to be a big thing with each state in the country putting on an air show next September. The Industry wants you to head the whole thing up, Jim."

"I have a pretty full schedule," Doolittle said doubtfully.

"You can always make room for one more job," Lanphier laughed. "I'll tell them it's okay."

When Doolittle is sixty he can retire from the Shell Company. He and Jo bought a piece of property at Carmel in California some time ago and Jo has already designed the kind of house to which she and Jim want to retire. But Jo hasn't as yet given the word to the builder to start construction. Her husband talks with great enthusiasm of the day when he can give it all up and live in California and tinker in a garden and do a little fishing and go after a deer in the autumn.

Jo listens quietly and says, "Yes, Doolittle, it'll be just wonderful," but in her heart she really knows better.

The amazing Mr. Doolittle will never retire.

(1)

Literature and History of Aviation

AN ARNO PRESS COLLECTION

Arnold, H[enry] H.
Global Mission. 1949.

Bordeaux, Henry.
Georges Guynemer: Knight of the Air. Translated by Louise Morgan Sill. 1918.

Boyington, "Pappy" (Col. Gregory Boyington).
Baa Baa Black Sheep. 1958.

Buckley, Harold.
Squadron 95. 1933.

Caidin, Martin.
Golden Wings. 1960.

"Contact" (Capt. Alan Bott).
Cavalry of the Clouds. 1917.

Crossfield, A. Scott and Clay Blair, Jr.
Always Another Dawn. 1960.

Fokker, Anthony H. G. and Bruce Gould.
Flying Dutchman: The Life of Anthony Fokker. 1931.

Gibson, Guy.
Enemy Coast Ahead. 1946.

Goldberg, Alfred, editor.
A History of the United States Air Force 1907-1957. 1957.

Gurney, Gene.
Five Down and Glory. Edited by Mark P. Friedlander, Jr. 1958.

Hall, Norman S.
The Balloon Buster: Frank Luke of Arizona. 1928.

Josephson, Matthew.
Empire of the Air: Juan Trippe and the Struggle for World Airways. 1944.

Kelly, Charles J., Jr.
The Sky's the Limit: The History of the Airlines. 1963.
New Introduction by Charles J. Kelly, Jr.

Kelly, Fred C., editor.
Miracle at Kitty Hawk. 1951.

La Farge, Oliver.
The Eagle in the Egg. 1949.

Levine, Isaac Don.
Mitchell: Pioneer of Air Power. 1943.

Lougheed, Victor.
Vehicles of the Air. 1909.

McFarland, Marvin W., editor.
The Papers of Wilbur and Orville Wright. 2 volumes. 1953.

McKee, Alexander.
Strike From the Sky: The Story of the Battle of Britain. 1960.

Macmillan, Norman.
Into the Blue. 1969.

Magoun, F. Alexander and Eric Hodgins.
A History of Aircraft. 1931.

Parsons, Edwin C.
I Flew with the Lafayette Escadrille. 1963.

Penrose, Harald.
No Echo in the Sky. 1958.

Reynolds, Quentin.
The Amazing Mr. Doolittle. 1953.

Saunders, Hilary St. George.
Per Ardua: The Rise of British Air Power 1911-1939. 1945.

Stilwell, Hart and Slats Rodgers.
Old Soggy No. 1. 1954.

Studer, Clara.
Sky Storming Yankee: The Life of Glenn Curtiss. 1937.

Turnbull, Archibald D. and Clifford L. Lord.
History of United States Naval Aviation. 1949.

Turner, C. C.
The Old Flying Days. 1927.

Von Richthofen, Manfred F.
The Red Air Fighter. 1918.

Werner, Johannes.
Knight of Germany: Oswald Boelcke, German Ace. Translated by Claud W. Sykes. 1933.

Wise, John.
Through the Air. 1873.

Wolff, Leon.
Low Level Mission. 1957.

Yakovlev, Alexander.
Notes of an Aircraft Designer. Translated by Albert Zdornykh. n.d.